RAY BRADBURY'S
FAHRENHEIT 451

RAY BRADBURY'S FAHRENHEIT 451
THE AUTHORIZED ADAPTATION

TIM HAMILTON
INTRODUCTION BY RAY BRADBURY

A NOVEL GRAPHIC FROM HILL AND WANG

A DIVISION OF FARRAR, STRAUS AND GIROUX
NEW YORK

TO DAVID PASSALACQUA,
WHOSE VOICE IS STILL IN MY HEAD EVERY DAY

AND I WOULD LIKE TO THANK THE FOLLOWING:
RAY BRADBURY, THOMAS LeBIEN, DEEP6 STUDIOS,
CHRIS SINDERSON, TORY SICA,
HOWARD ZIMMERMAN, DEAN MOTTER,
MY MOM, AND JEAN LEE

—TIM HAMILTON

HILL AND WANG
A DIVISION OF FARRAR, STRAUS AND GIROUX
18 WEST 18TH STREET, NEW YORK 10011

THIS IS A Z FILE, INC. BOOK
FAHRENHEIT 451 COPYRIGHT © 1953, RENEWED 1981 BY RAY BRADBURY
INTRODUCTION COPYRIGHT © 2009 BY RAY BRADBURY
ARTWORK COPYRIGHT © 2009 BY Z FILE, INC.
ALL RIGHTS RESERVED
DISTRIBUTED IN CANADA BY DOUGLAS & MCINTYRE LTD.
PRINTED IN THE UNITED STATES OF AMERICA
PUBLISHED SIMULTANEOUSLY IN HARDCOVER AND PAPERBACK
FIRST EDITION, 2009

PORTIONS OF THIS BOOK PREVIOUSLY APPEARED IN *PLAYBOY*.

LIBRARY OF CONGRESS CATALOGING-IN-PUBLICATION DATA
Hamilton, Tim.
    Ray Bradbury's Fahrenheit 451 : the authorized adaptation / by Tim Hamilton. -- 1st ed.
    p. cm
    "A novel graphic from Hill and Wang."
    ISBN: 978-0-8090-5100-7 (alk. paper)
    1. Book burning—Comic books, strips, etc. 2. Totalitarianism—Comic books, strips etc.
3. Graphic novels. I. Bradbury, Ray, 1920--Fahrenheit 451. II. Title.
PN6727.H28R39 2009
741.5'973--dc22
                                                                2009004804

Paperback ISBN: 978-0-8090-5101-4

ART BY TIM HAMILTON
EDITED BY HOWARD ZIMMERMAN
DESIGNED BY DEAN MOTTER
PRODUCTION ASSISTANT: ELIZABETH MAPLES

WWW.FSGBOOKS.COM

1 3 5 7 9 10 8 6 4 2

C O N T E N T S

INTRODUCTION

BY RAY BRADBURY

BACK IN 1950, I DINED OUT ONE NIGHT WITH A FRIEND. LATER IN THE EVENING WE WERE WALKING ALONG WILSHIRE BOULEVARD WHEN A POLICE CAR STOPPED AND AN OFFICER GOT OUT AND ASKED US WHAT WE WERE DOING.

"PUTTING ONE FOOT IN FRONT OF THE OTHER," I SAID, NOT VERY HELPFULLY.

THE POLICEMAN KEPT QUESTIONING US AS TO WHY WE WERE BEING PEDESTRIANS, AS IF BY TAKING A LATE-NIGHT STROLL WE WERE COMING PERILOUSLY CLOSE TO BREAKING THE LAW. IRRITATED, I WENT HOME AND WROTE A STORY CALLED "THE PEDESTRIAN."

SEVERAL WEEKS LATER, I TOOK MY PEDESTRIAN OUT FOR A LITERARY WALK WHERE HE ENCOUNTERED A YOUNG GIRL NAMED CLARISSE McCLELLAN. SEVEN DAYS LATER, THE FIRST DRAFT OF *THE FIREMAN* WAS FINISHED, WHICH WAS THE NOVELLA THAT TURNED INTO *FAHRENHEIT 451* NOT LONG AFTER.

SOME YEARS LATER, LOOKING BACK, I THOUGHT "THE PEDESTRIAN" WAS THE TRUE SOURCE OF *FAHRENHEIT 451*, BUT MY MEMORY WAS INCORRECT. I NOW REALIZE OTHER THINGS WERE AT WORK IN MY SUBCONSCIOUS.

IT IS ONLY NOW, SOME FIFTY YEARS AFTER THAT L.A. POLICE OFFICER CHALLENGED MY RIGHT TO BE A PEDESTRIAN, THAT I SEE THE ODD IDEAS THAT ROSE TO PERFORM IN SHORT STORIES, WHICH WENT UNNOTICED AS I WROTE THEM.

I WROTE A TALE ABOUT THE GREATEST FANTASY AUTHORS IN HISTORY BEING EXILED TO MARS WHILE THEIR BOOKS WERE BURNED ON EARTH. THAT BECAME A STORY CALLED "THE EXILES."

I WROTE ANOTHER TALE, "USHER II," IN WHICH MY HERO COMPLAINS THAT HE, AS A FANTASY WRITER, IS REJECTED BY THE INTELLECTUALS ON EARTH WHO MAKE FUN OF THE GROTESQUES THAT SPRANG UP IN THE TALES OF EDGAR ALLAN POE AND OTHER SIMILAR AUTHORS.

AND YEARS BEFORE THAT, I PUBLISHED ANOTHER NOVELLA, CALLED *PILLAR OF FIRE,* IN WHICH A DEAD MAN RISES FROM THE GRAVE TO REENACT THE STRANGE LIVES OF DRACULA AND FRANKENSTEIN'S MONSTER.

ALL OF THESE STORIES WERE FORGOTTEN WHEN I FIRST WROTE *FAHRENHEIT 451*. BUT THEY WERE STILL THERE, SOMEWHERE, PERCOLATING IN MY SUBCONSCIOUS.

WHAT YOU HAVE BEFORE YOU NOW IS A FURTHER REJUVENATION OF A BOOK THAT WAS ONCE A SHORT NOVEL THAT WAS ONCE A SHORT STORY THAT WAS ONCE A WALK AROUND THE BLOCK, A RISING UP IN A GRAVEYARD, AND A FINAL FALL OF THE HOUSE OF USHER.

MY SUBCONSCIOUS IS MORE COMPLICATED THAN I EVER IMAGINED. I'VE LEARNED OVER THE YEARS TO LET IT RUN RAMPANT AND OFFER ME ITS IDEAS AS THEY COME, GIVING THEM NO PREFERENCE AND NO SPECIAL TREATMENT. WHEN THE TIME IS RIGHT, SOMEHOW THEY COALESCE AND ERUPT FROM MY SUBCONSCIOUS AND SPILL ONTO THE PAGE.

IN THE CASE OF THE FINAL VERSION OF *FAHRENHEIT 451*, ILLUSTRATED HERE, I BROUGHT ALL MY CHARACTERS ONSTAGE AGAIN AND RAN THEM THROUGH MY TYPEWRITER, LETTING MY FINGERS TELL THE STORIES AND BRING FORTH THE GHOSTS OF OTHER TALES FROM OTHER TIMES.

I AM THE HERO, MONTAG, AND A GOOD PART OF ME IS ALSO CLARISSE McCLELLAN. A DARKER SIDE OF ME IS THE FIRE CHIEF, BEATTY, AND MY PHILOSOPHICAL CAPACITIES ARE REPRESENTED BY THE PHILOSOPHER FABER.

I PUT THEM ALL TOGETHER, SHOOK THEM UP, AND POURED THEM FORTH, PRETENDING NOT TO NOTICE WHAT I WAS DOING. AT THE END OF A NUMBER OF DAYS AND A FURTHER NUMBER OF WEEKS, I HAD A NOVEL.

THANK GOD THAT I DIDN'T, AT ANY TIME IN THE LAST TWENTY OR THIRTY YEARS, KNOW EXACTLY WHAT I WAS DOING, SO THAT EACH OF THESE PARTS OF ME WAS ABLE TO STEP FORTH AND DECLARE ITSELF. EACH CHARACTER IN *FAHRENHEIT 451* HAS HIS OR HER MOMENT OF TRUTH; I STAYED QUIETLY IN THE BACKGROUND AND LET THEM DECLAIM AND NEVER INTERRUPTED.

SO WHAT YOU HAVE HERE, NOW, IS A PASTICHE OF MY FORMER LIVES, MY FORMER FEARS, MY INHIBITIONS, AND MY STRANGE AND MYSTERIOUS AND UNRECOGNIZED PREDICTIONS OF THE FUTURE.

I SAY ALL THIS TO INFORM ANY TEACHERS OR STUDENTS READING THIS BOOK THAT WHAT I DID WAS NAME A METAPHOR AND LET MYSELF RUN FREE, ALLOWING MY SUBCONSCIOUS TO SURFACE WITH ALL KINDS OF WILD IDEAS.

SIMILARLY, IN THE FUTURE, IF SOME TEACHER SUGGESTS TO HIS OR HER STUDENTS THAT THEY CONCEIVE METAPHORS AND WRITE ESSAYS OR STORIES ABOUT THEM, THE YOUNG WRITERS SHOULD TAKE CARE NOT TO INTELLECTUALIZE OR BE SELF-CONSCIOUS OR OVERANALYZE THEIR METAPHORS; THEY SHOULD LET THE METAPHORS RACE AS FAST AND FURIOUS AND FREELY AS POSSIBLE SO THAT WHAT IS STIRRED UP ARE ALL THE HIDDEN TRUTHS AT THE BOTTOM OF THE WRITER'S MIND.

IT WOULD NOT BE PROPER FOR ME, FIFTY YEARS ON, TO OVERANALYZE AND PONTIFICATE ABOUT MY BOOK, BECAUSE IT WAS WRITTEN BY THE OTHER ME, BY THE INNER SELF, BY THE FUN-LOVING AND FREE-RANGING YOUNG RAY BRADBURY.

FINALLY, MAY I SUGGEST THAT ANYONE READING THIS INTRODUCTION SHOULD TAKE THE TIME TO NAME THE ONE BOOK THAT HE OR SHE WOULD MOST WANT TO MEMORIZE AND PROTECT FROM ANY CENSORS OR "FIREMEN." AND NOT ONLY NAME THE BOOK, BUT GIVE THE REASONS WHY THEY WOULD WISH TO MEMORIZE IT AND WHY IT WOULD BE A VALUABLE ASSET TO BE RECITED AND REMEMBERED IN THE FUTURE. I THINK THIS WOULD MAKE FOR A LIVELY SESSION WHEN MY READERS MEET AND TELL THE BOOKS THEY NAMED AND MEMORIZED, AND WHY.

RAY BRADBURY
JULY 2009

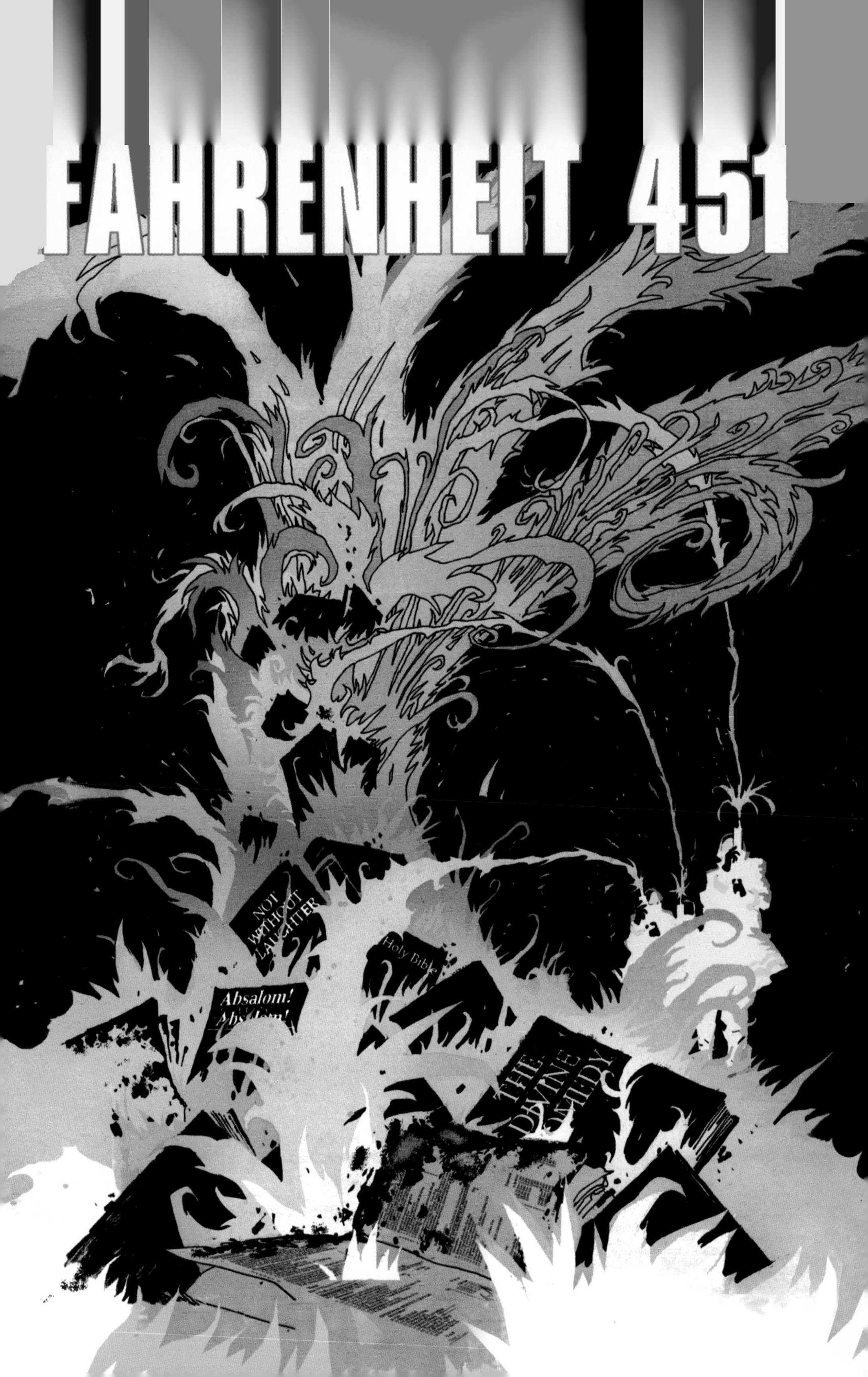
FAHRENHEIT 451
NOT WITHOUT LAUGHTER
Holy Bible
Absalom!
THE DIVINE

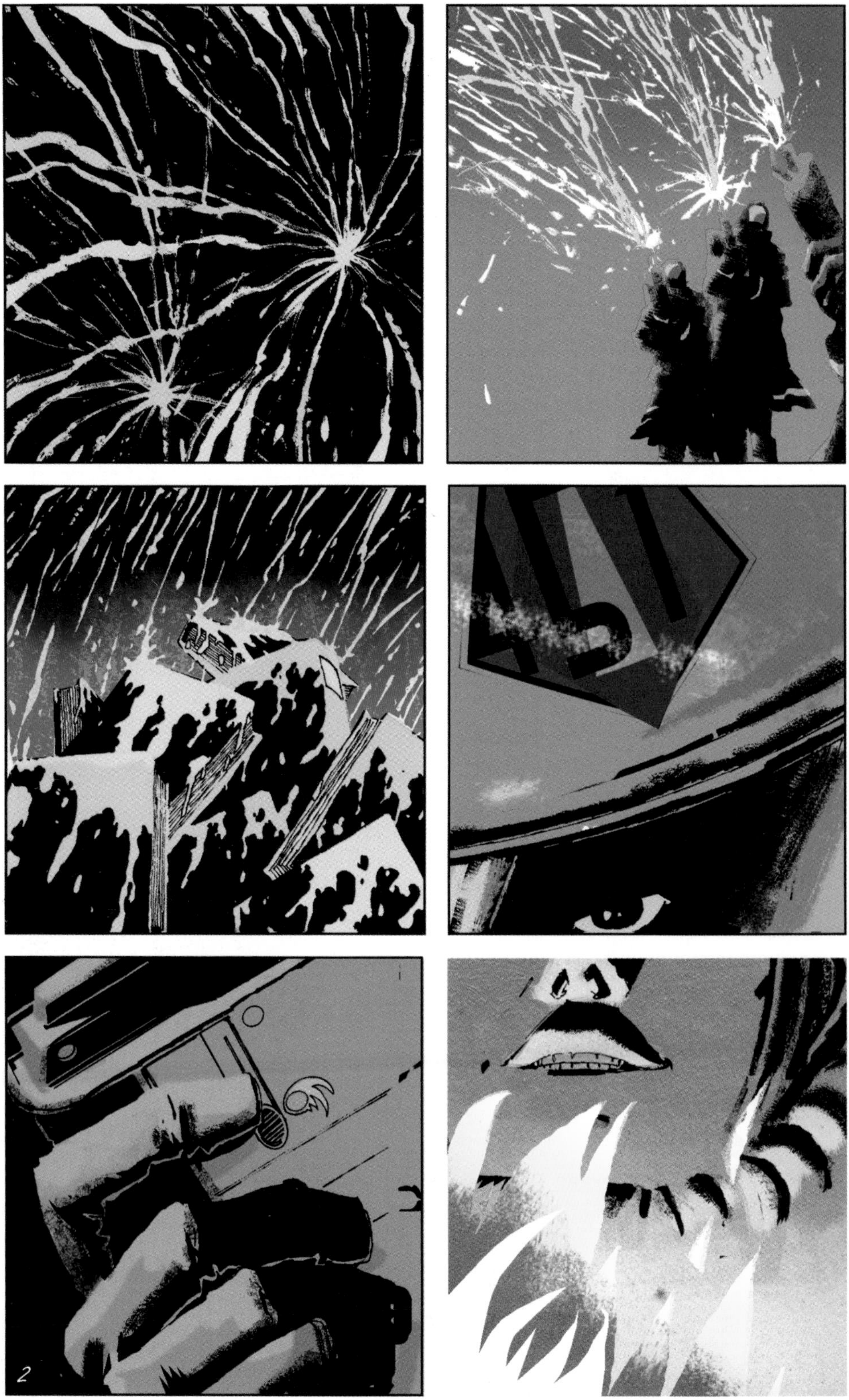
A51

PART ONE: THE HEARTH AND THE SALAMANDER

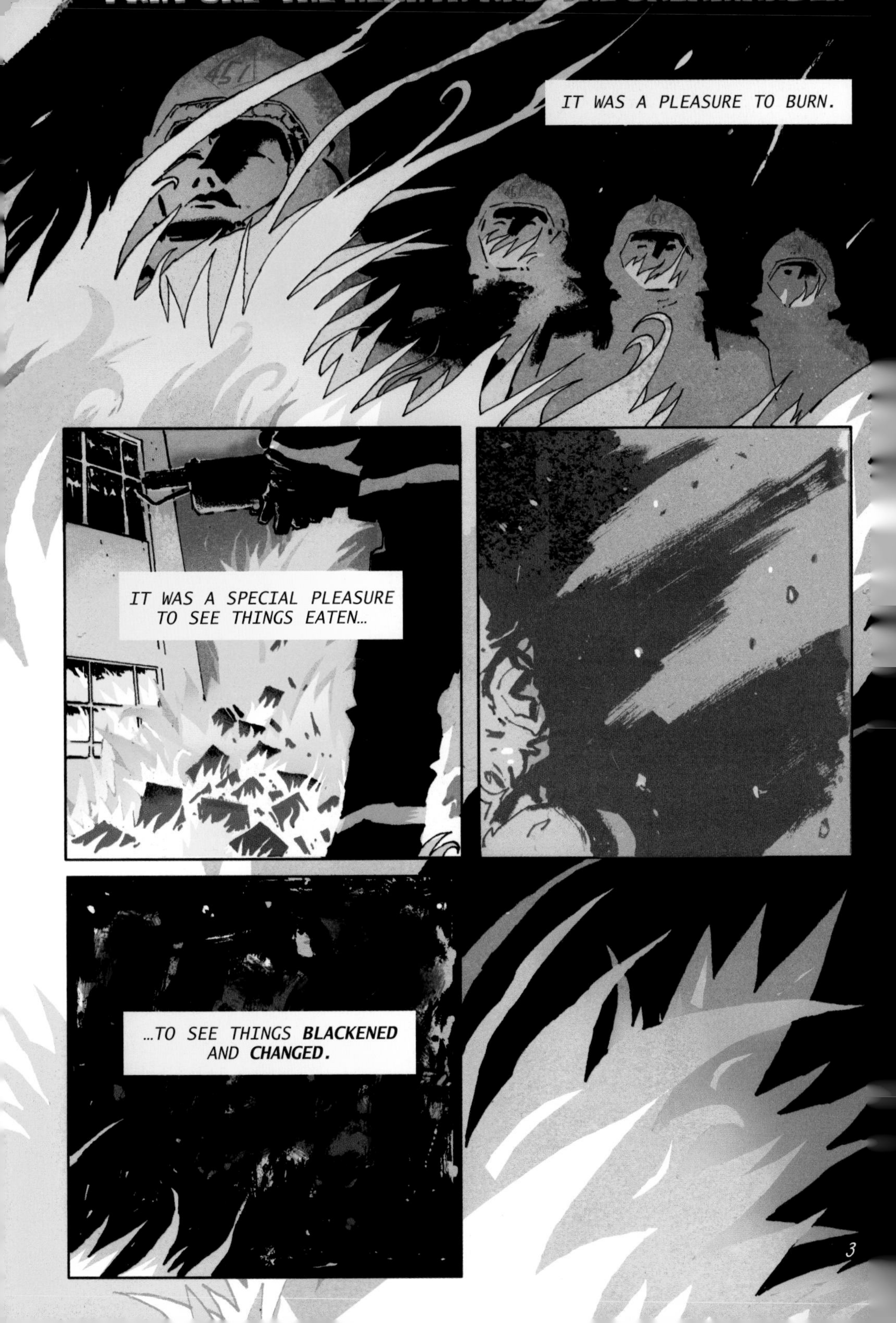
IT WAS A PLEASURE TO BURN.
IT WAS A SPECIAL PLEASURE TO SEE THINGS EATEN...
...TO SEE THINGS **BLACKENED** AND **CHANGED.**

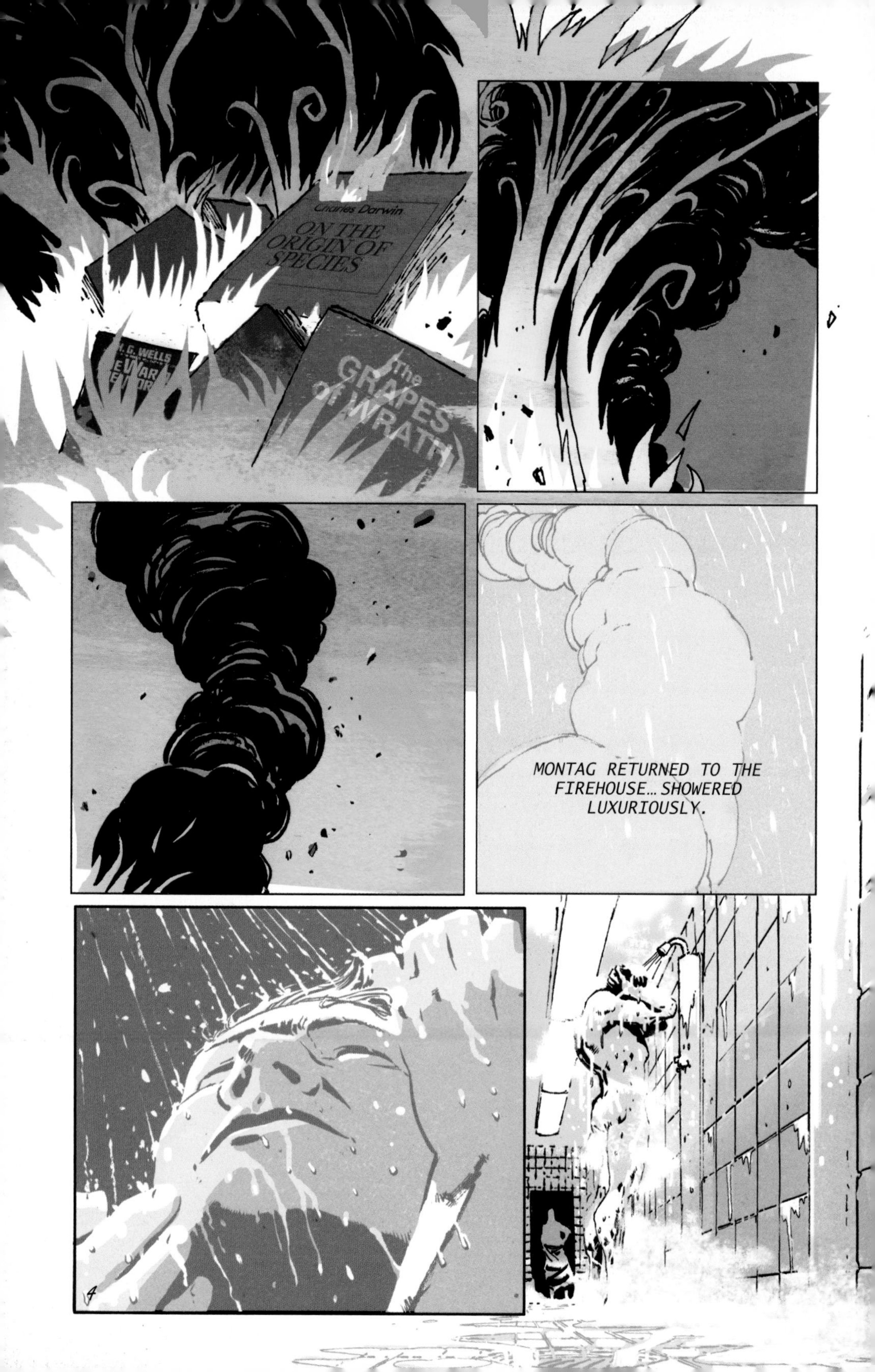
Charles Darwin
ON THE ORIGIN OF SPECIES
The GRAPES of WRATH
MONTAG RETURNED TO THE FIREHOUSE... SHOWERED LUXURIOUSLY.

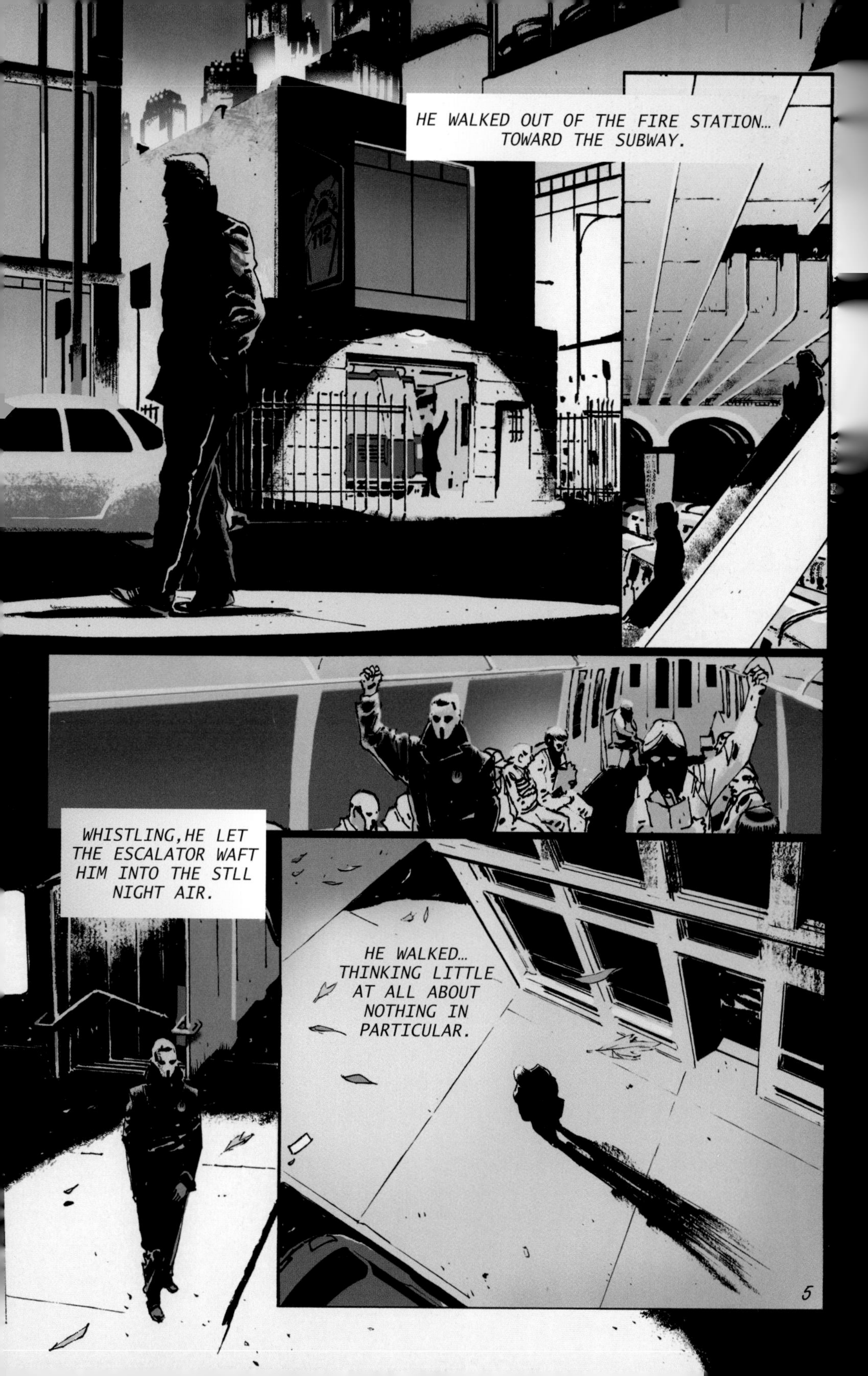
HE WALKED OUT OF THE FIRE STATION... TOWARD THE SUBWAY.
112
WHISTLING,HE LET THE ESCALATOR WAFT HIM INTO THE STLL NIGHT AIR.
HE WALKED... THINKING LITTLE AT ALL ABOUT NOTHING IN PARTICULAR.

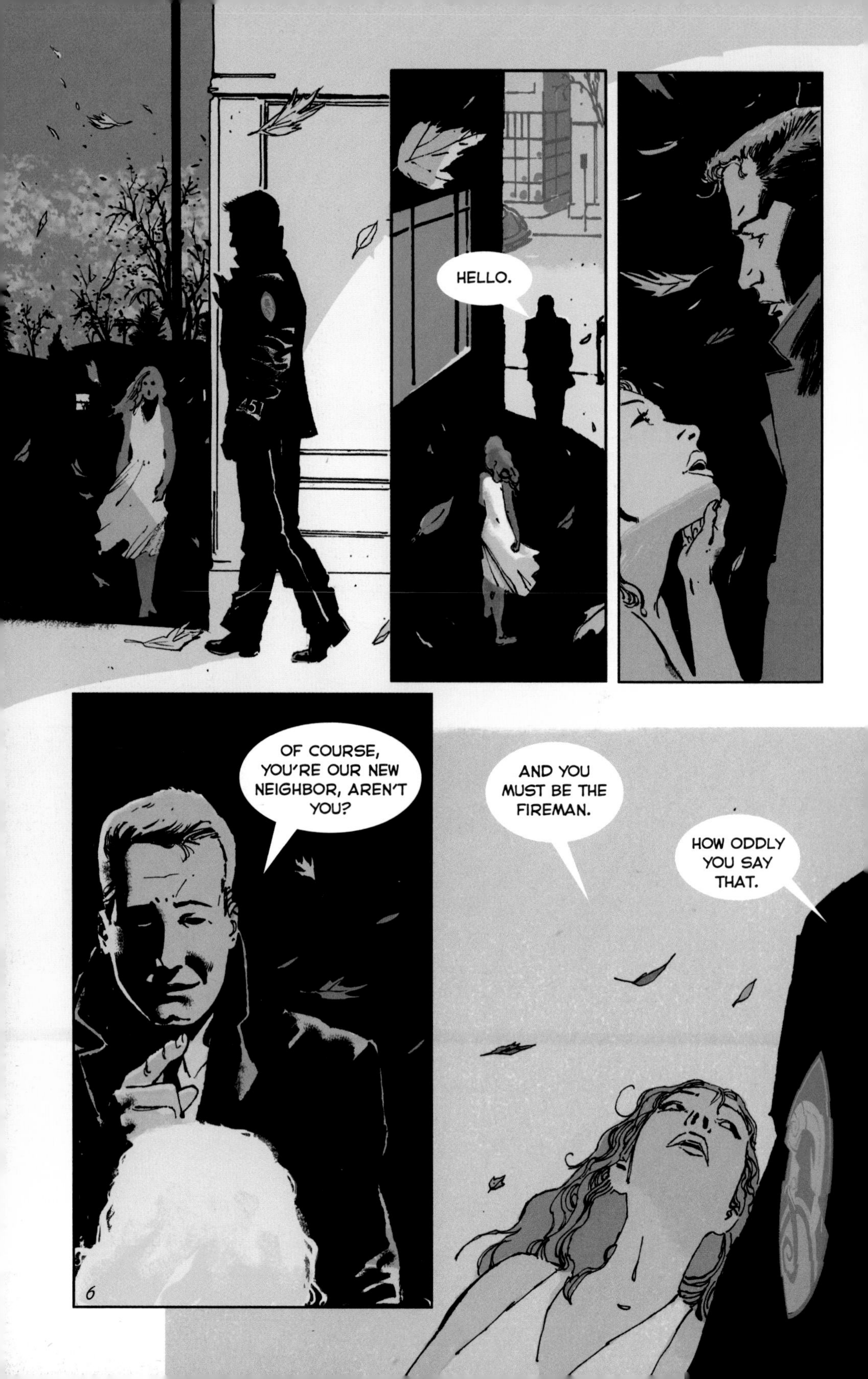
HELLO.
OF COURSE, YOU'RE OUR NEW NEIGHBOR, AREN'T YOU?
AND YOU MUST BE THE FIREMAN.
HOW ODDLY YOU SAY THAT.

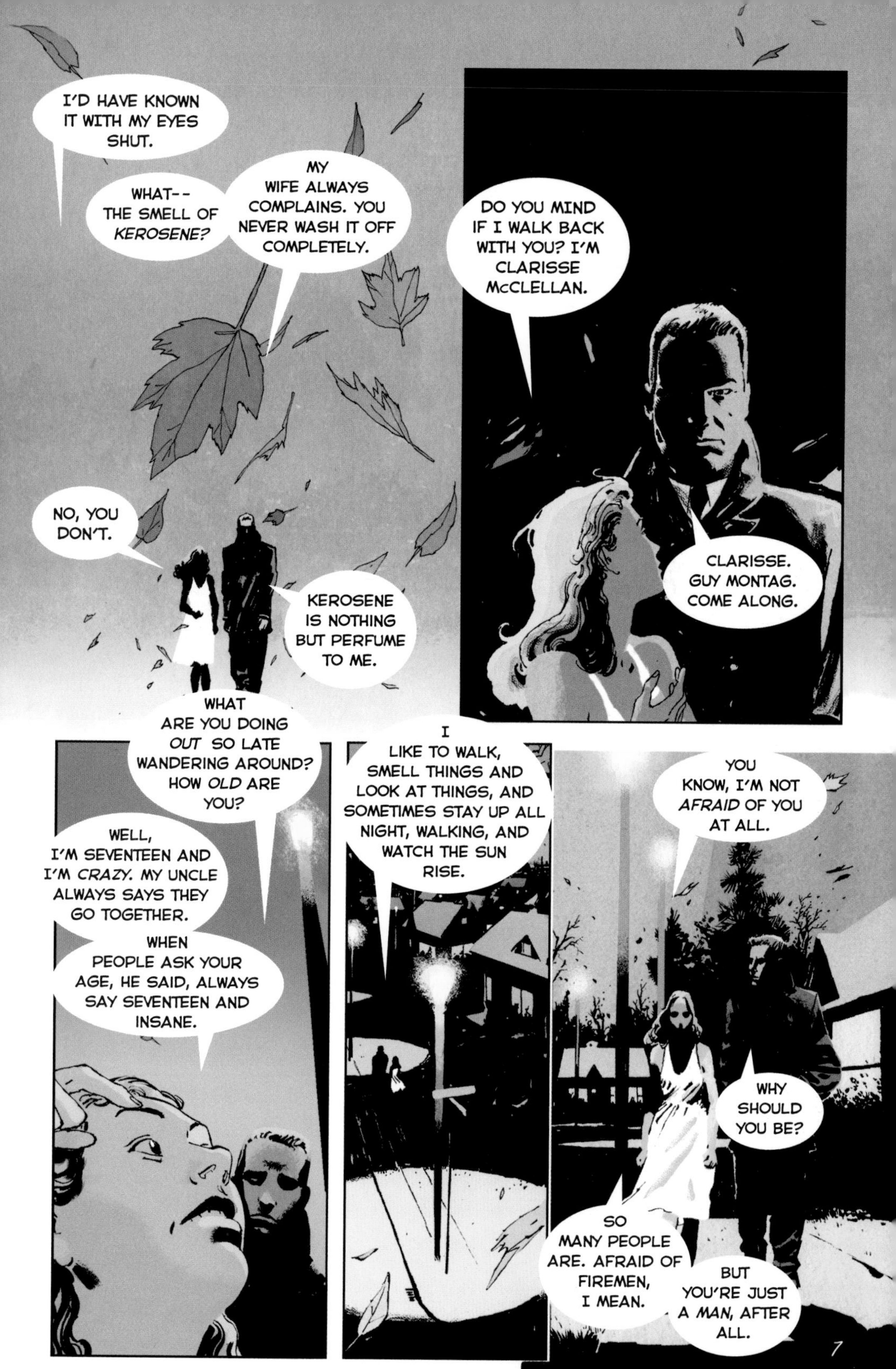

I'D HAVE KNOWN IT WITH MY EYES SHUT.
WHAT-- THE SMELL OF *KEROSENE?*
MY WIFE ALWAYS COMPLAINS. YOU NEVER WASH IT OFF COMPLETELY.
NO, YOU DON'T.
KEROSENE IS NOTHING BUT PERFUME TO ME.
DO YOU MIND IF I WALK BACK WITH YOU? I'M CLARISSE McCLELLAN.
CLARISSE. GUY MONTAG. COME ALONG.
WHAT ARE YOU DOING *OUT* SO LATE WANDERING AROUND? HOW *OLD* ARE YOU?
WELL, I'M SEVENTEEN AND I'M *CRAZY*. MY UNCLE ALWAYS SAYS THEY GO TOGETHER.
WHEN PEOPLE ASK YOUR AGE, HE SAID, ALWAYS SAY SEVENTEEN AND INSANE.
I LIKE TO WALK, SMELL THINGS AND LOOK AT THINGS, AND SOMETIMES STAY UP ALL NIGHT, WALKING, AND WATCH THE SUN RISE.
YOU KNOW, I'M NOT *AFRAID* OF YOU AT ALL.
WHY SHOULD YOU BE?
SO MANY PEOPLE ARE. AFRAID OF FIREMEN, I MEAN.
BUT YOU'RE JUST A *MAN*, AFTER ALL.

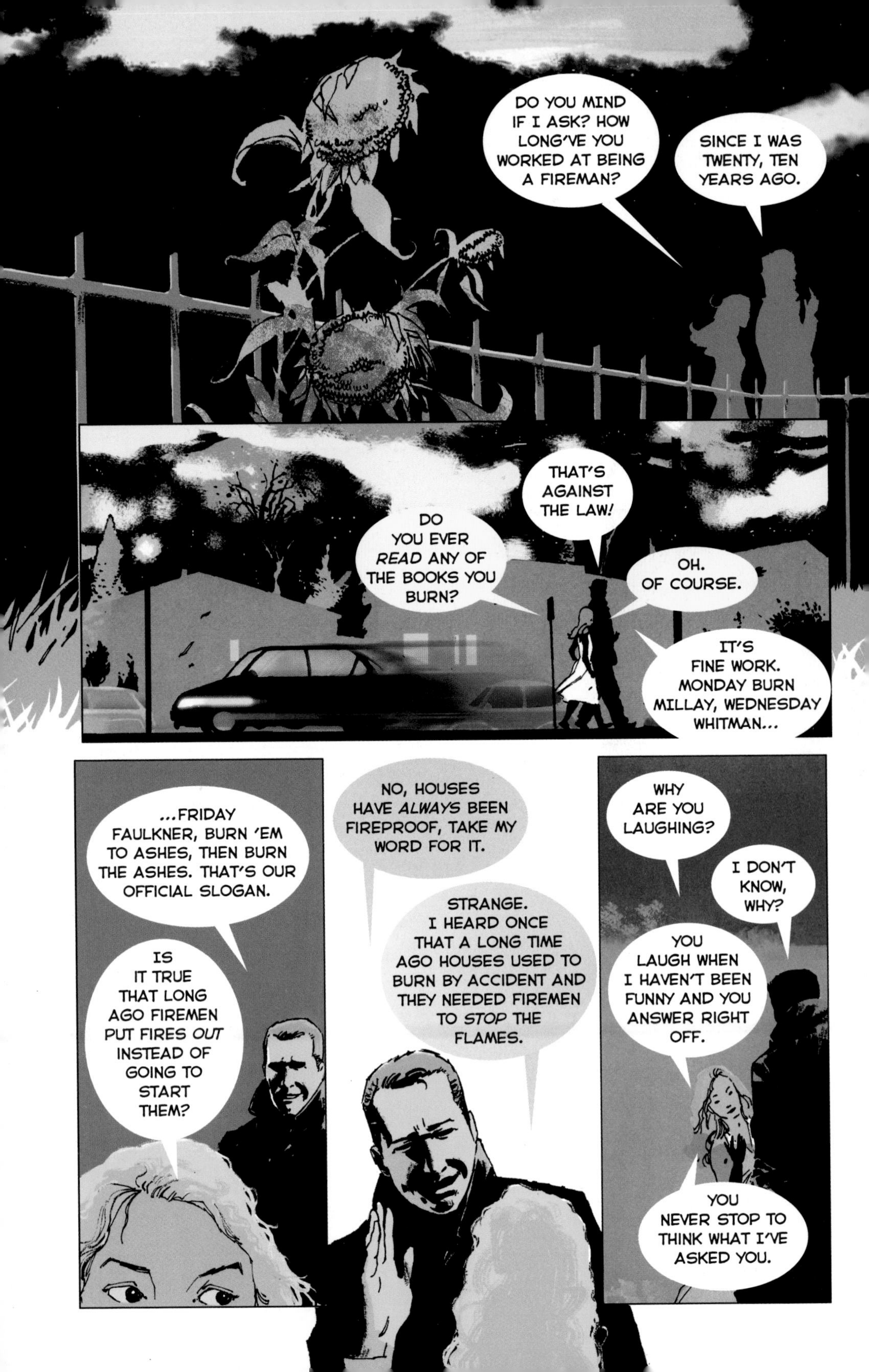
DO YOU MIND IF I ASK? HOW LONG'VE YOU WORKED AT BEING A FIREMAN?
SINCE I WAS TWENTY, TEN YEARS AGO.
DO YOU EVER *READ* ANY OF THE BOOKS YOU BURN?
THAT'S AGAINST THE LAW!
OH. OF COURSE.
IT'S FINE WORK. MONDAY BURN MILLAY, WEDNESDAY WHITMAN...
...FRIDAY FAULKNER, BURN 'EM TO ASHES, THEN BURN THE ASHES. THAT'S OUR OFFICIAL SLOGAN.
IS IT TRUE THAT LONG AGO FIREMEN PUT FIRES *OUT* INSTEAD OF GOING TO START THEM?
NO, HOUSES HAVE *ALWAYS* BEEN FIREPROOF, TAKE MY WORD FOR IT.
STRANGE. I HEARD ONCE THAT A LONG TIME AGO HOUSES USED TO BURN BY ACCIDENT AND THEY NEEDED FIREMEN TO *STOP* THE FLAMES.
WHY ARE YOU LAUGHING?
I DON'T KNOW, WHY?
YOU LAUGH WHEN I HAVEN'T BEEN FUNNY AND YOU ANSWER RIGHT OFF.
YOU NEVER STOP TO THINK WHAT I'VE ASKED YOU.

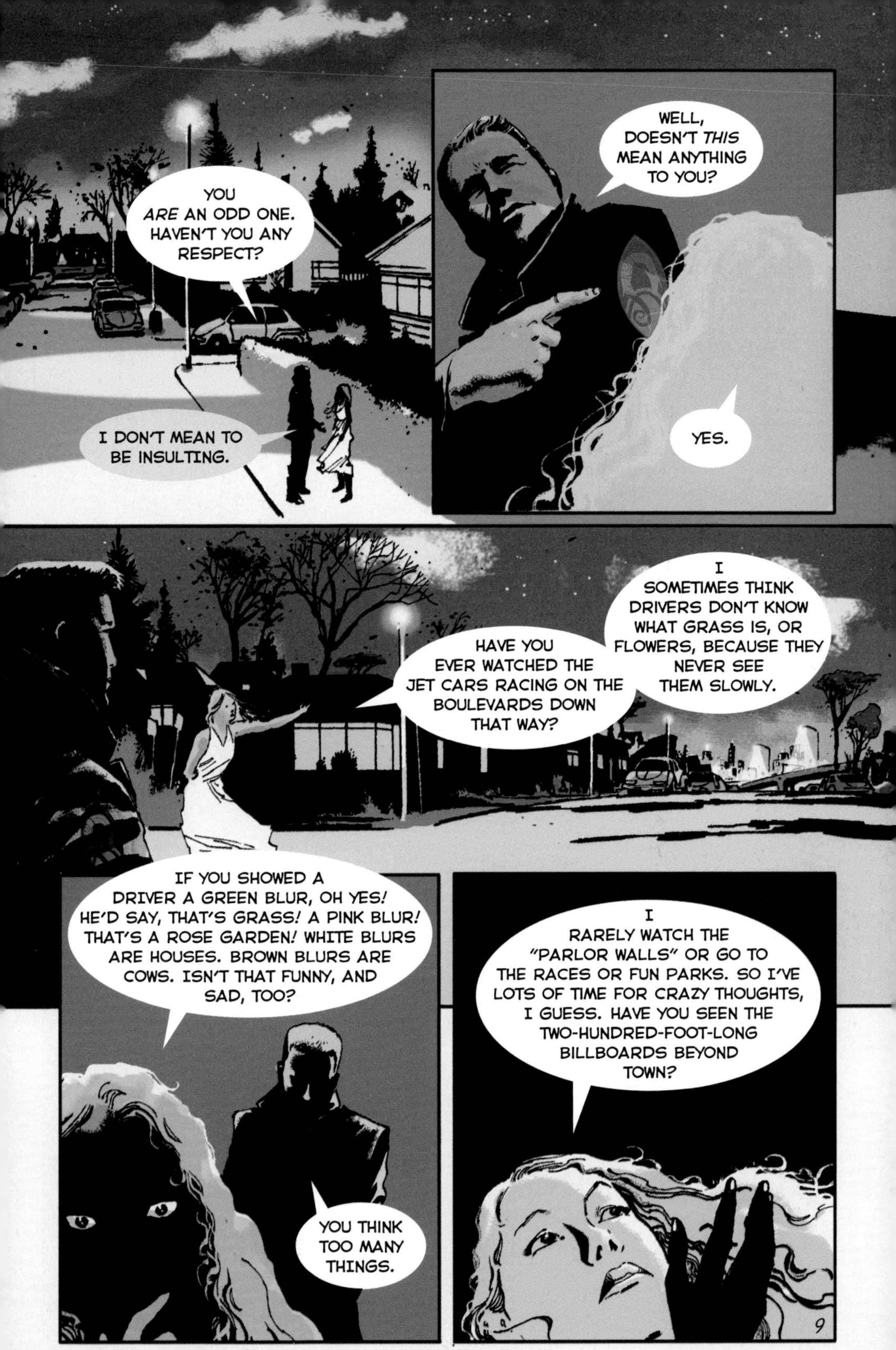
YOU ARE AN ODD ONE. HAVEN'T YOU ANY RESPECT?
I DON'T MEAN TO BE INSULTING.
WELL, DOESN'T THIS MEAN ANYTHING TO YOU?
YES.
HAVE YOU EVER WATCHED THE JET CARS RACING ON THE BOULEVARDS DOWN THAT WAY?
I SOMETIMES THINK DRIVERS DON'T KNOW WHAT GRASS IS, OR FLOWERS, BECAUSE THEY NEVER SEE THEM SLOWLY.
IF YOU SHOWED A DRIVER A GREEN BLUR, OH YES! HE'D SAY, THAT'S GRASS! A PINK BLUR! THAT'S A ROSE GARDEN! WHITE BLURS ARE HOUSES. BROWN BLURS ARE COWS. ISN'T THAT FUNNY, AND SAD, TOO?
YOU THINK TOO MANY THINGS.
I RARELY WATCH THE "PARLOR WALLS" OR GO TO THE RACES OR FUN PARKS. SO I'VE LOTS OF TIME FOR CRAZY THOUGHTS, I GUESS. HAVE YOU SEEN THE TWO-HUNDRED-FOOT-LONG BILLBOARDS BEYOND TOWN?

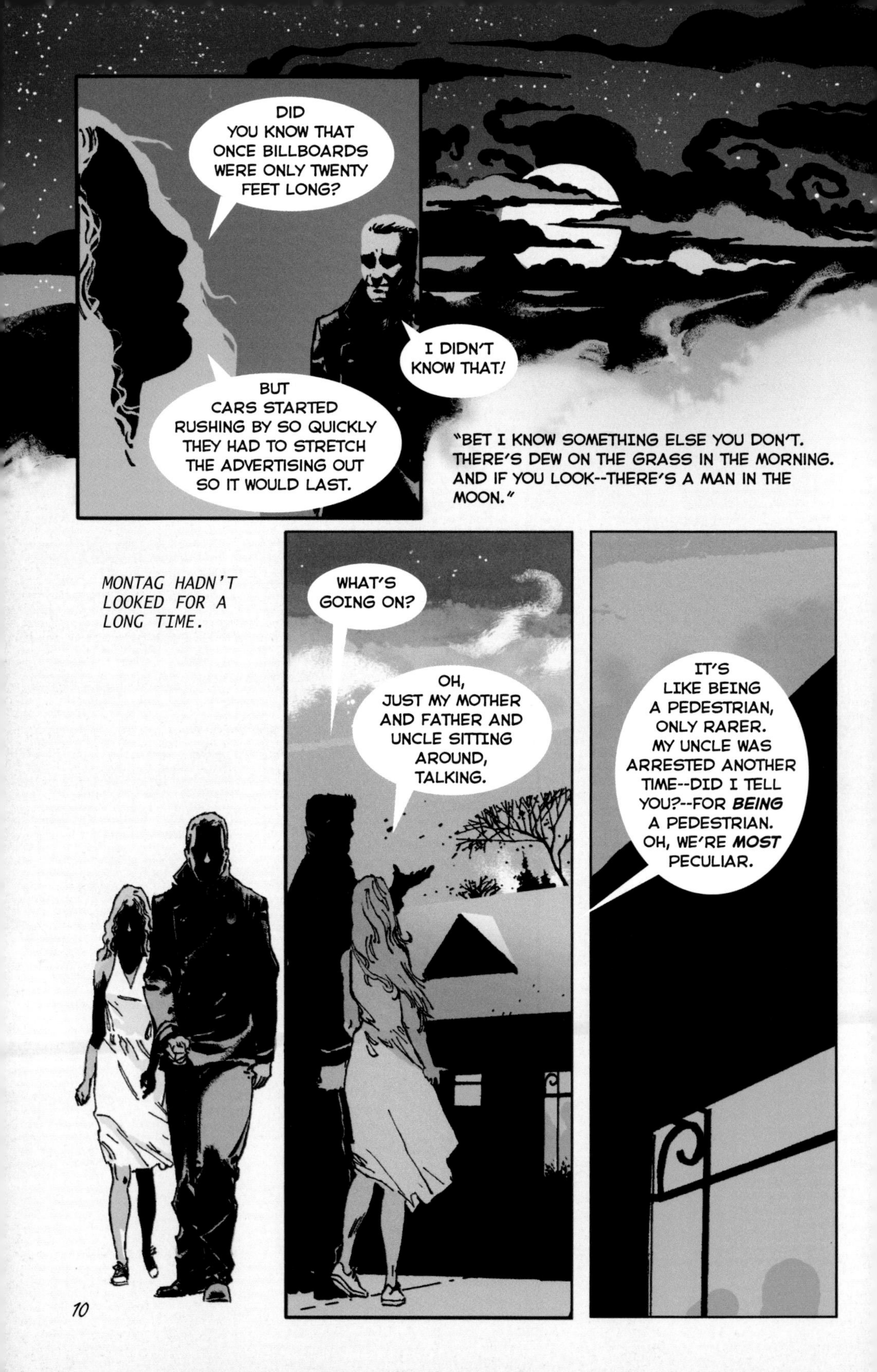
DID YOU KNOW THAT ONCE BILLBOARDS WERE ONLY TWENTY FEET LONG?
I DIDN'T KNOW THAT!
BUT CARS STARTED RUSHING BY SO QUICKLY THEY HAD TO STRETCH THE ADVERTISING OUT SO IT WOULD LAST.
"BET I KNOW SOMETHING ELSE YOU DON'T. THERE'S DEW ON THE GRASS IN THE MORNING. AND IF YOU LOOK--THERE'S A MAN IN THE MOON."
MONTAG HADN'T LOOKED FOR A LONG TIME.
WHAT'S GOING ON?
OH, JUST MY MOTHER AND FATHER AND UNCLE SITTING AROUND, TALKING.
IT'S LIKE BEING A PEDESTRIAN, ONLY RARER. MY UNCLE WAS ARRESTED ANOTHER TIME--DID I TELL YOU?--FOR *BEING* A PEDESTRIAN. OH, WE'RE *MOST* PECULIAR.

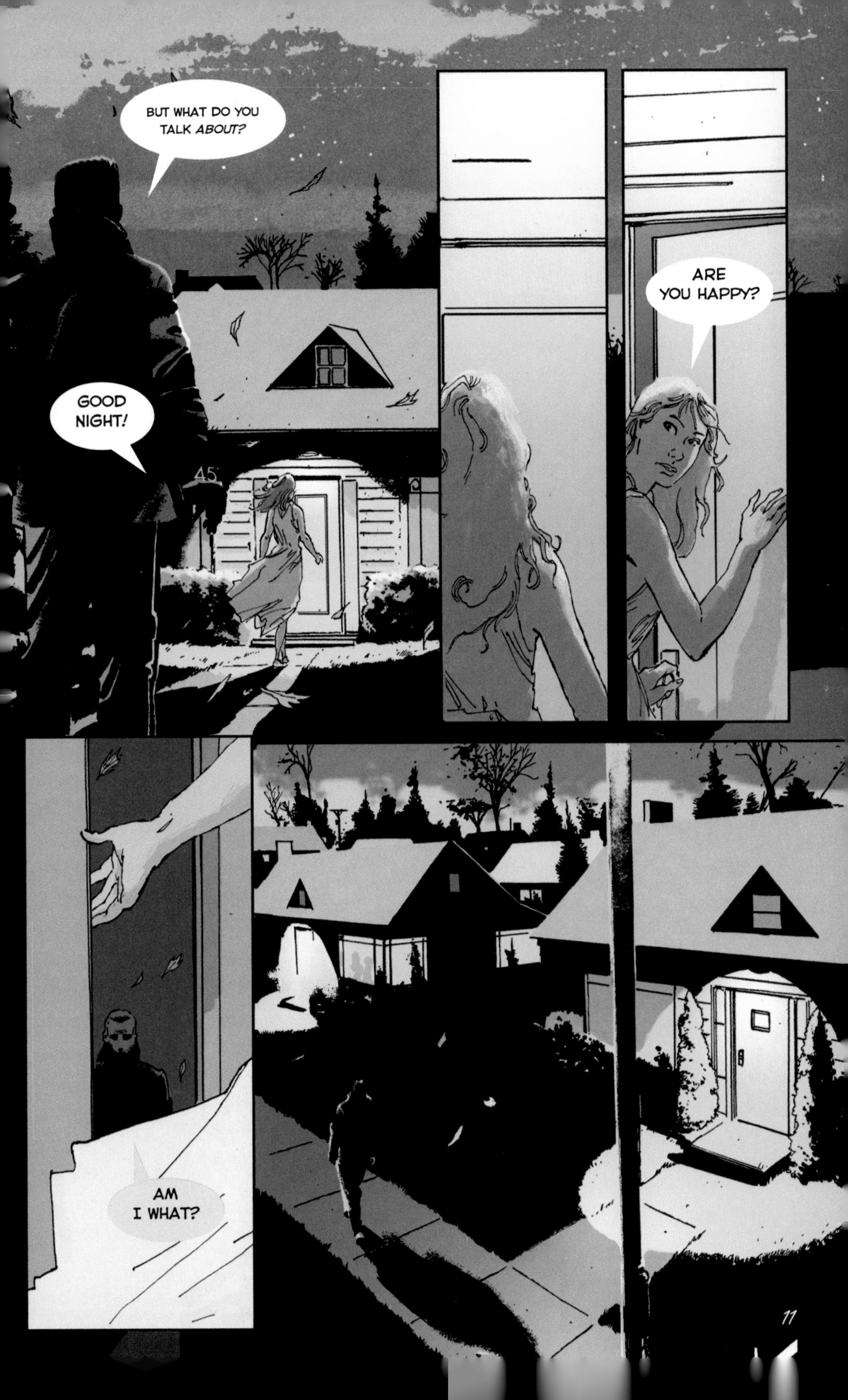
BUT WHAT DO YOU TALK *ABOUT?*
GOOD NIGHT!
ARE YOU HAPPY?
AM I WHAT?

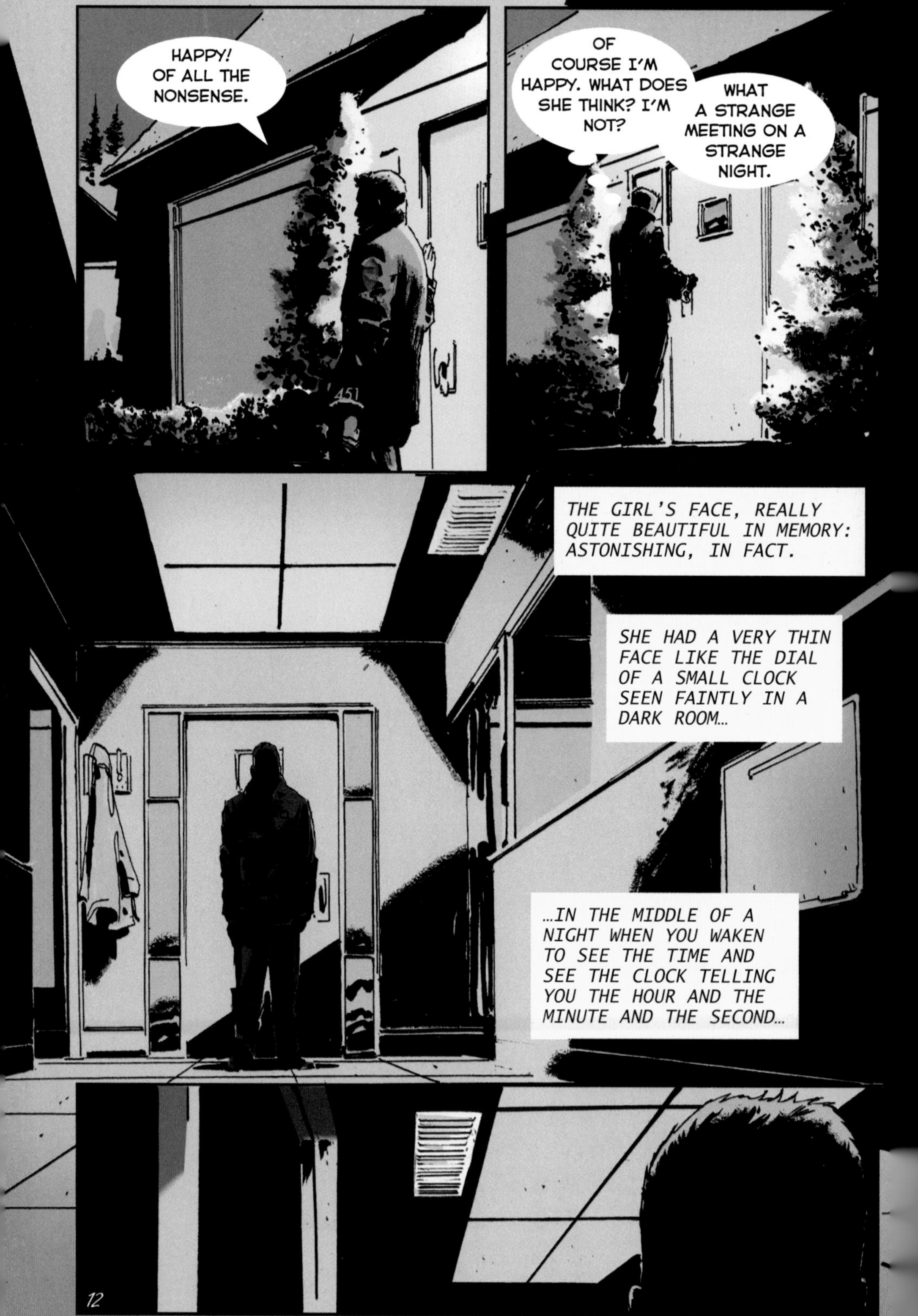
HAPPY! OF ALL THE NONSENSE.
OF COURSE I'M HAPPY. WHAT DOES SHE THINK? I'M NOT?
WHAT A STRANGE MEETING ON A STRANGE NIGHT.
451
THE GIRL'S FACE, REALLY QUITE BEAUTIFUL IN MEMORY: ASTONISHING, IN FACT.
SHE HAD A VERY THIN FACE LIKE THE DIAL OF A SMALL CLOCK SEEN FAINTLY IN A DARK ROOM…
…IN THE MIDDLE OF A NIGHT WHEN YOU WAKEN TO SEE THE TIME AND SEE THE CLOCK TELLING YOU THE HOUR AND THE MINUTE AND THE SECOND…

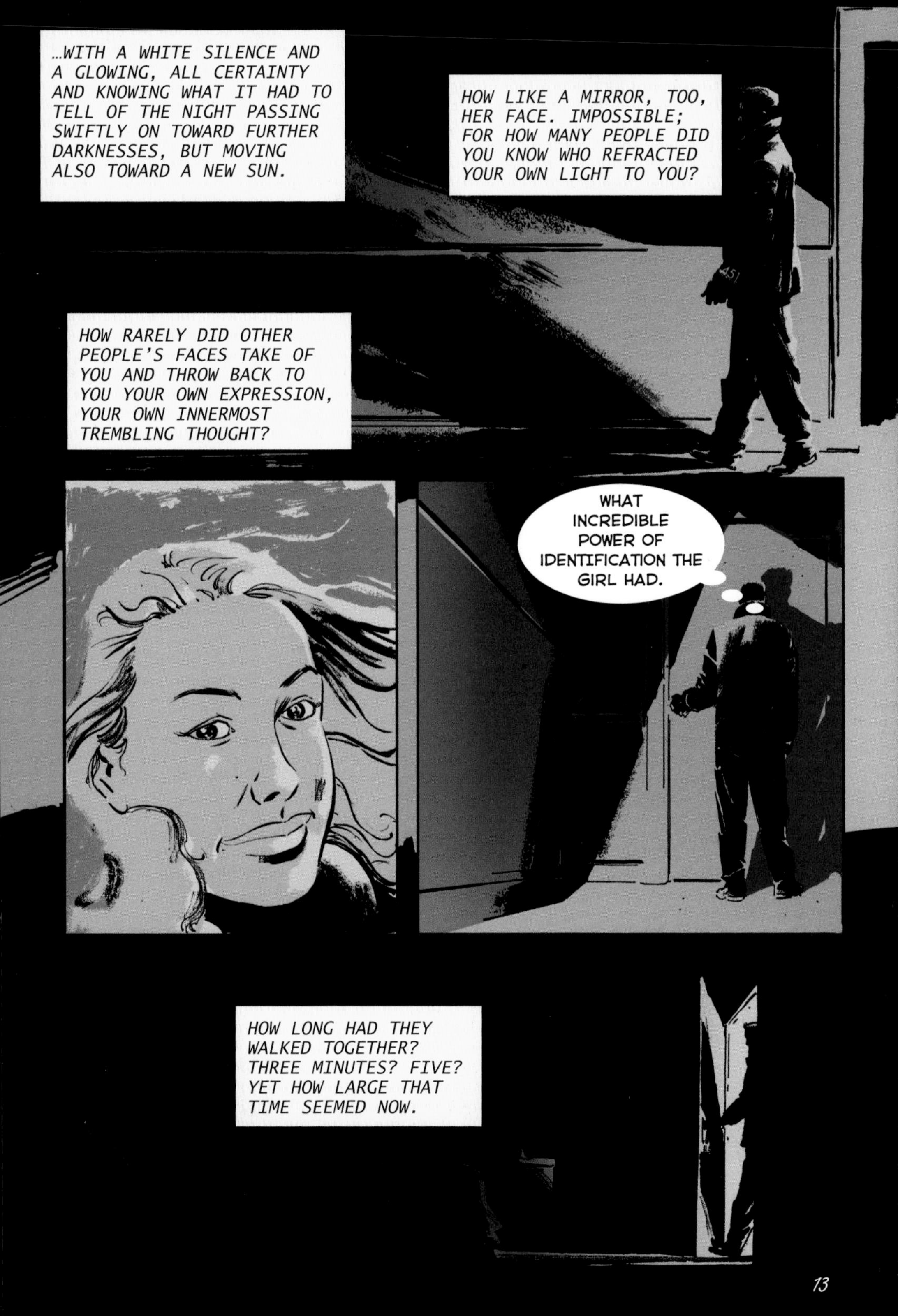
...WITH A WHITE SILENCE AND A GLOWING, ALL CERTAINTY AND KNOWING WHAT IT HAD TO TELL OF THE NIGHT PASSING SWIFTLY ON TOWARD FURTHER DARKNESSES, BUT MOVING ALSO TOWARD A NEW SUN.
HOW LIKE A MIRROR, TOO, HER FACE. IMPOSSIBLE; FOR HOW MANY PEOPLE DID YOU KNOW WHO REFRACTED YOUR OWN LIGHT TO YOU?
451
HOW RARELY DID OTHER PEOPLE'S FACES TAKE OF YOU AND THROW BACK TO YOU YOUR OWN EXPRESSION, YOUR OWN INNERMOST TREMBLING THOUGHT?
WHAT INCREDIBLE POWER OF IDENTIFICATION THE GIRL HAD.
HOW LONG HAD THEY WALKED TOGETHER? THREE MINUTES? FIVE? YET HOW LARGE THAT TIME SEEMED NOW.

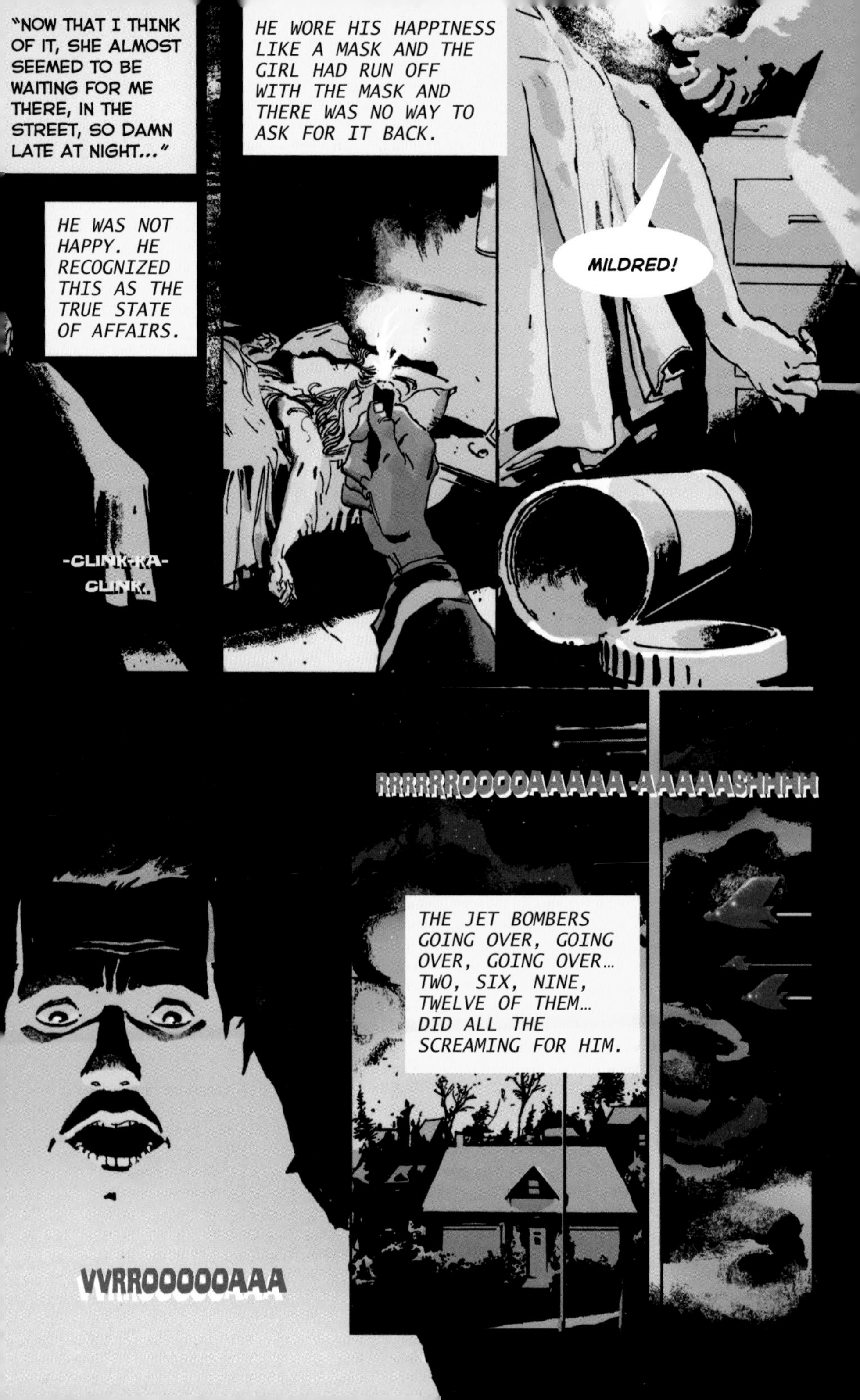
"NOW THAT I THINK OF IT, SHE ALMOST SEEMED TO BE WAITING FOR ME THERE, IN THE STREET, SO DAMN LATE AT NIGHT..."
HE WORE HIS HAPPINESS LIKE A MASK AND THE GIRL HAD RUN OFF WITH THE MASK AND THERE WAS NO WAY TO ASK FOR IT BACK.
HE WAS NOT HAPPY. HE RECOGNIZED THIS AS THE TRUE STATE OF AFFAIRS.
MILDRED!
-CLINK-KA-CLINK.
RRRRRROOOOOAAAAA-AAAAASHHHH
THE JET BOMBERS GOING OVER, GOING OVER, GOING OVER... TWO, SIX, NINE, TWELVE OF THEM... DID ALL THE SCREAMING FOR HIM.
VVRROOOOOAAA

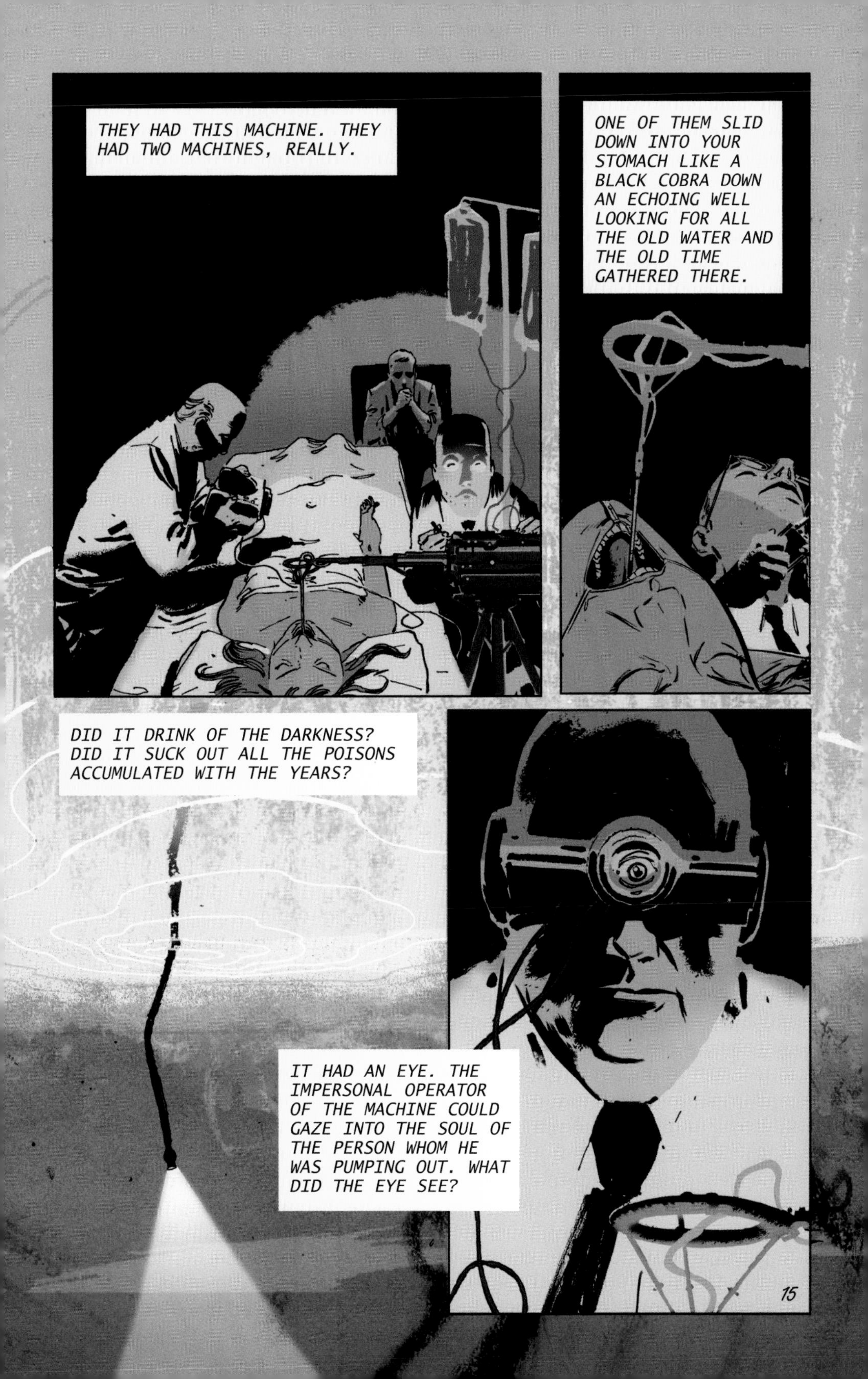
THEY HAD THIS MACHINE. THEY HAD TWO MACHINES, REALLY.
ONE OF THEM SLID DOWN INTO YOUR STOMACH LIKE A BLACK COBRA DOWN AN ECHOING WELL LOOKING FOR ALL THE OLD WATER AND THE OLD TIME GATHERED THERE.
DID IT DRINK OF THE DARKNESS? DID IT SUCK OUT ALL THE POISONS ACCUMULATED WITH THE YEARS?
IT HAD AN EYE. THE IMPERSONAL OPERATOR OF THE MACHINE COULD GAZE INTO THE SOUL OF THE PERSON WHOM HE WAS PUMPING OUT. WHAT DID THE EYE SEE?

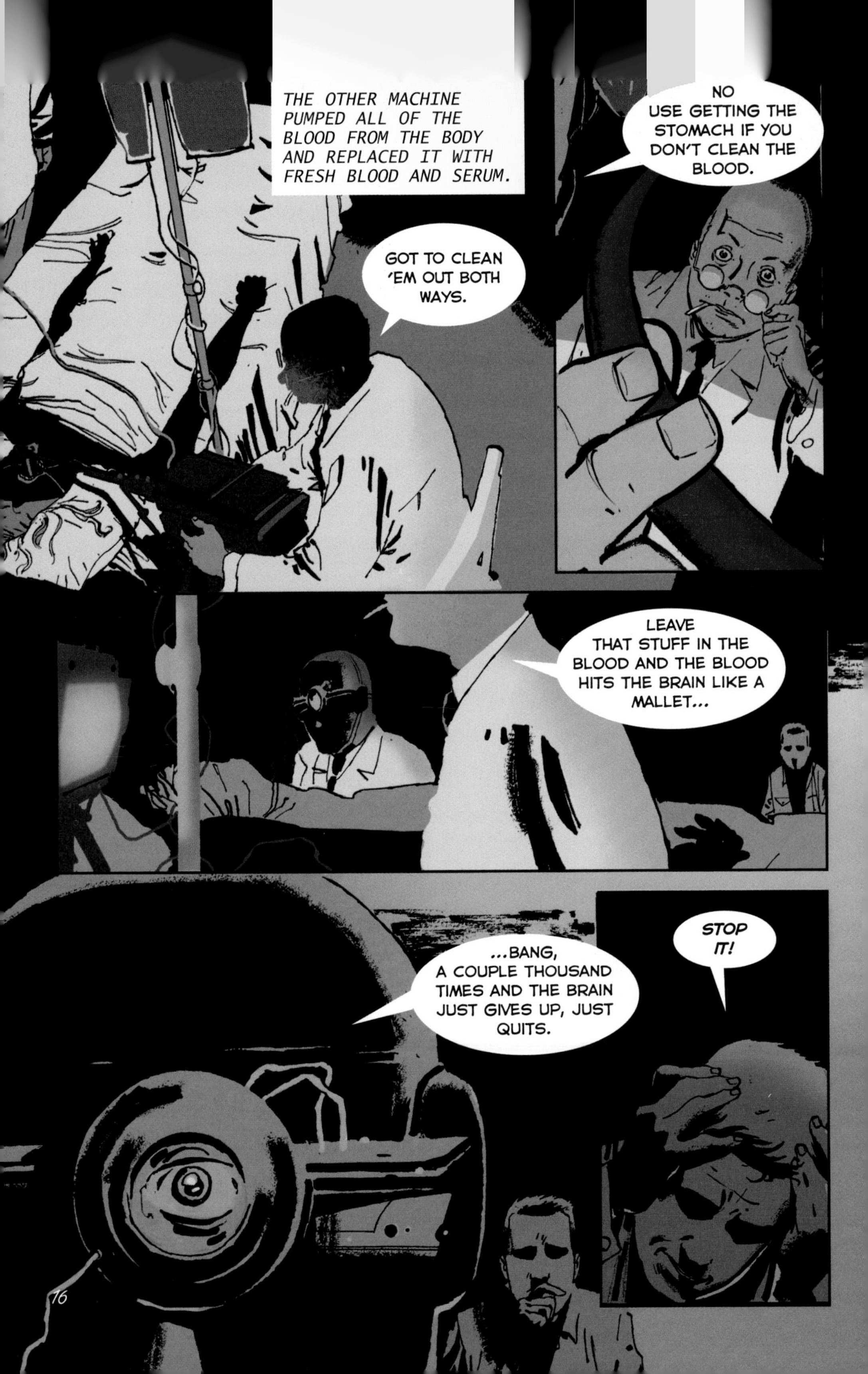
THE OTHER MACHINE PUMPED ALL OF THE BLOOD FROM THE BODY AND REPLACED IT WITH FRESH BLOOD AND SERUM.
NO USE GETTING THE STOMACH IF YOU DON'T CLEAN THE BLOOD.
GOT TO CLEAN 'EM OUT BOTH WAYS.
LEAVE THAT STUFF IN THE BLOOD AND THE BLOOD HITS THE BRAIN LIKE A MALLET...
...BANG, A COUPLE THOUSAND TIMES AND THE BRAIN JUST GIVES UP, JUST QUITS.
STOP IT!

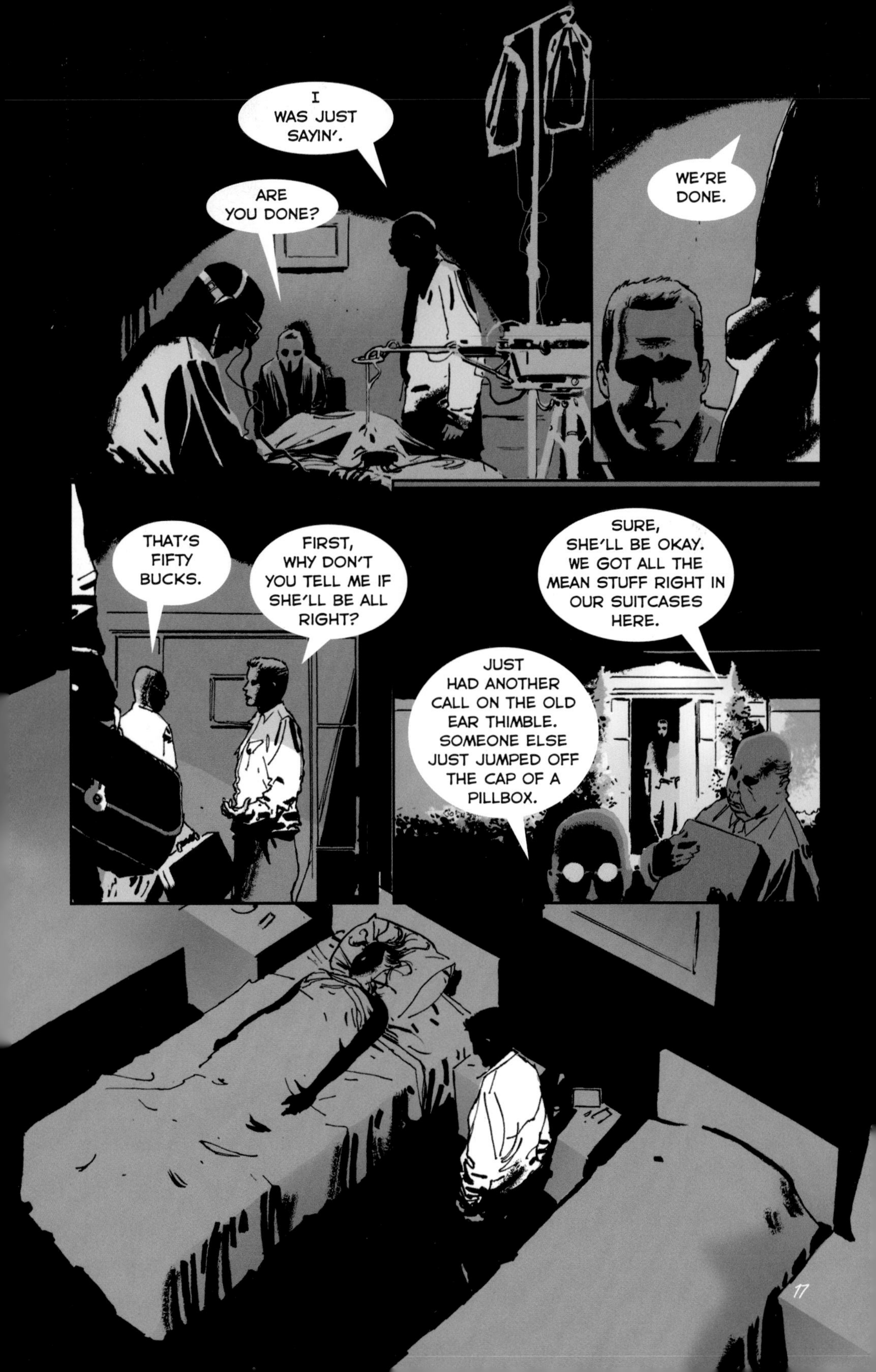
I WAS JUST SAYIN'.
ARE YOU DONE?
WE'RE DONE.
THAT'S FIFTY BUCKS.
FIRST, WHY DON'T YOU TELL ME IF SHE'LL BE ALL RIGHT?
SURE, SHE'LL BE OKAY. WE GOT ALL THE MEAN STUFF RIGHT IN OUR SUITCASES HERE.
JUST HAD ANOTHER CALL ON THE OLD EAR THIMBLE. SOMEONE ELSE JUST JUMPED OFF THE CAP OF A PILLBOX.

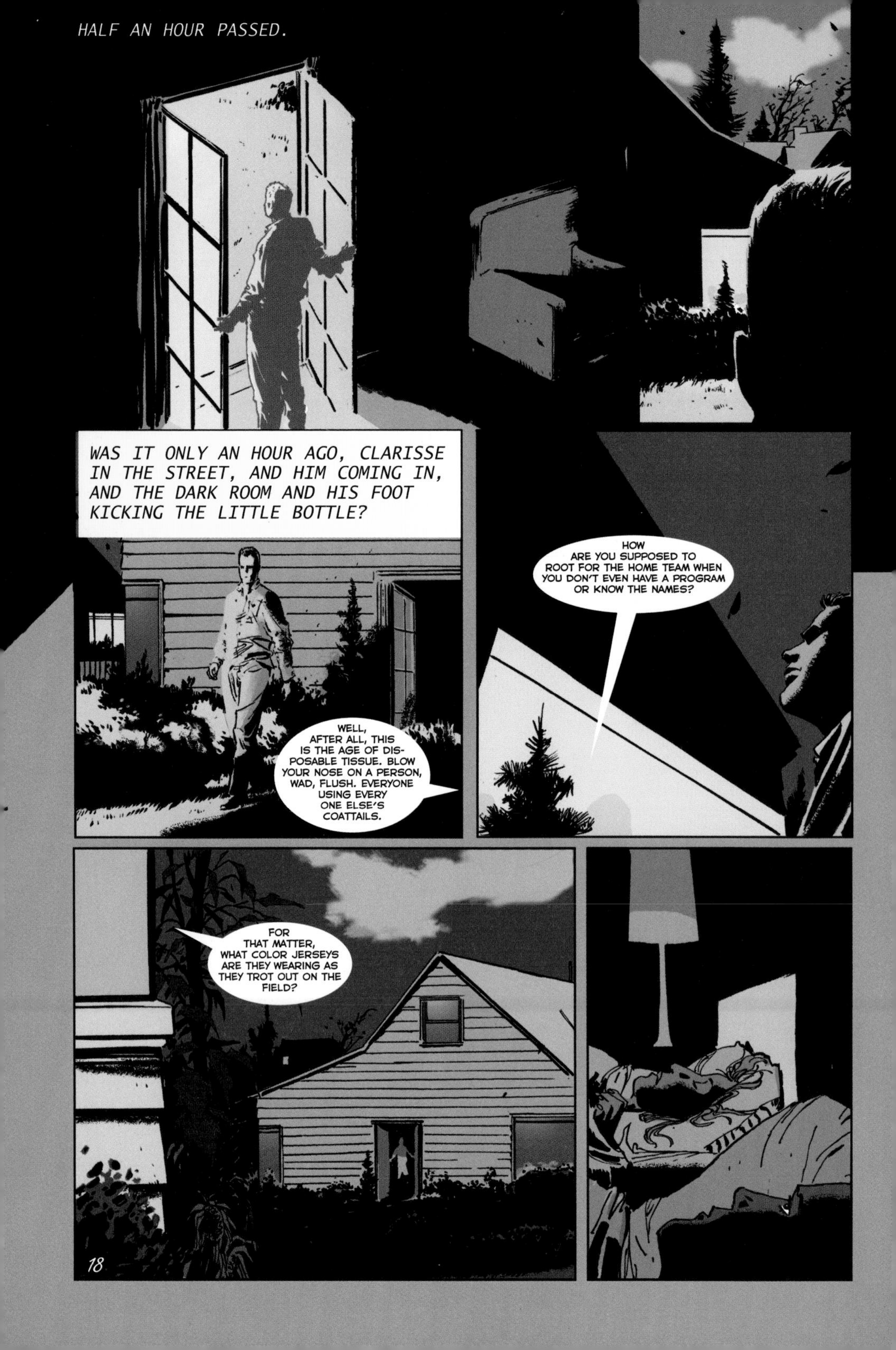
HALF AN HOUR PASSED.
WAS IT ONLY AN HOUR AGO, CLARISSE IN THE STREET, AND HIM COMING IN, AND THE DARK ROOM AND HIS FOOT KICKING THE LITTLE BOTTLE?
WELL, AFTER ALL, THIS IS THE AGE OF DIS-POSABLE TISSUE. BLOW YOUR NOSE ON A PERSON, WAD, FLUSH. EVERYONE USING EVERY ONE ELSE'S COATTAILS.
HOW ARE YOU SUPPOSED TO ROOT FOR THE HOME TEAM WHEN YOU DON'T EVEN HAVE A PROGRAM OR KNOW THE NAMES?
FOR THAT MATTER, WHAT COLOR JERSEYS ARE THEY WEARING AS THEY TROT OUT ON THE FIELD?

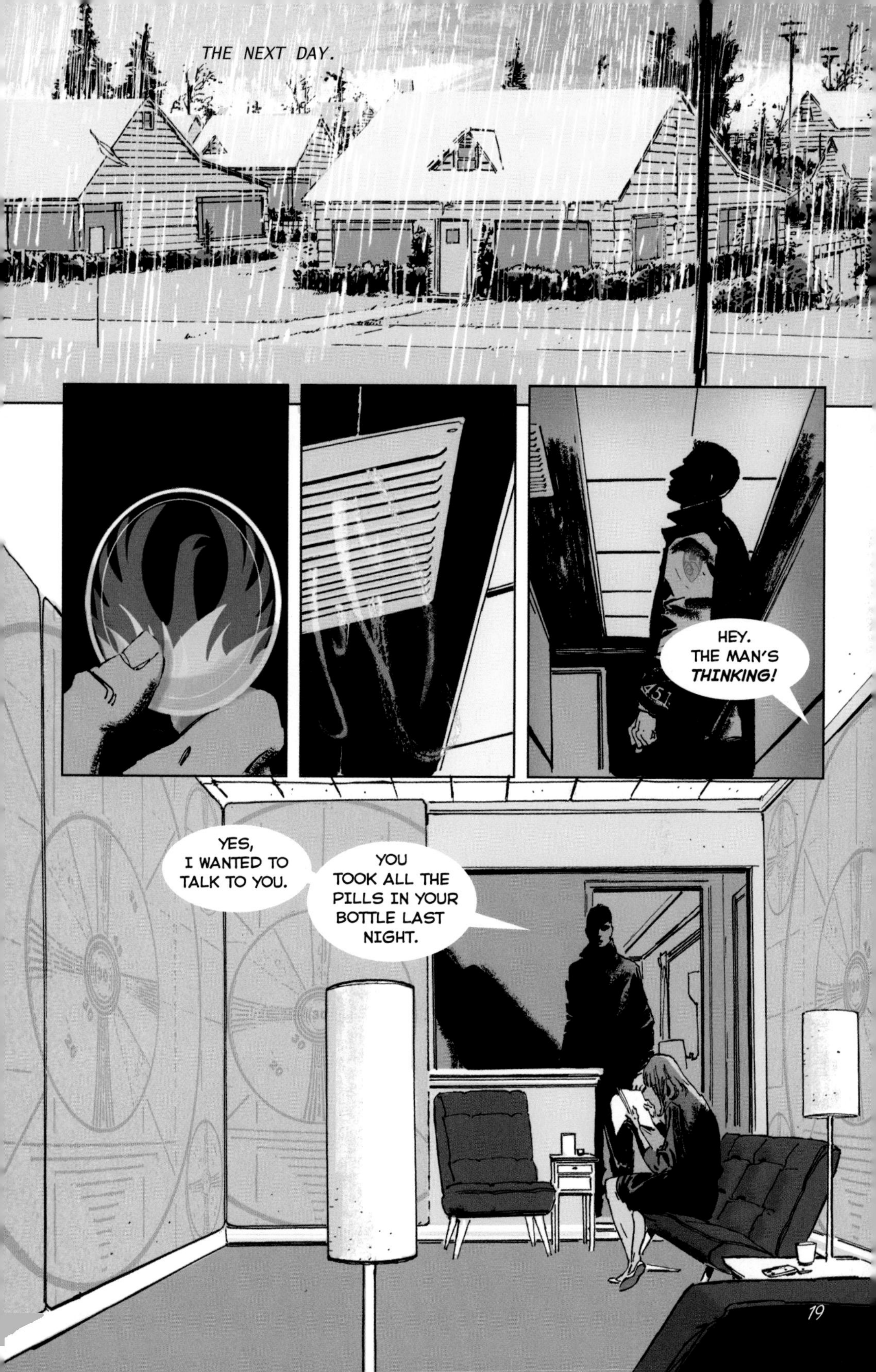
THE NEXT DAY.
HEY. THE MAN'S *THINKING!*
YES, I WANTED TO TALK TO YOU.
YOU TOOK ALL THE PILLS IN YOUR BOTTLE LAST NIGHT.

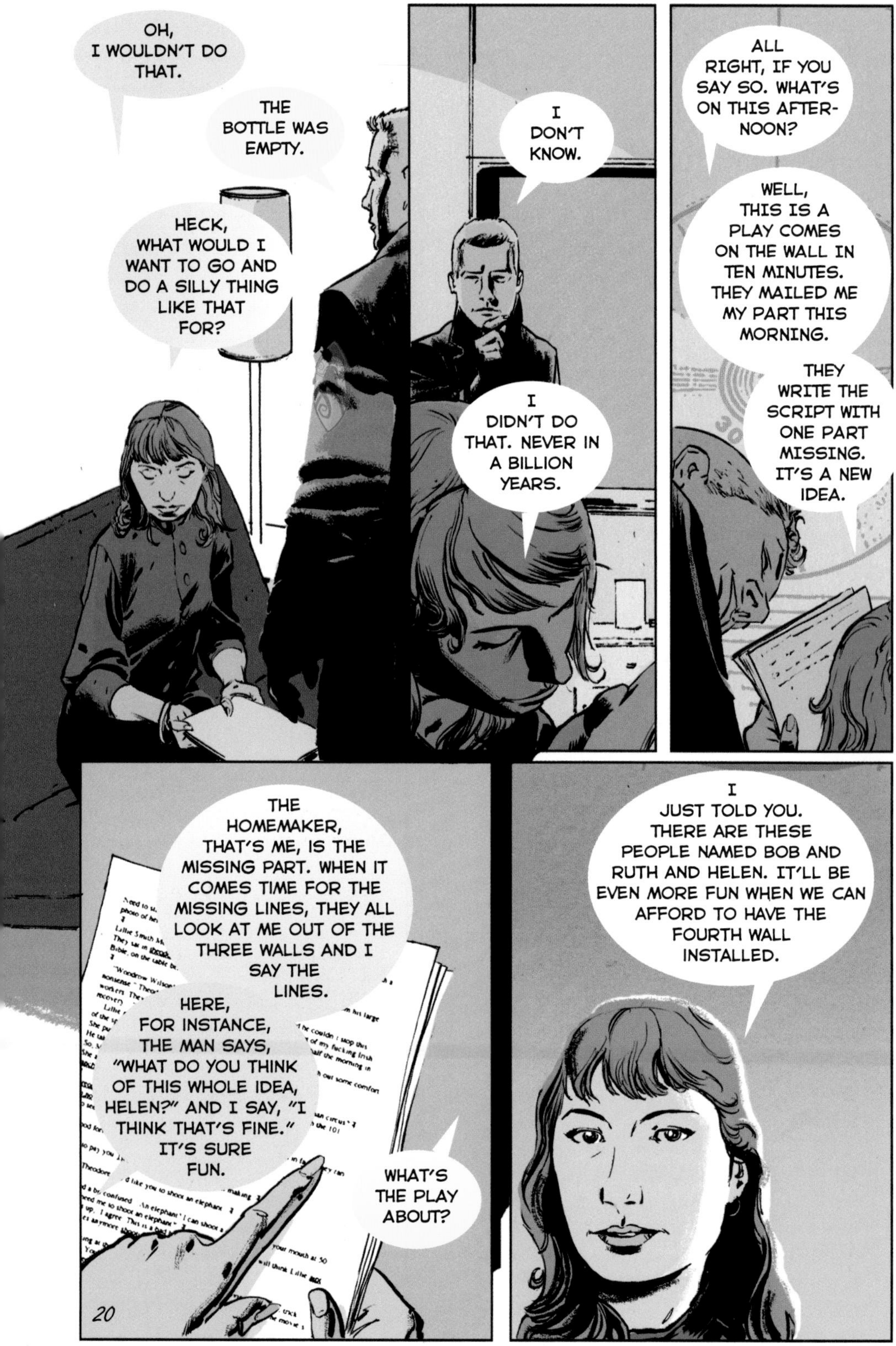
OH, I WOULDN'T DO THAT.
THE BOTTLE WAS EMPTY.
HECK, WHAT WOULD I WANT TO GO AND DO A SILLY THING LIKE THAT FOR?
I DON'T KNOW.
I DIDN'T DO THAT. NEVER IN A BILLION YEARS.
ALL RIGHT, IF YOU SAY SO. WHAT'S ON THIS AFTERNOON?
WELL, THIS IS A PLAY COMES ON THE WALL IN TEN MINUTES. THEY MAILED ME MY PART THIS MORNING.
THEY WRITE THE SCRIPT WITH ONE PART MISSING. IT'S A NEW IDEA.
THE HOMEMAKER, THAT'S ME, IS THE MISSING PART. WHEN IT COMES TIME FOR THE MISSING LINES, THEY ALL LOOK AT ME OUT OF THE THREE WALLS AND I SAY THE LINES.
HERE, FOR INSTANCE, THE MAN SAYS, "WHAT DO YOU THINK OF THIS WHOLE IDEA, HELEN?" AND I SAY, "I THINK THAT'S FINE." IT'S SURE FUN.
WHAT'S THE PLAY ABOUT?
I JUST TOLD YOU. THERE ARE THESE PEOPLE NAMED BOB AND RUTH AND HELEN. IT'LL BE EVEN MORE FUN WHEN WE CAN AFFORD TO HAVE THE FOURTH WALL INSTALLED.

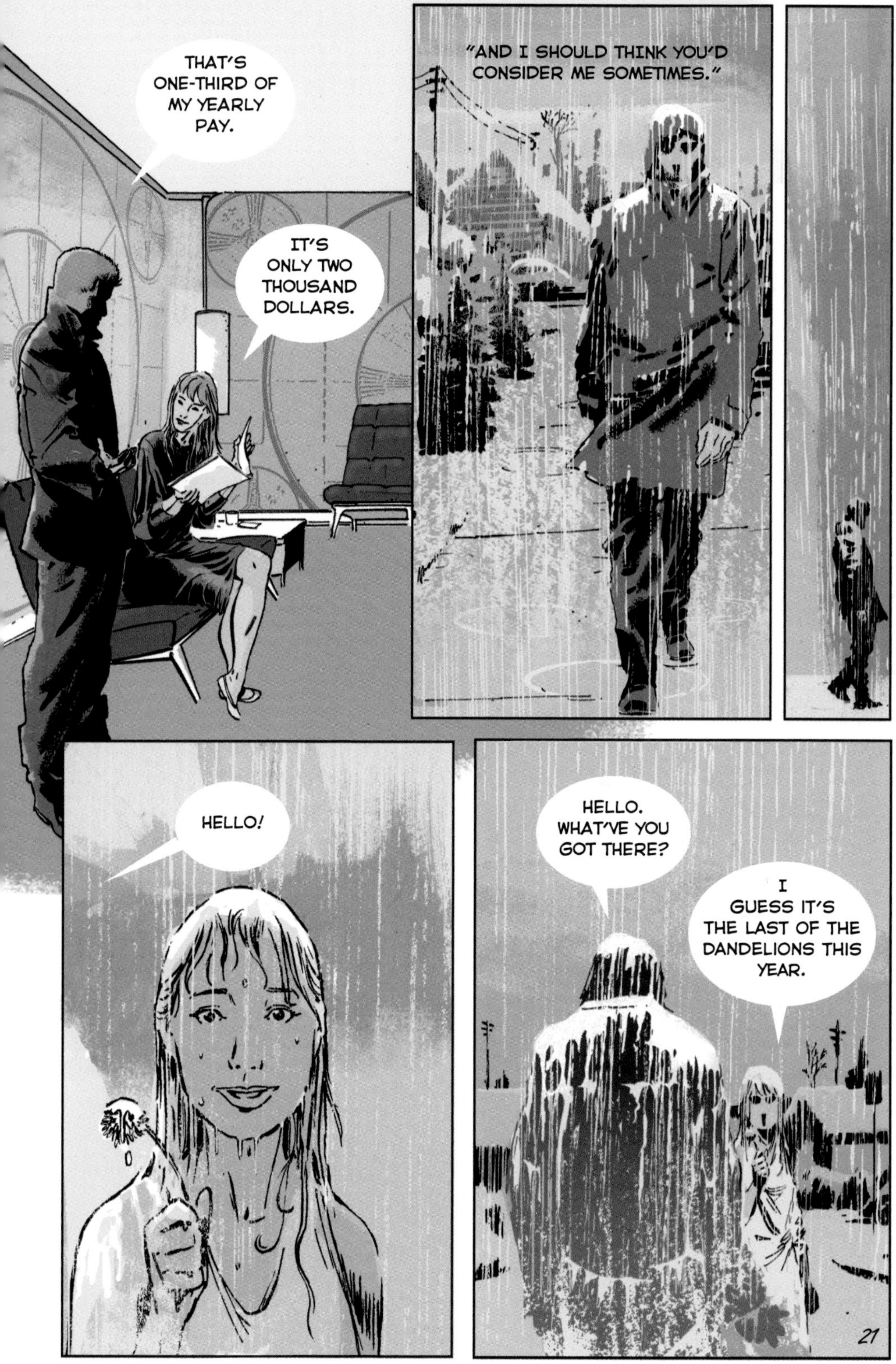
THAT'S ONE-THIRD OF MY YEARLY PAY.
IT'S ONLY TWO THOUSAND DOLLARS.
"AND I SHOULD THINK YOU'D CONSIDER ME SOMETIMES."
HELLO!
HELLO. WHAT'VE YOU GOT THERE?
I GUESS IT'S THE LAST OF THE DANDELIONS THIS YEAR.

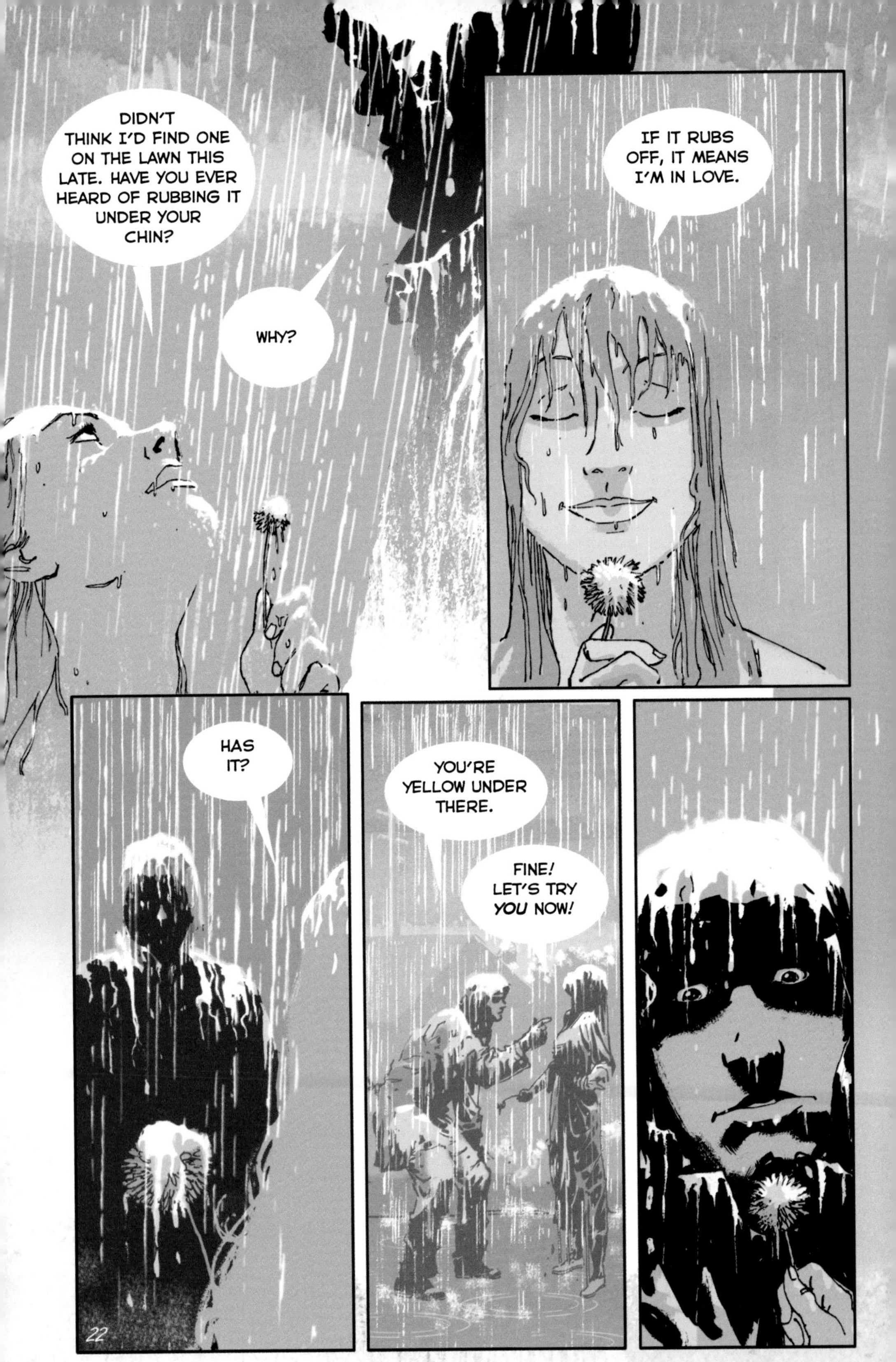
DIDN'T THINK I'D FIND ONE ON THE LAWN THIS LATE. HAVE YOU EVER HEARD OF RUBBING IT UNDER YOUR CHIN?
WHY?
IF IT RUBS OFF, IT MEANS I'M IN LOVE.
HAS IT?
YOU'RE YELLOW UNDER THERE.
FINE! LET'S TRY *YOU* NOW!

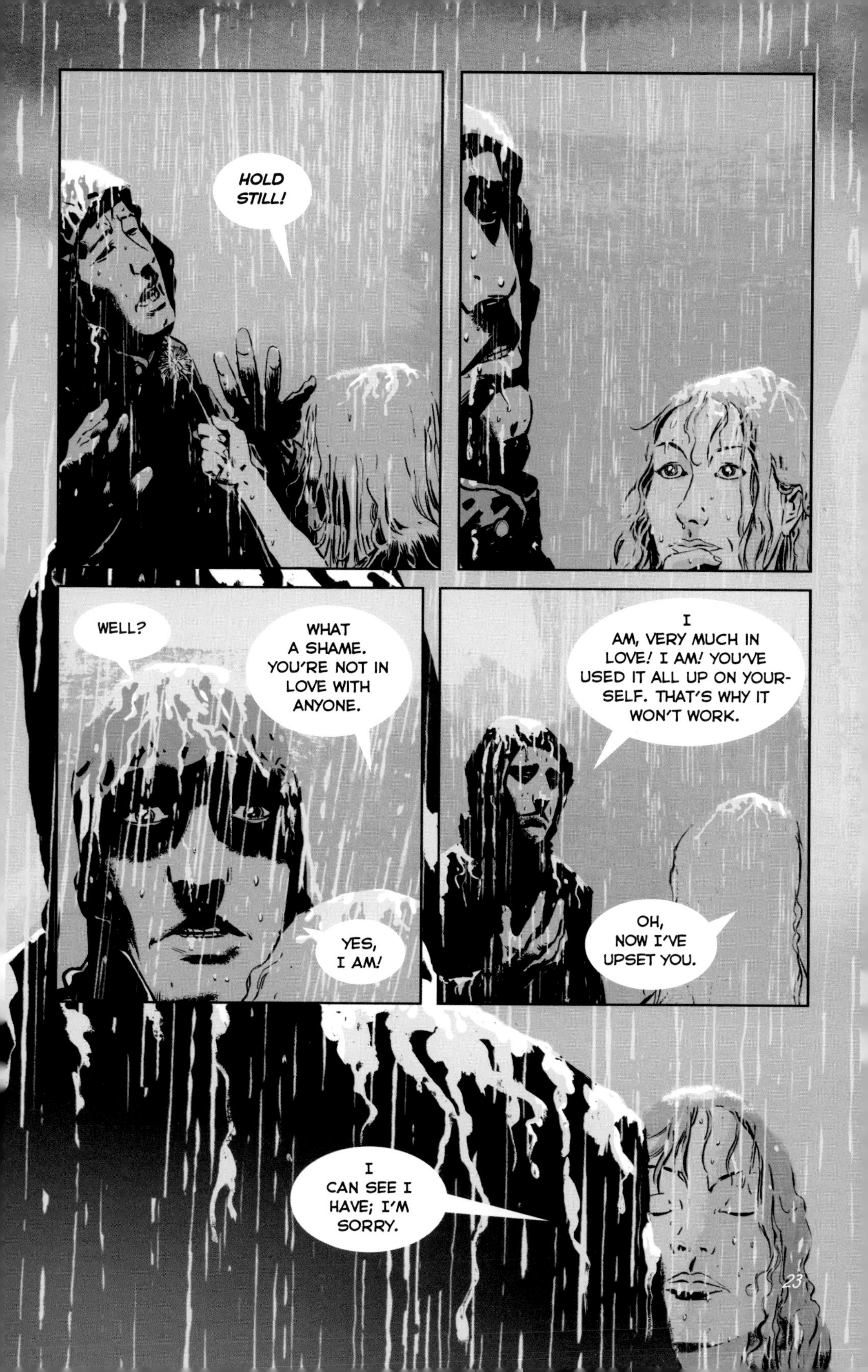

HOLD STILL!
WELL?
WHAT A SHAME. YOU'RE NOT IN LOVE WITH ANYONE.
YES, I AM!
I AM, VERY MUCH IN LOVE! I AM! YOU'VE USED IT ALL UP ON YOURSELF. THAT'S WHY IT WON'T WORK.
OH, NOW I'VE UPSET YOU.
I CAN SEE I HAVE; I'M SORRY.

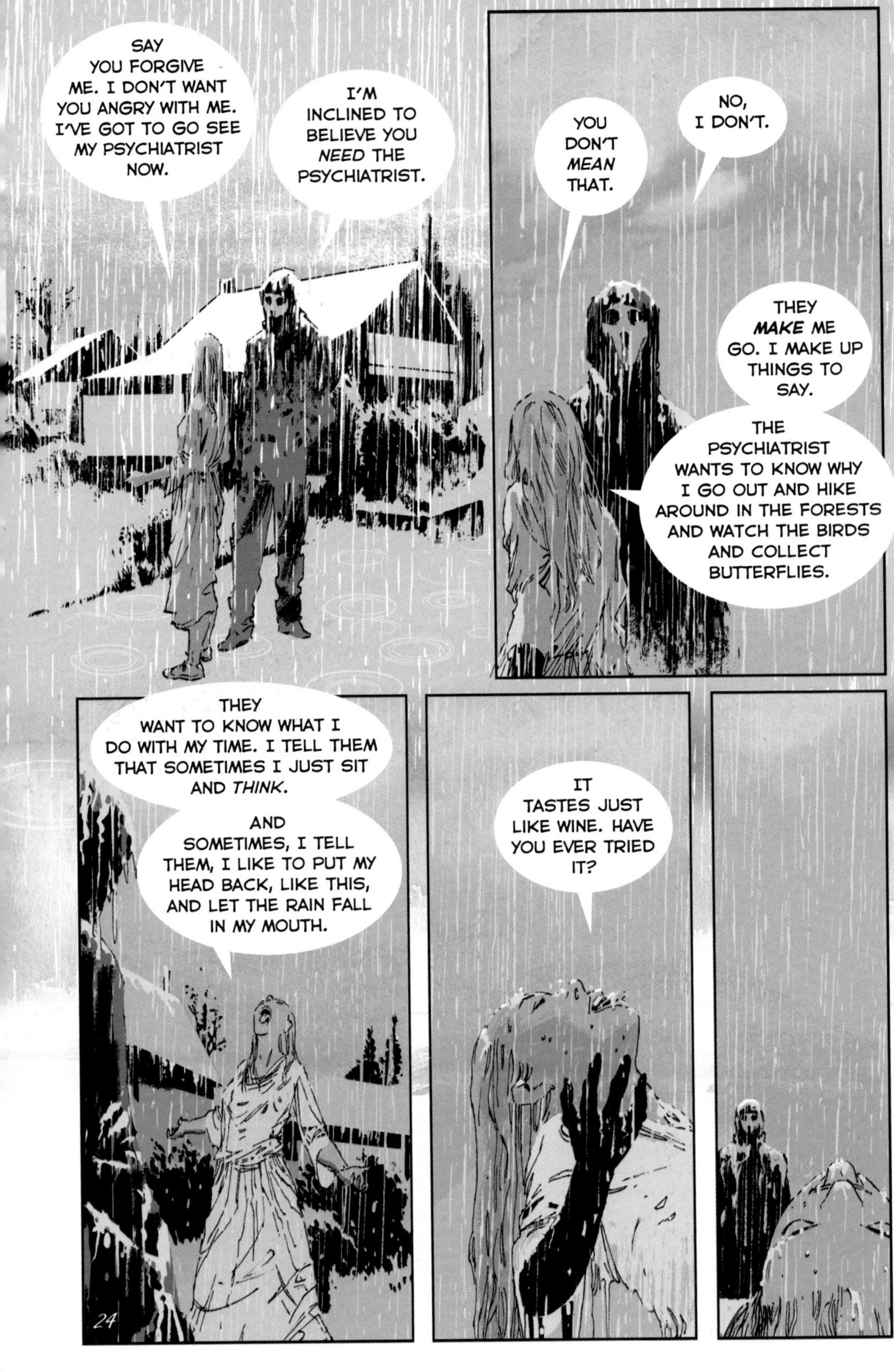
SAY YOU FORGIVE ME. I DON'T WANT YOU ANGRY WITH ME. I'VE GOT TO GO SEE MY PSYCHIATRIST NOW.
I'M INCLINED TO BELIEVE YOU *NEED* THE PSYCHIATRIST.
YOU DON'T *MEAN* THAT.
NO, I DON'T.
THEY ***MAKE*** ME GO. I MAKE UP THINGS TO SAY.
THE PSYCHIATRIST WANTS TO KNOW WHY I GO OUT AND HIKE AROUND IN THE FORESTS AND WATCH THE BIRDS AND COLLECT BUTTERFLIES.
THEY WANT TO KNOW WHAT I DO WITH MY TIME. I TELL THEM THAT SOMETIMES I JUST SIT AND *THINK*.
AND SOMETIMES, I TELL THEM, I LIKE TO PUT MY HEAD BACK, LIKE THIS, AND LET THE RAIN FALL IN MY MOUTH.
IT TASTES JUST LIKE WINE. HAVE YOU EVER TRIED IT?

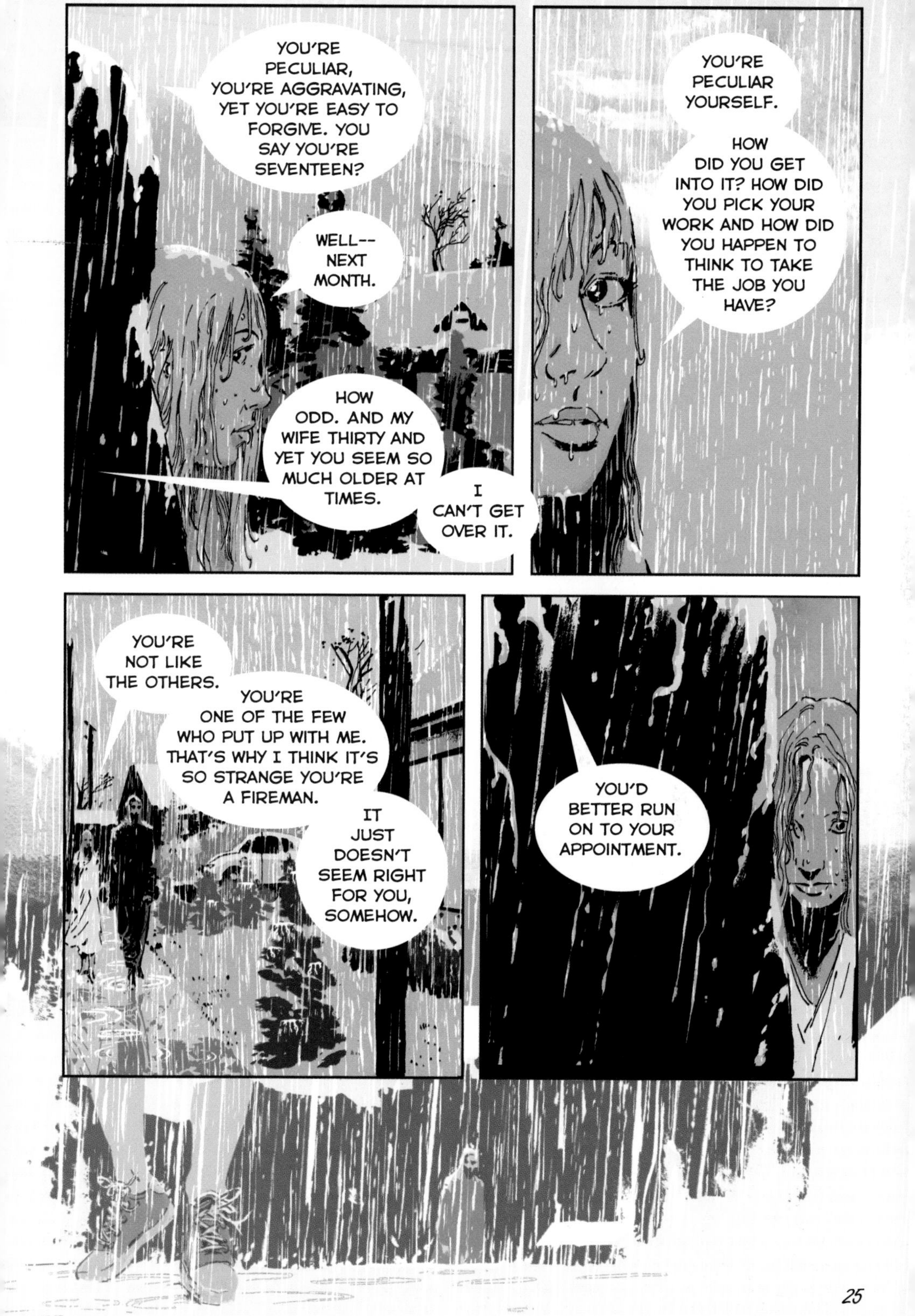
YOU'RE PECULIAR, YOU'RE AGGRAVATING, YET YOU'RE EASY TO FORGIVE. YOU SAY YOU'RE SEVENTEEN?
WELL-- NEXT MONTH.
HOW ODD. AND MY WIFE THIRTY AND YET YOU SEEM SO MUCH OLDER AT TIMES.
I CAN'T GET OVER IT.
YOU'RE PECULIAR YOURSELF.
HOW DID YOU GET INTO IT? HOW DID YOU PICK YOUR WORK AND HOW DID YOU HAPPEN TO THINK TO TAKE THE JOB YOU HAVE?
YOU'RE NOT LIKE THE OTHERS.
YOU'RE ONE OF THE FEW WHO PUT UP WITH ME. THAT'S WHY I THINK IT'S SO STRANGE YOU'RE A FIREMAN.
IT JUST DOESN'T SEEM RIGHT FOR YOU, SOMEHOW.
YOU'D BETTER RUN ON TO YOUR APPOINTMENT.

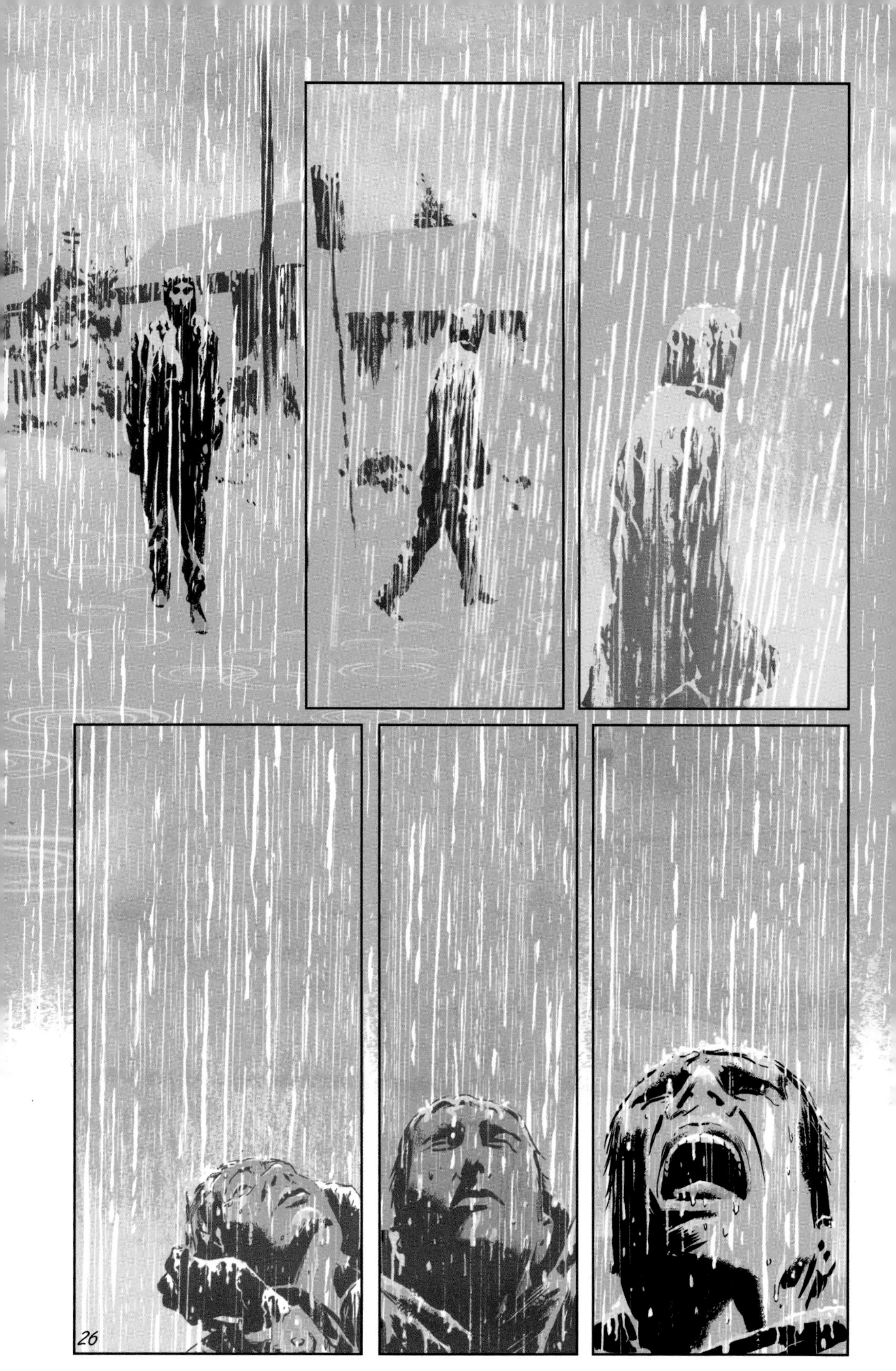

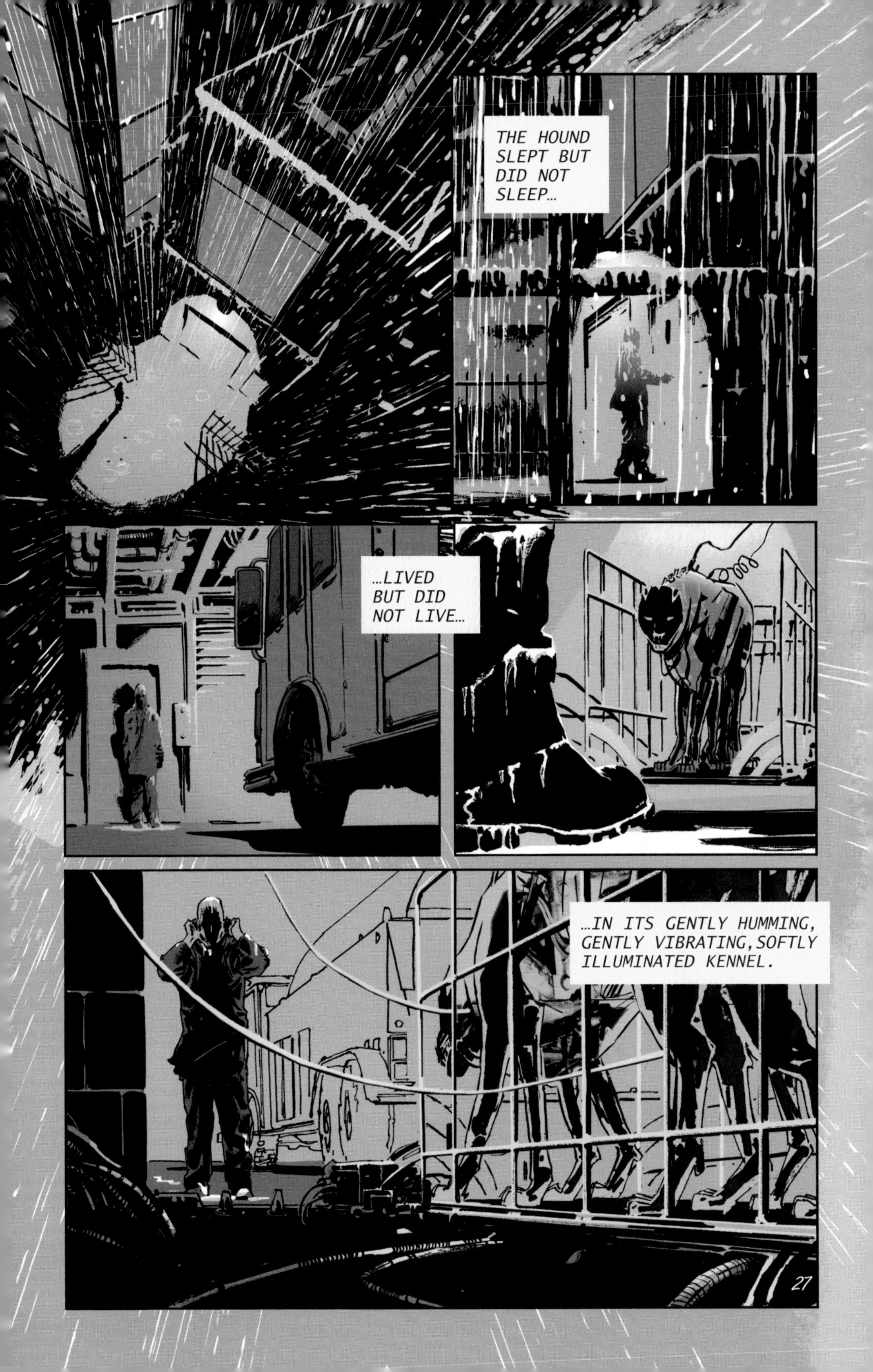

THE HOUND SLEPT BUT DID NOT SLEEP...
...LIVED BUT DID NOT LIVE...
...IN ITS GENTLY HUMMING, GENTLY VIBRATING, SOFTLY ILLUMINATED KENNEL.

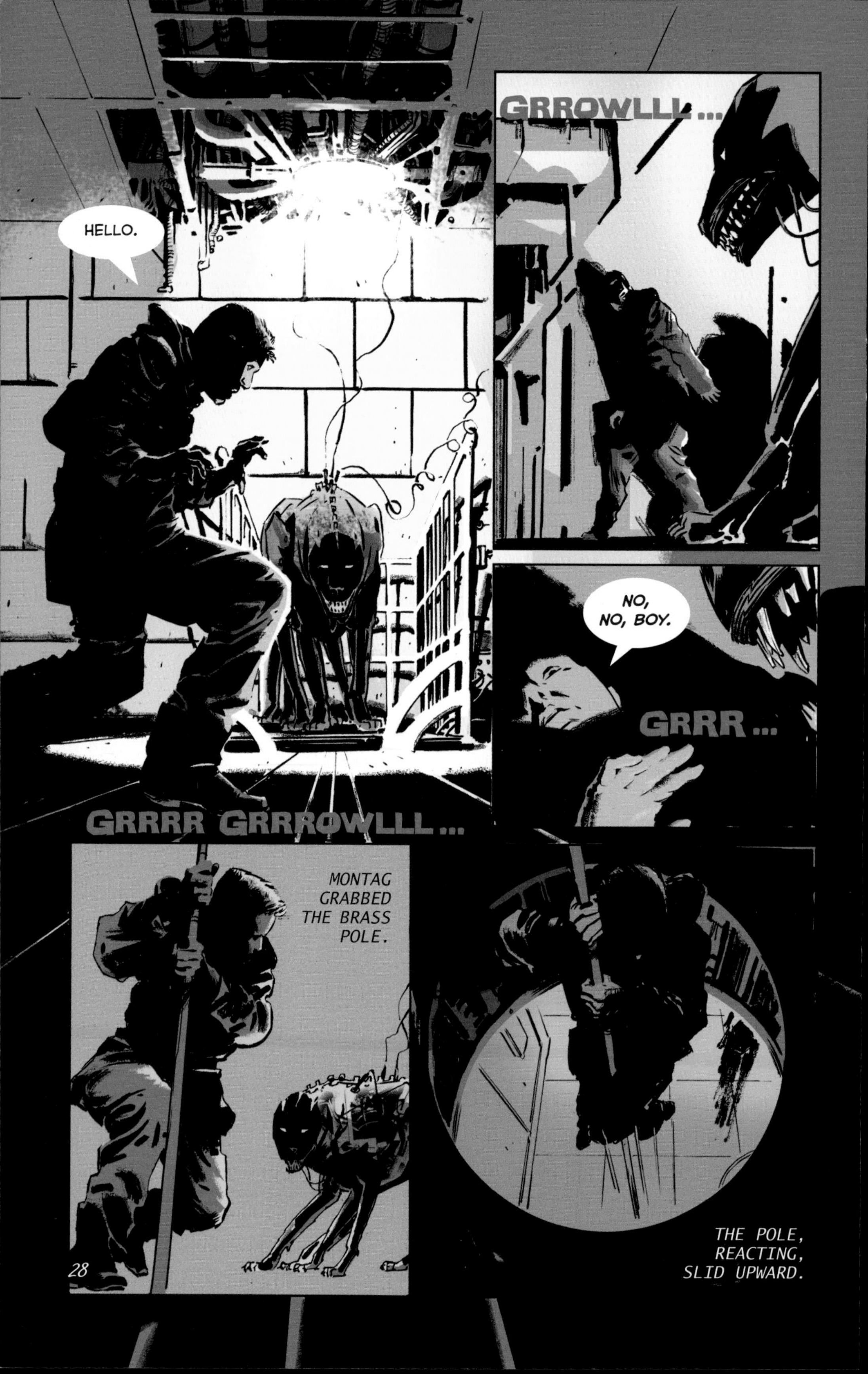
HELLO.
GRROWLLL...
NO, NO, BOY.
GRRR...
GRRRR GRRROWLLL...
MONTAG GRABBED THE BRASS POLE.
THE POLE, REACTING, SLID UPWARD.

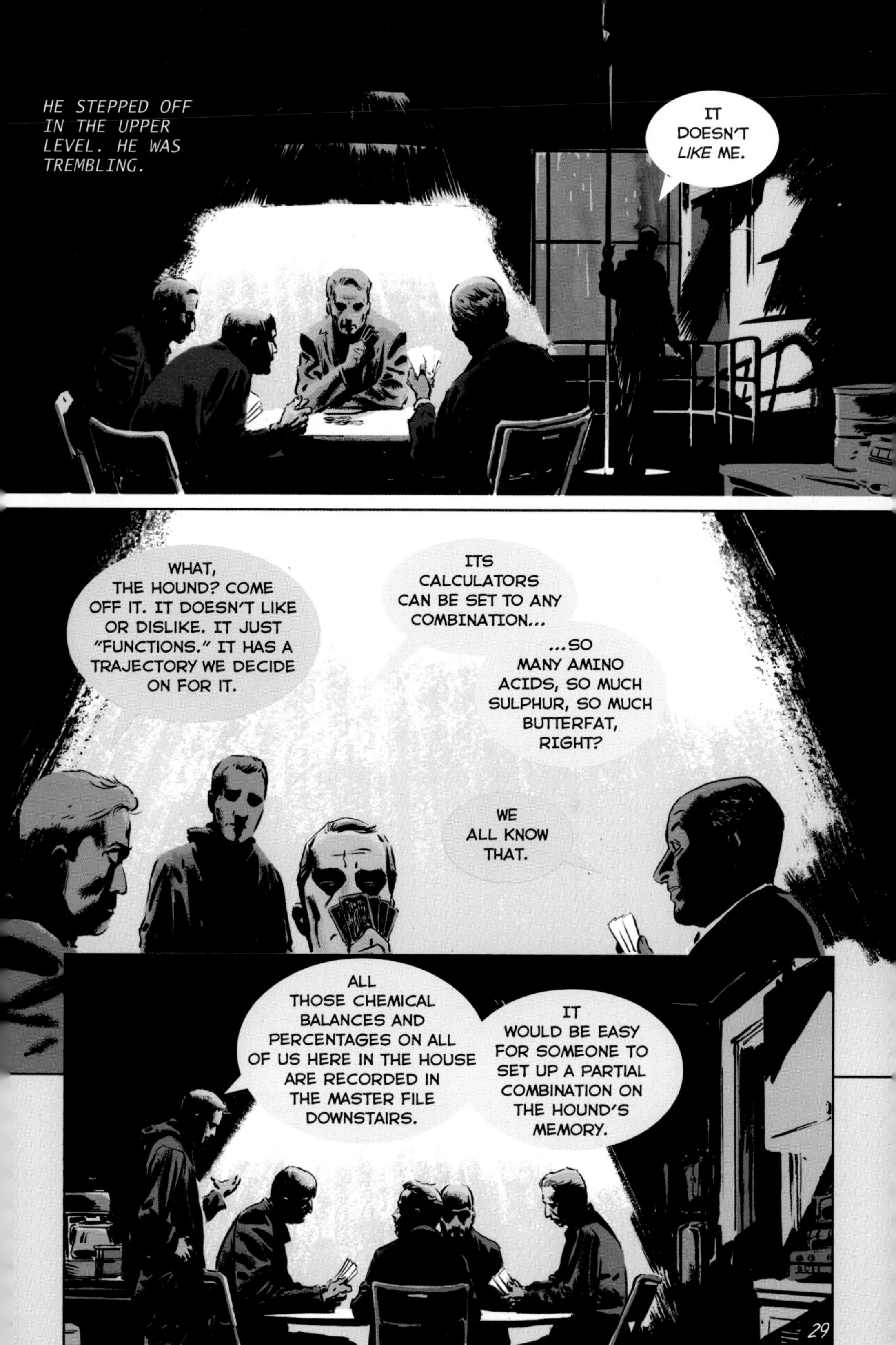
HE STEPPED OFF IN THE UPPER LEVEL. HE WAS TREMBLING.
IT DOESN'T LIKE ME.
WHAT, THE HOUND? COME OFF IT. IT DOESN'T LIKE OR DISLIKE. IT JUST "FUNCTIONS." IT HAS A TRAJECTORY WE DECIDE ON FOR IT.
ITS CALCULATORS CAN BE SET TO ANY COMBINATION...
...SO MANY AMINO ACIDS, SO MUCH SULPHUR, SO MUCH BUTTERFAT, RIGHT?
WE ALL KNOW THAT.
ALL THOSE CHEMICAL BALANCES AND PERCENTAGES ON ALL OF US HERE IN THE HOUSE ARE RECORDED IN THE MASTER FILE DOWNSTAIRS.
IT WOULD BE EASY FOR SOMEONE TO SET UP A PARTIAL COMBINATION ON THE HOUND'S MEMORY.

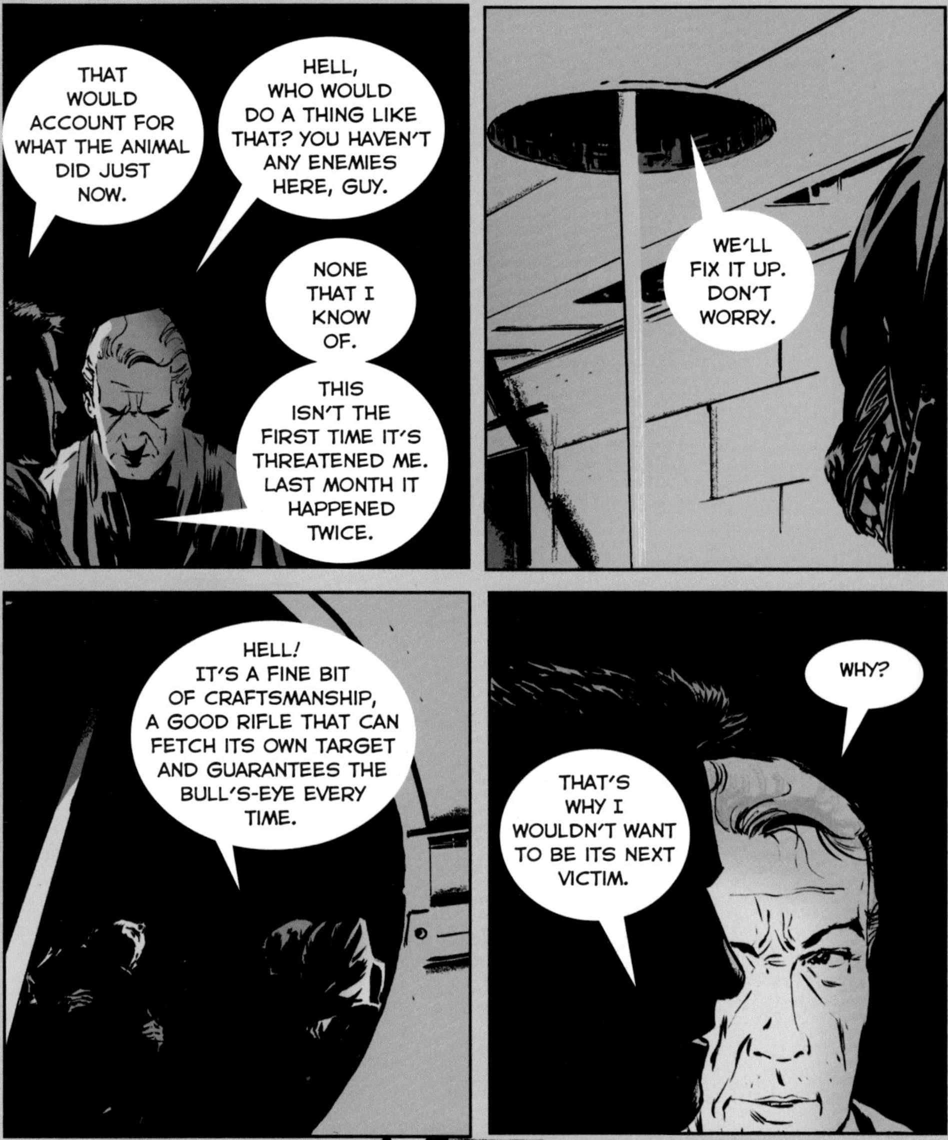
THAT WOULD ACCOUNT FOR WHAT THE ANIMAL DID JUST NOW.
HELL, WHO WOULD DO A THING LIKE THAT? YOU HAVEN'T ANY ENEMIES HERE, GUY.
NONE THAT I KNOW OF.
THIS ISN'T THE FIRST TIME IT'S THREATENED ME. LAST MONTH IT HAPPENED TWICE.
WE'LL FIX IT UP. DON'T WORRY.
HELL! IT'S A FINE BIT OF CRAFTSMANSHIP, A GOOD RIFLE THAT CAN FETCH ITS OWN TARGET AND GUARANTEES THE BULL'S-EYE EVERY TIME.
WHY?
THAT'S WHY I WOULDN'T WANT TO BE ITS NEXT VICTIM.

"YOU GOT A GUILTY CONSCIENCE ABOUT SOMETHING?"

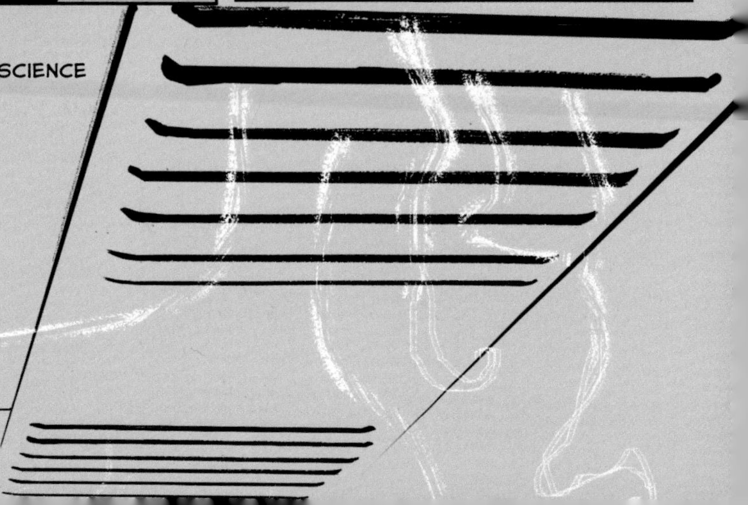

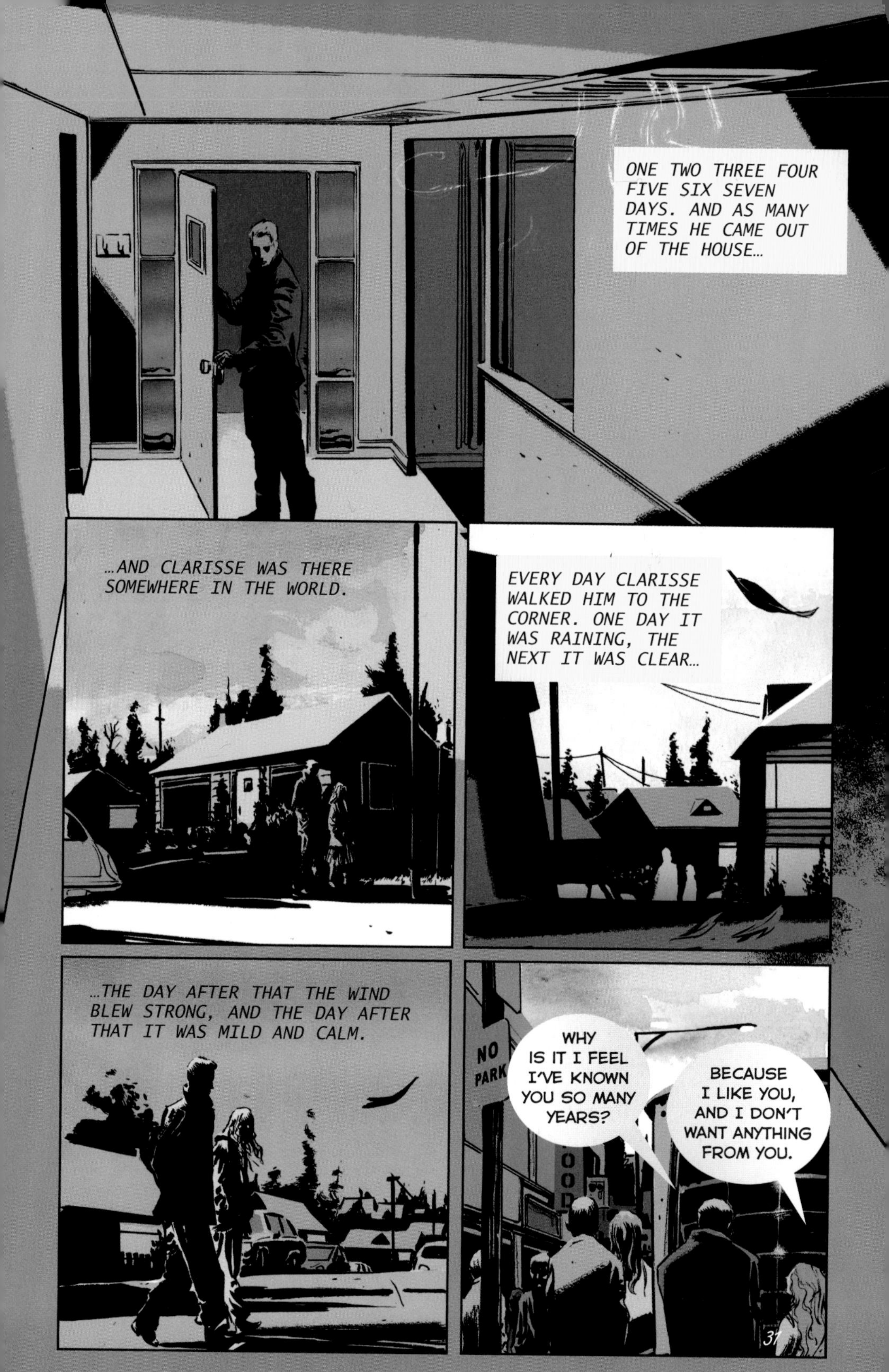
ONE TWO THREE FOUR FIVE SIX SEVEN DAYS. AND AS MANY TIMES HE CAME OUT OF THE HOUSE...
...AND CLARISSE WAS THERE SOMEWHERE IN THE WORLD.
EVERY DAY CLARISSE WALKED HIM TO THE CORNER. ONE DAY IT WAS RAINING, THE NEXT IT WAS CLEAR...
...THE DAY AFTER THAT THE WIND BLEW STRONG, AND THE DAY AFTER THAT IT WAS MILD AND CALM.
NO PARK
WHY IS IT I FEEL I'VE KNOWN YOU SO MANY YEARS?
BECAUSE I LIKE YOU, AND I DON'T WANT ANYTHING FROM YOU.

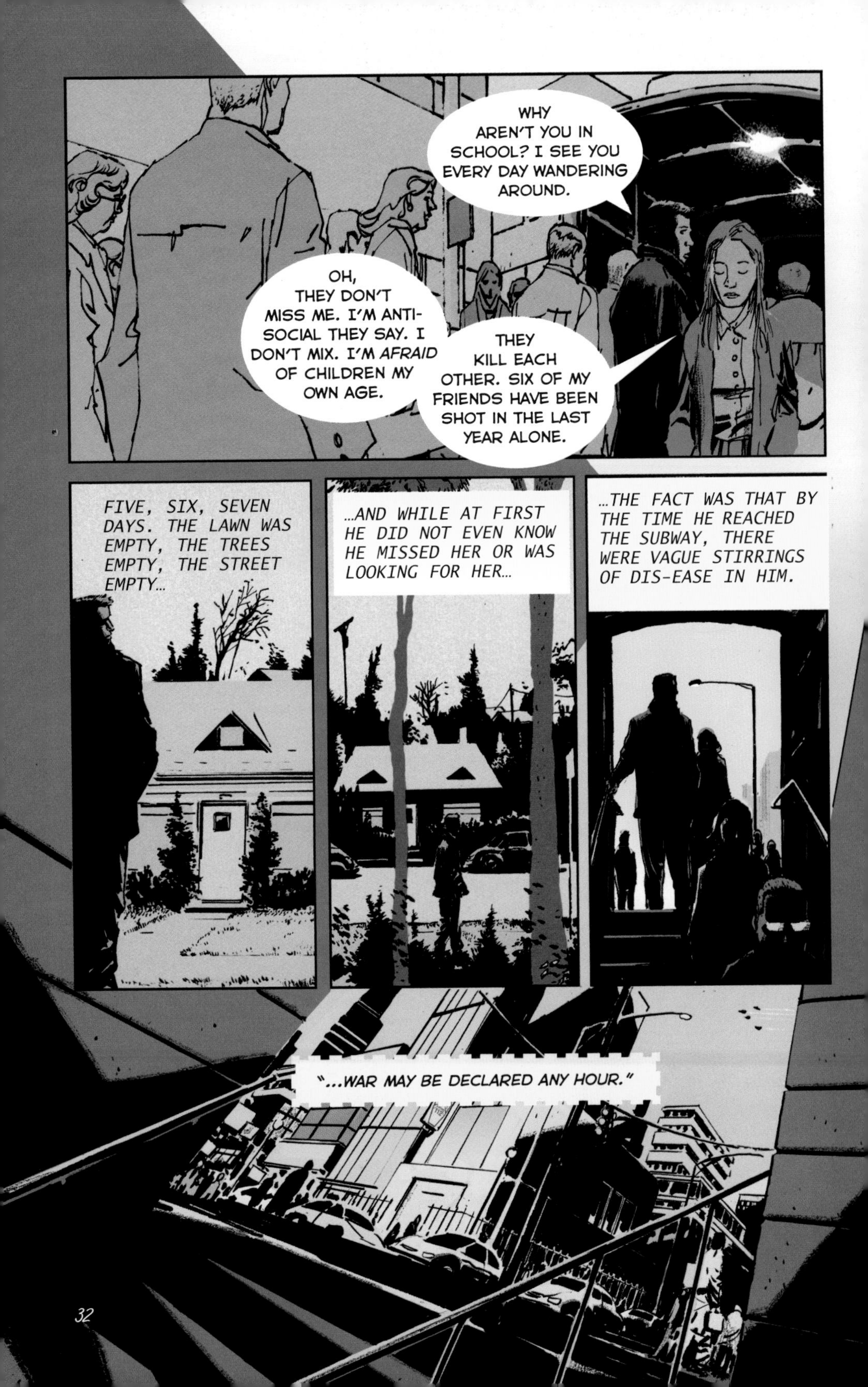
WHY AREN'T YOU IN SCHOOL? I SEE YOU EVERY DAY WANDERING AROUND.
OH, THEY DON'T MISS ME. I'M ANTI-SOCIAL THEY SAY. I DON'T MIX. I'M *AFRAID* OF CHILDREN MY OWN AGE.
THEY KILL EACH OTHER. SIX OF MY FRIENDS HAVE BEEN SHOT IN THE LAST YEAR ALONE.
FIVE, SIX, SEVEN DAYS. THE LAWN WAS EMPTY, THE TREES EMPTY, THE STREET EMPTY...
...AND WHILE AT FIRST HE DID NOT EVEN KNOW HE MISSED HER OR WAS LOOKING FOR HER...
...THE FACT WAS THAT BY THE TIME HE REACHED THE SUBWAY, THERE WERE VAGUE STIRRINGS OF DIS-EASE IN HIM.
"...WAR MAY BE DECLARED ANY HOUR."

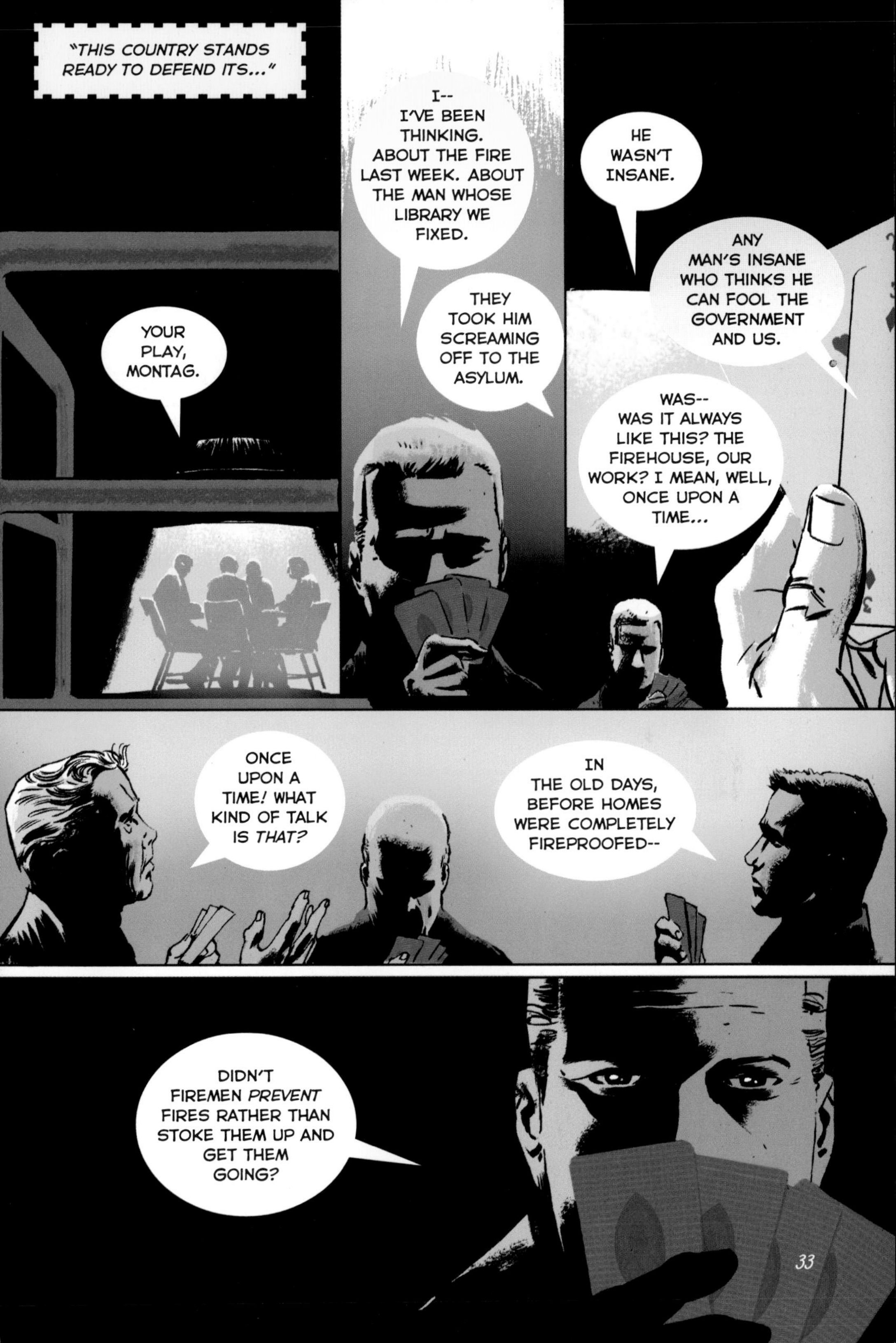
"THIS COUNTRY STANDS READY TO DEFEND ITS..."
YOUR PLAY, MONTAG.
I-- I'VE BEEN THINKING. ABOUT THE FIRE LAST WEEK. ABOUT THE MAN WHOSE LIBRARY WE FIXED.
THEY TOOK HIM SCREAMING OFF TO THE ASYLUM.
HE WASN'T INSANE.
ANY MAN'S INSANE WHO THINKS HE CAN FOOL THE GOVERNMENT AND US.
WAS-- WAS IT ALWAYS LIKE THIS? THE FIREHOUSE, OUR WORK? I MEAN, WELL, ONCE UPON A TIME...
ONCE UPON A TIME! WHAT KIND OF TALK IS *THAT?*
IN THE OLD DAYS, BEFORE HOMES WERE COMPLETELY FIREPROOFED--
DIDN'T FIREMEN *PREVENT* FIRES RATHER THAN STOKE THEM UP AND GET THEM GOING?

THAT'S RICH!

STONEMAN AND BLACK DREW FORTH THEIR RULE BOOKS ...AND LAID THEM OUT WHERE MONTAG MIGHT READ:

Established 1790, to burn English-influenced books in the Colonies. First Fireman: Benjamin Franklin

RULE: 1. Answer the alarm swiftly.
2. Start the fire swiftly.
3. Burn everything.
4. Report back to firehouse immediately.
5. Stand alert for other alarms.

CLANG!
CLANG!
CLANG!

CLANG!
CLANG!
CLANG!

THE ALARM SOUNDED. THE CARDS FELL IN A FLURRY...THE MEN WERE GONE.

WHEEEEOOO O-AAOOO

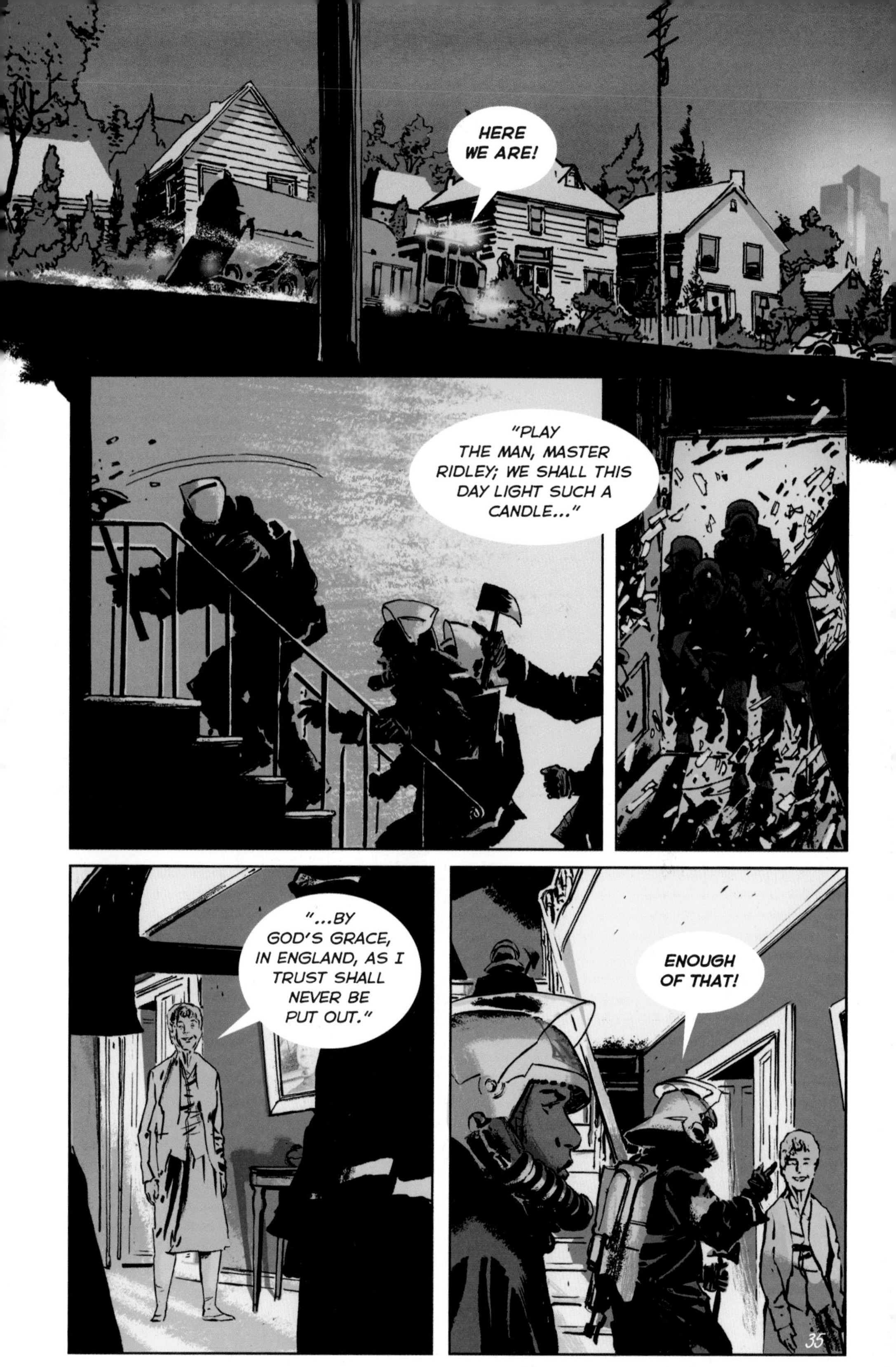
HERE WE ARE!
"PLAY THE MAN, MASTER RIDLEY; WE SHALL THIS DAY LIGHT SUCH A CANDLE..."
"...BY GOD'S GRACE, IN ENGLAND, AS I TRUST SHALL NEVER BE PUT OUT."
ENOUGH OF THAT!

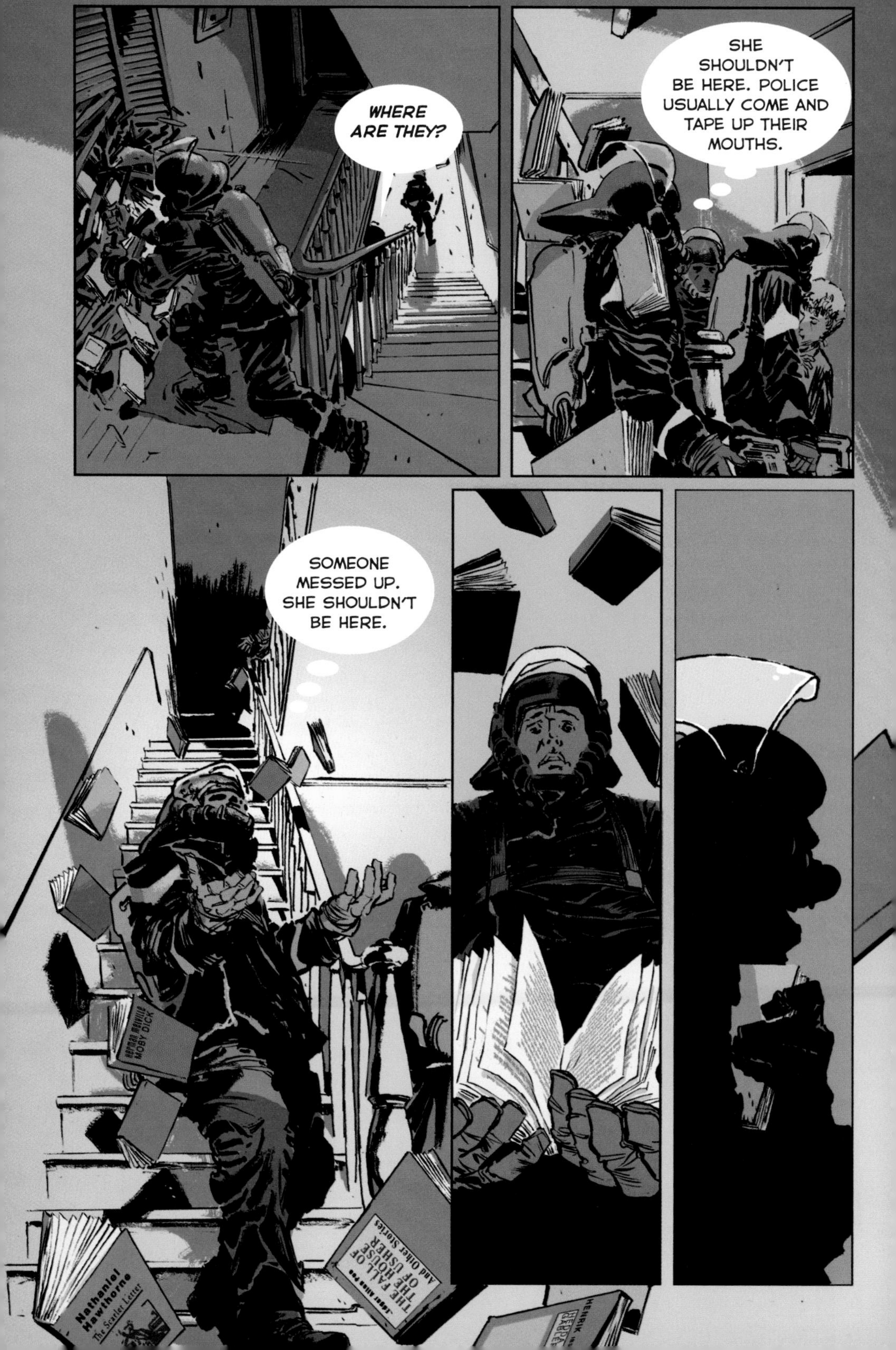
WHERE ARE THEY?
SHE SHOULDN'T BE HERE. POLICE USUALLY COME AND TAPE UP THEIR MOUTHS.
SOMEONE MESSED UP. SHE SHOULDN'T BE HERE.
Herman Melville
MOBY DICK
THE FALL OF THE HOUSE OF USHER
And Other Stories
Edgar Allan Poe
Nathaniel Hawthorne
The Scarlet Letter

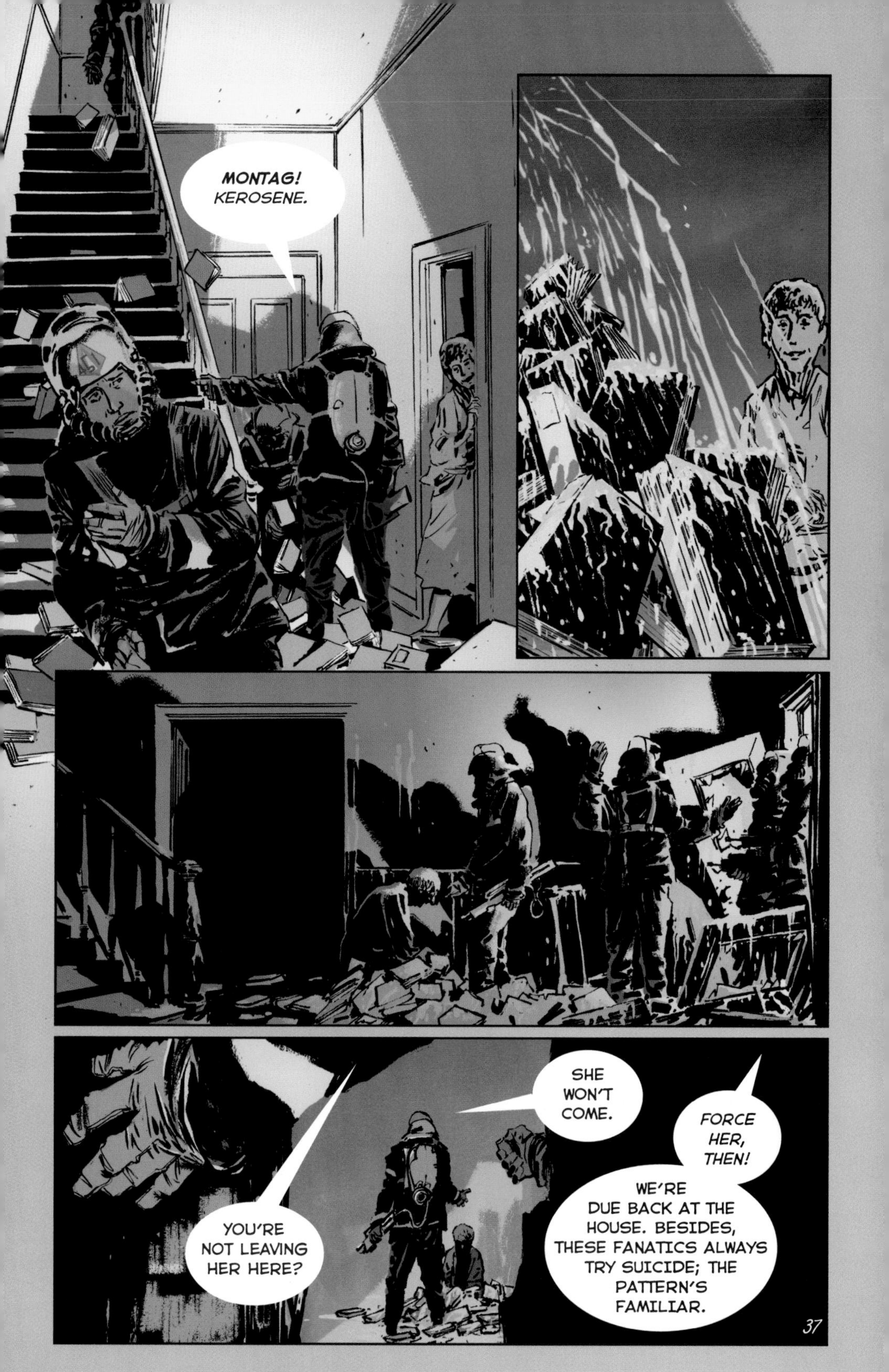
MONTAG! KEROSENE.
YOU'RE NOT LEAVING HER HERE?
SHE WON'T COME.
FORCE HER, THEN!
WE'RE DUE BACK AT THE HOUSE. BESIDES, THESE FANATICS ALWAYS TRY SUICIDE; THE PATTERN'S FAMILIAR.

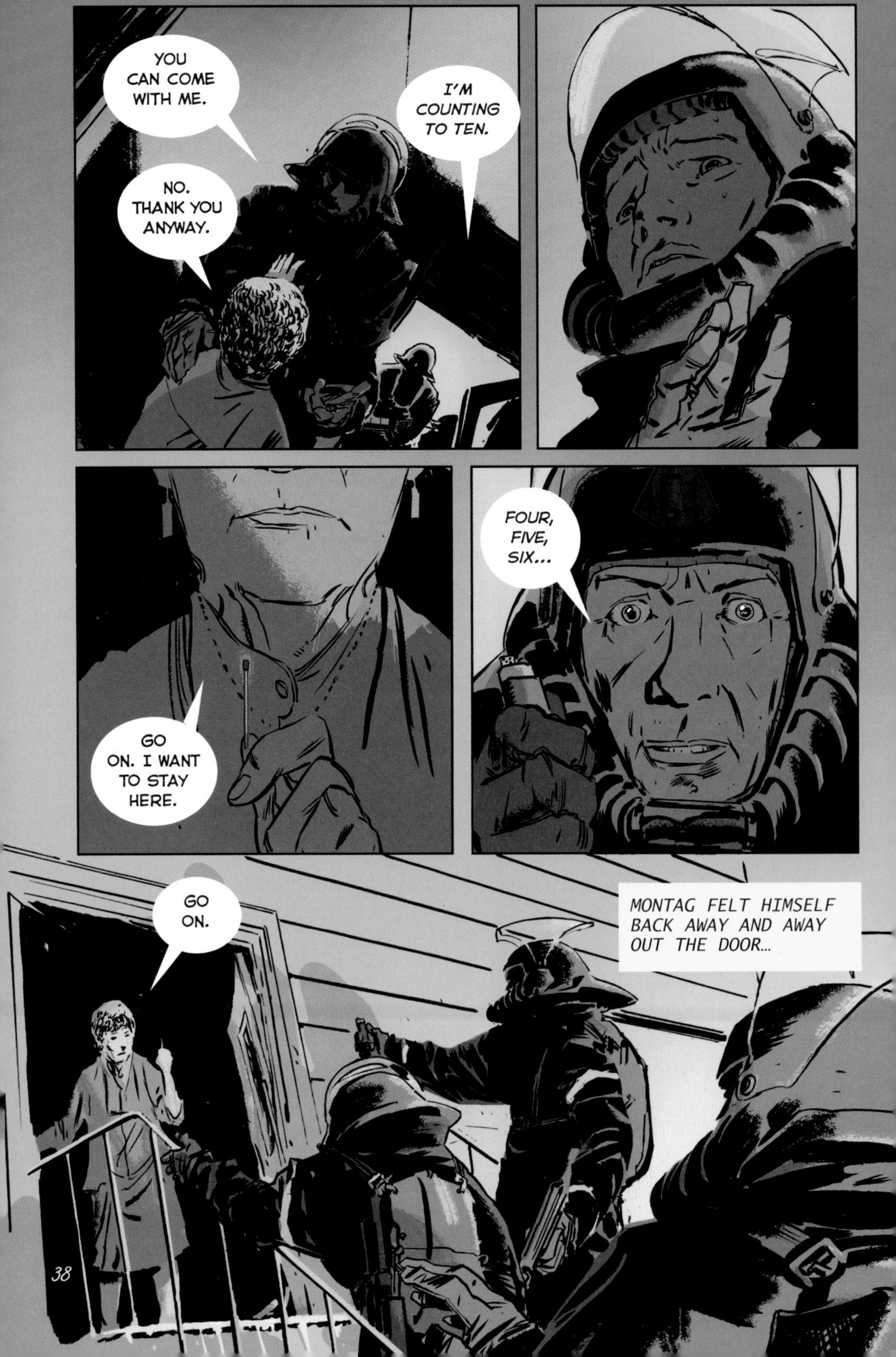
YOU CAN COME WITH ME.
I'M COUNTING TO TEN.
NO. THANK YOU ANYWAY.
GO ON. I WANT TO STAY HERE.
FOUR, FIVE, SIX...
GO ON.
MONTAG FELT HIMSELF BACK AWAY AND AWAY OUT THE DOOR...

...ACROSS THE LAWN, WHERE THE PATH OF KEROSENE LAY LIKE THE TRACK OF SOME EVIL SNAIL.

BEATTY FLICKED HIS FINGERS TO SPARK THE KEROSENE.

HE WAS TOO LATE.

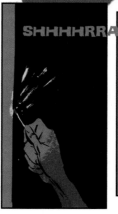

SHHHHRRAAAATCH!

39

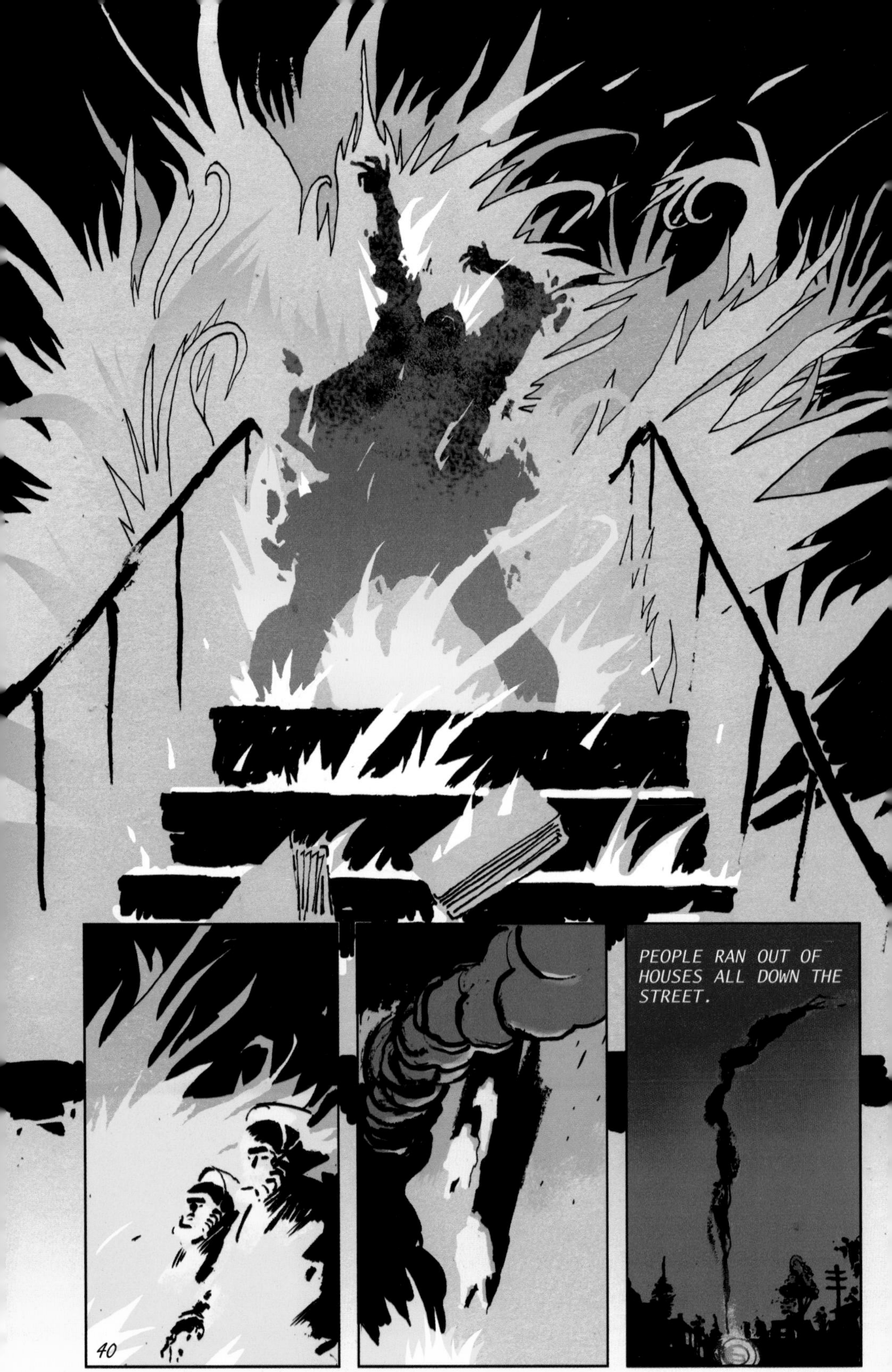
PEOPLE RAN OUT OF HOUSES ALL DOWN THE STREET.

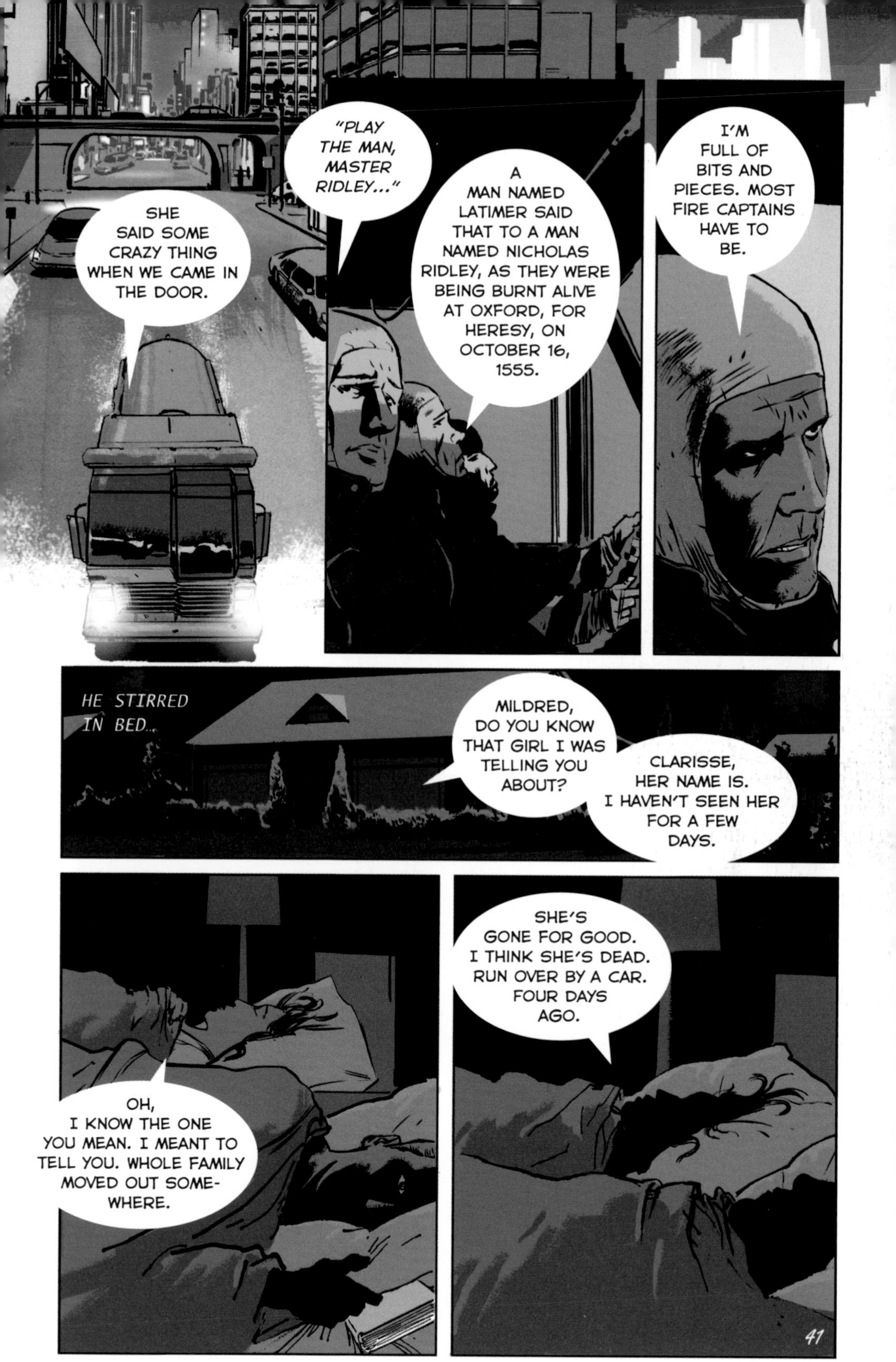
SHE SAID SOME CRAZY THING WHEN WE CAME IN THE DOOR.
"PLAY THE MAN, MASTER RIDLEY..."
A MAN NAMED LATIMER SAID THAT TO A MAN NAMED NICHOLAS RIDLEY, AS THEY WERE BEING BURNT ALIVE AT OXFORD, FOR HERESY, ON OCTOBER 16, 1555.
I'M FULL OF BITS AND PIECES. MOST FIRE CAPTAINS HAVE TO BE.
HE STIRRED IN BED...
MILDRED, DO YOU KNOW THAT GIRL I WAS TELLING YOU ABOUT?
CLARISSE, HER NAME IS. I HAVEN'T SEEN HER FOR A FEW DAYS.
OH, I KNOW THE ONE YOU MEAN. I MEANT TO TELL YOU. WHOLE FAMILY MOVED OUT SOME-WHERE.
SHE'S GONE FOR GOOD. I THINK SHE'S DEAD. RUN OVER BY A CAR. FOUR DAYS AGO.

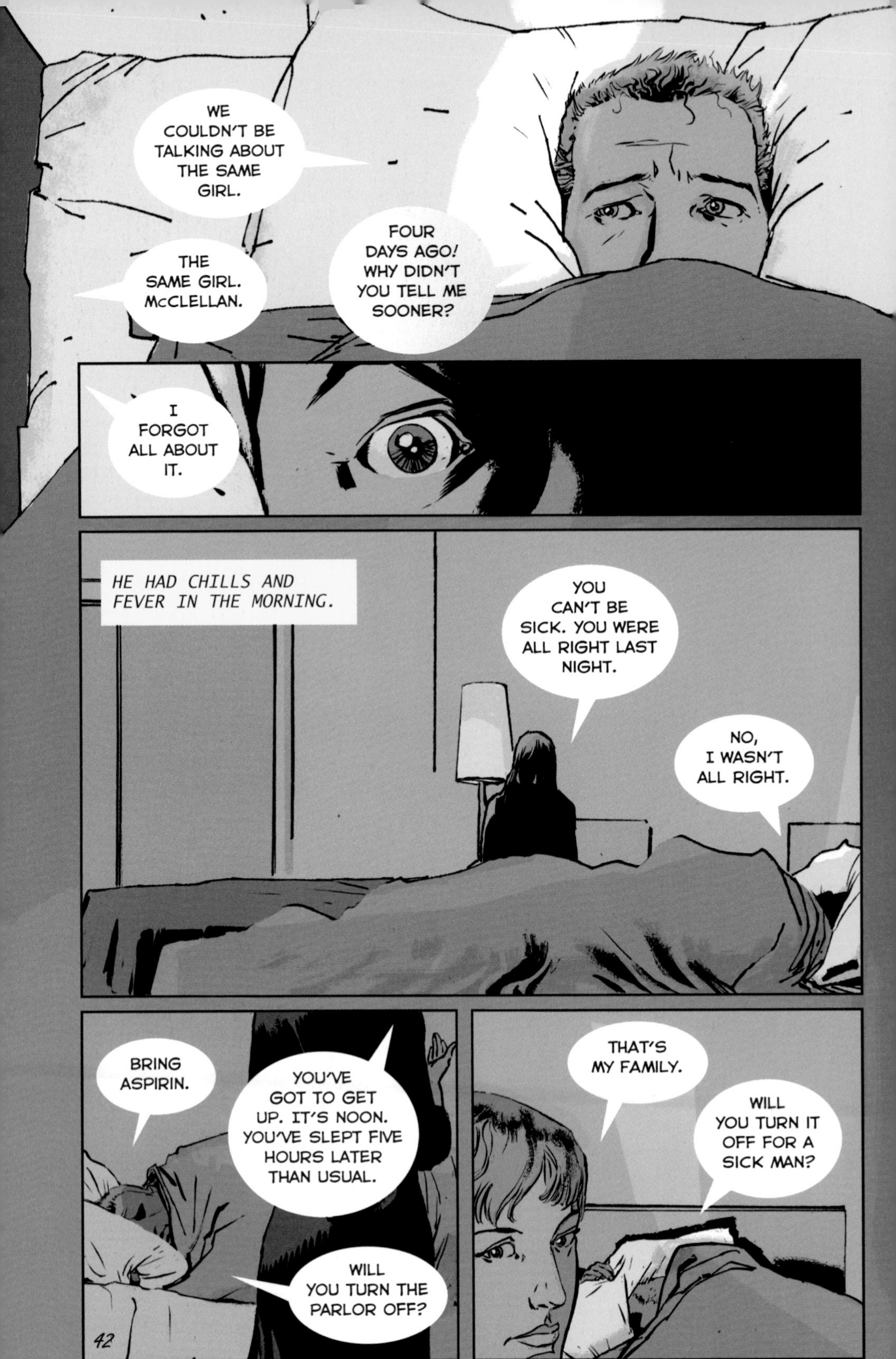
WE COULDN'T BE TALKING ABOUT THE SAME GIRL.
THE SAME GIRL. McCLELLAN.
FOUR DAYS AGO! WHY DIDN'T YOU TELL ME SOONER?
I FORGOT ALL ABOUT IT.
HE HAD CHILLS AND FEVER IN THE MORNING.
YOU CAN'T BE SICK. YOU WERE ALL RIGHT LAST NIGHT.
NO, I WASN'T ALL RIGHT.
BRING ASPIRIN.
YOU'VE GOT TO GET UP. IT'S NOON. YOU'VE SLEPT FIVE HOURS LATER THAN USUAL.
WILL YOU TURN THE PARLOR OFF?
THAT'S MY FAMILY.
WILL YOU TURN IT OFF FOR A SICK MAN?

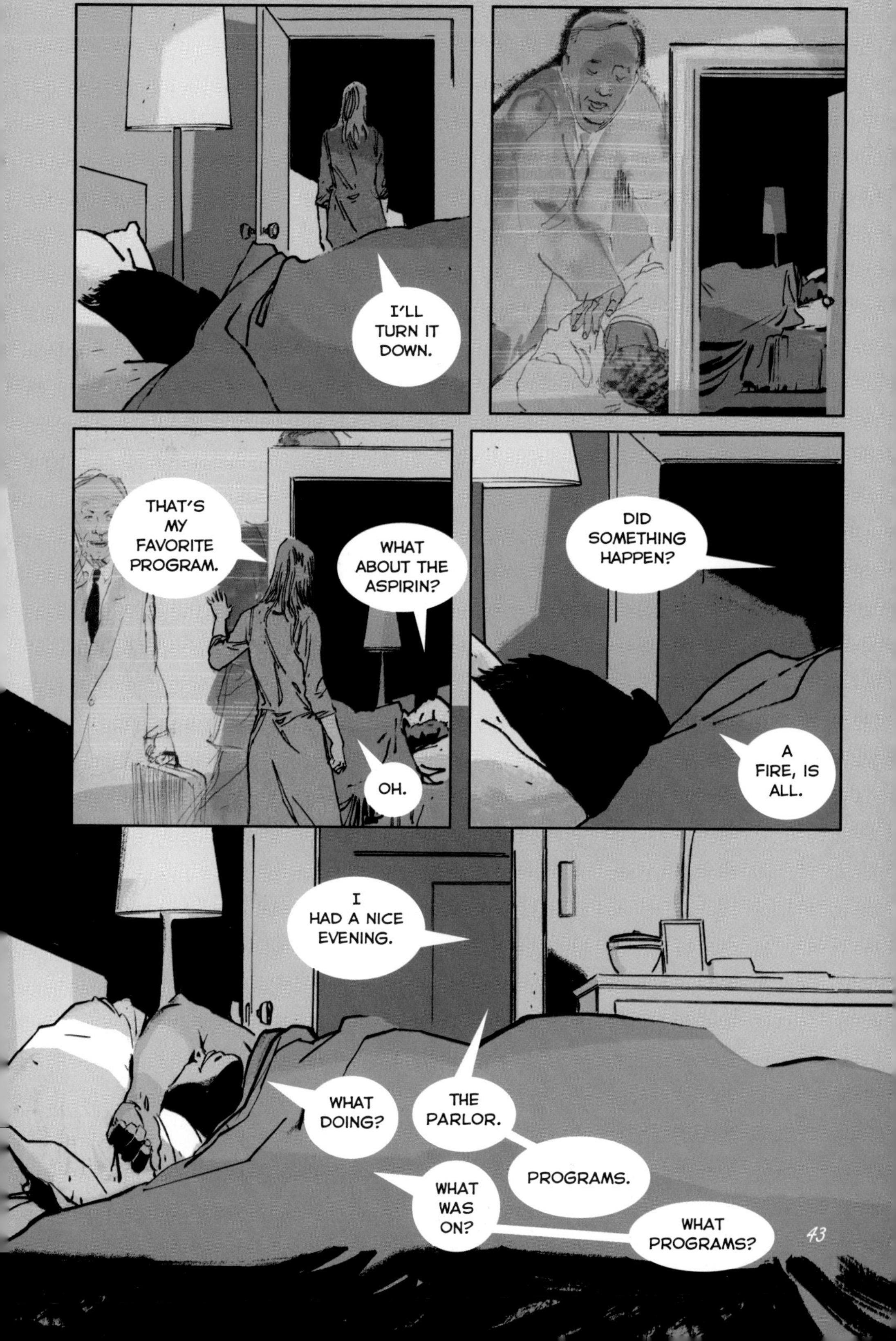
I'LL TURN IT DOWN.
THAT'S MY FAVORITE PROGRAM.
WHAT ABOUT THE ASPIRIN?
OH.
DID SOMETHING HAPPEN?
A FIRE, IS ALL.
I HAD A NICE EVENING.
WHAT DOING?
THE PARLOR.
PROGRAMS.
WHAT WAS ON?
WHAT PROGRAMS?

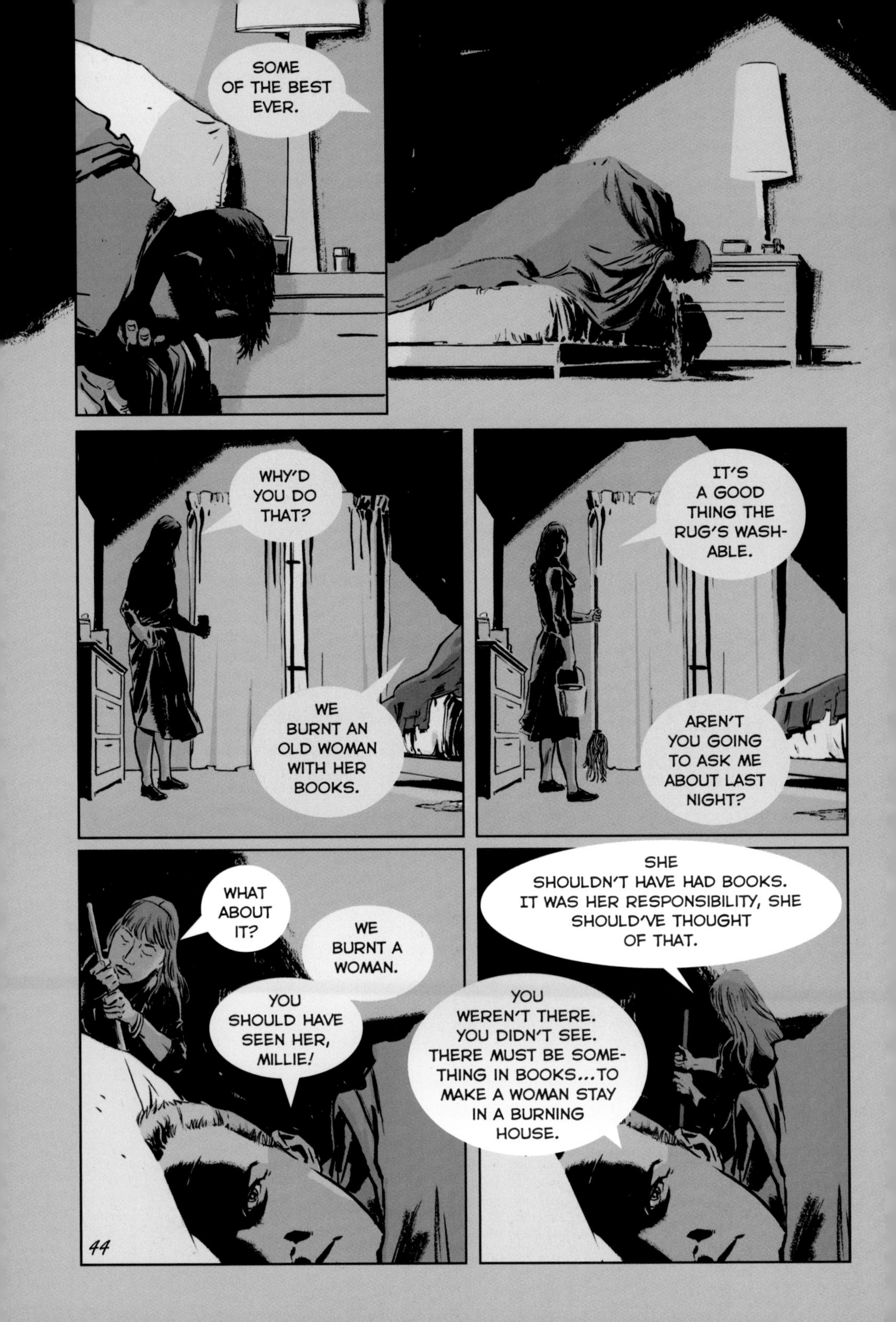
SOME OF THE BEST EVER.
WHY'D YOU DO THAT?
WE BURNT AN OLD WOMAN WITH HER BOOKS.
IT'S A GOOD THING THE RUG'S WASH-ABLE.
AREN'T YOU GOING TO ASK ME ABOUT LAST NIGHT?
WHAT ABOUT IT?
WE BURNT A WOMAN.
YOU SHOULD HAVE SEEN HER, MILLIE!
SHE SHOULDN'T HAVE HAD BOOKS. IT WAS HER RESPONSIBILITY, SHE SHOULD'VE THOUGHT OF THAT.
YOU WEREN'T THERE. YOU DIDN'T SEE. THERE MUST BE SOME-THING IN BOOKS...TO MAKE A WOMAN STAY IN A BURNING HOUSE.

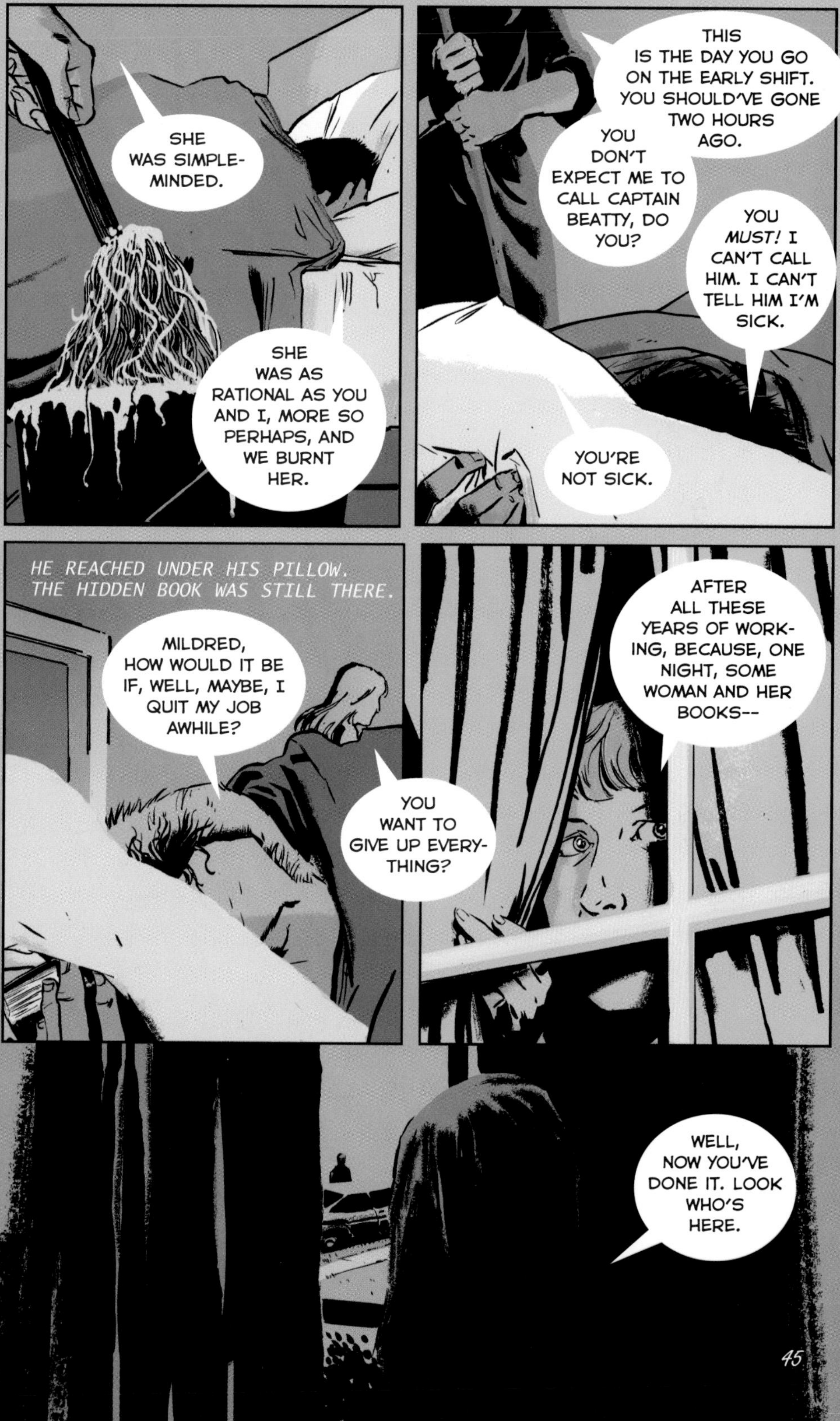
SHE WAS SIMPLE-MINDED.
SHE WAS AS RATIONAL AS YOU AND I, MORE SO PERHAPS, AND WE BURNT HER.
THIS IS THE DAY YOU GO ON THE EARLY SHIFT. YOU SHOULD'VE GONE TWO HOURS AGO.
YOU DON'T EXPECT ME TO CALL CAPTAIN BEATTY, DO YOU?
YOU *MUST!* I CAN'T CALL HIM. I CAN'T TELL HIM I'M SICK.
YOU'RE NOT SICK.
HE REACHED UNDER HIS PILLOW. THE HIDDEN BOOK WAS STILL THERE.
MILDRED, HOW WOULD IT BE IF, WELL, MAYBE, I QUIT MY JOB AWHILE?
YOU WANT TO GIVE UP EVERY-THING?
AFTER ALL THESE YEARS OF WORK-ING, BECAUSE, ONE NIGHT, SOME WOMAN AND HER BOOKS--
WELL, NOW YOU'VE DONE IT. LOOK WHO'S HERE.

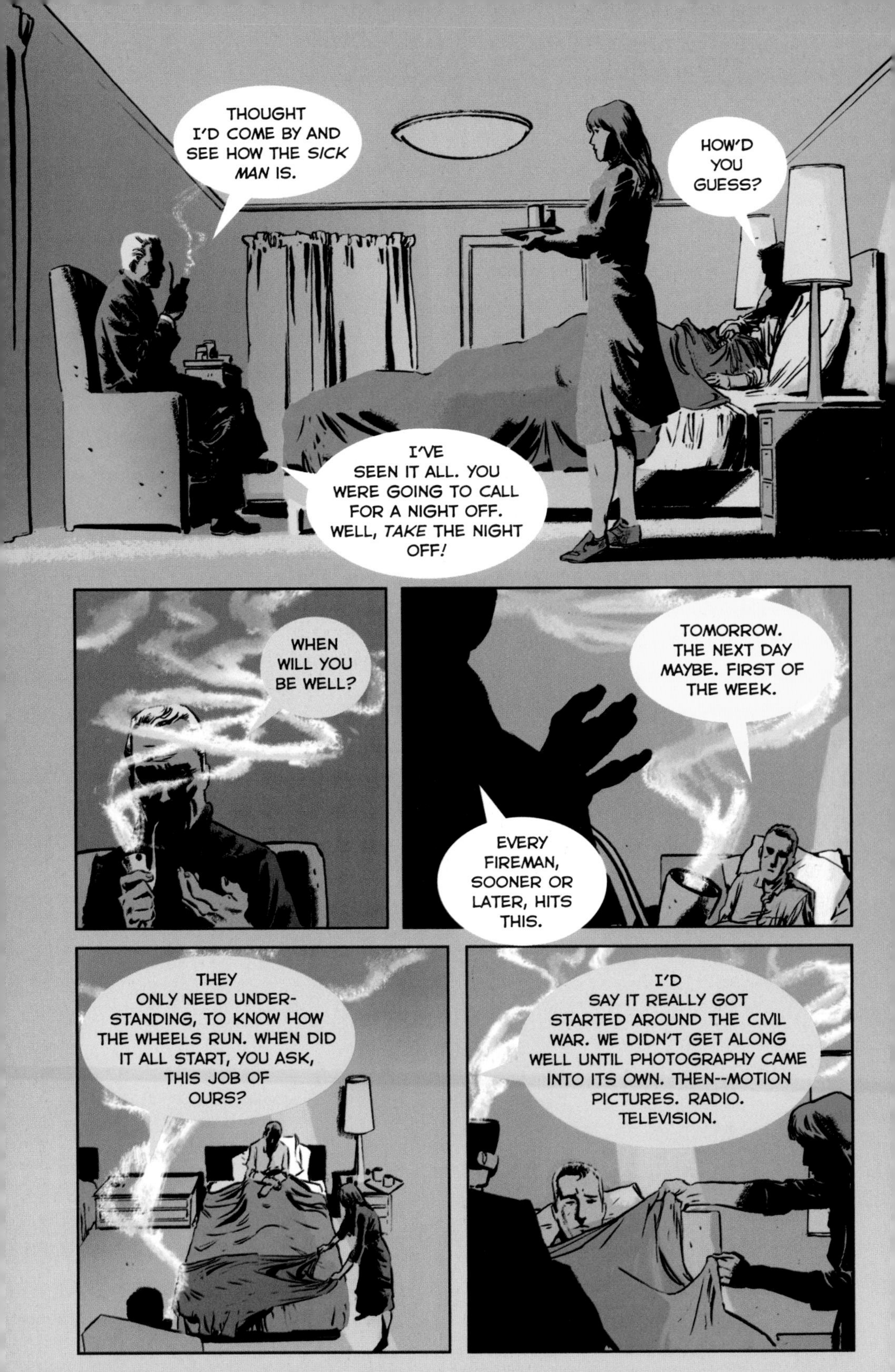
THOUGHT I'D COME BY AND SEE HOW THE *SICK MAN* IS.
HOW'D YOU GUESS?
I'VE SEEN IT ALL. YOU WERE GOING TO CALL FOR A NIGHT OFF. WELL, *TAKE* THE NIGHT OFF!
WHEN WILL YOU BE WELL?
TOMORROW. THE NEXT DAY MAYBE. FIRST OF THE WEEK.
EVERY FIREMAN, SOONER OR LATER, HITS THIS.
THEY ONLY NEED UNDER-STANDING, TO KNOW HOW THE WHEELS RUN. WHEN DID IT ALL START, YOU ASK, THIS JOB OF OURS?
I'D SAY IT REALLY GOT STARTED AROUND THE CIVIL WAR. WE DIDN'T GET ALONG WELL UNTIL PHOTOGRAPHY CAME INTO ITS OWN. THEN--MOTION PICTURES. RADIO. TELEVISION.

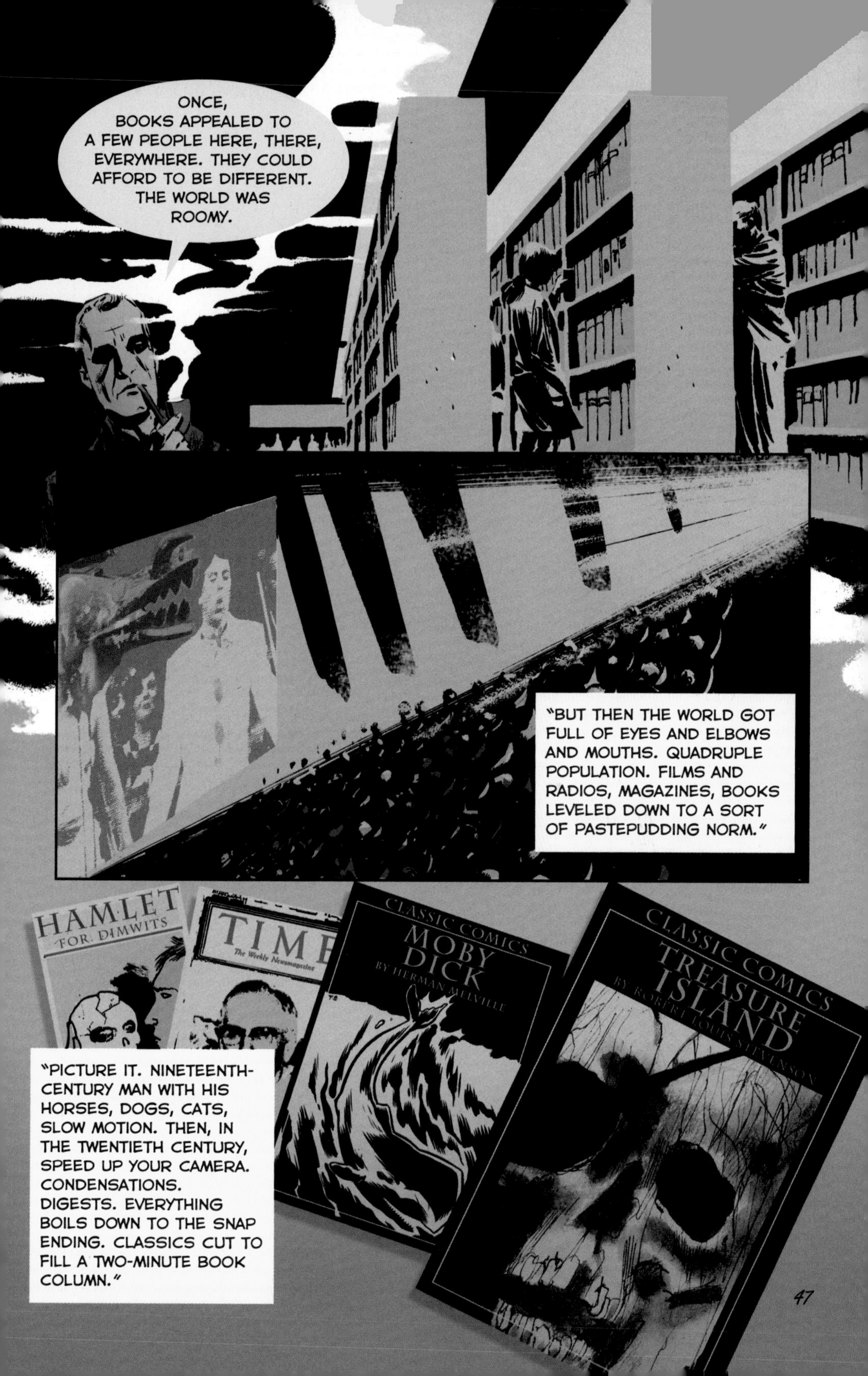
ONCE, BOOKS APPEALED TO A FEW PEOPLE HERE, THERE, EVERYWHERE. THEY COULD AFFORD TO BE DIFFERENT. THE WORLD WAS ROOMY.
"BUT THEN THE WORLD GOT FULL OF EYES AND ELBOWS AND MOUTHS. QUADRUPLE POPULATION. FILMS AND RADIOS, MAGAZINES, BOOKS LEVELED DOWN TO A SORT OF PASTEPUDDING NORM."
HAMLET FOR DIMWITS
TIME
The Weekly Newsmagazine
CLASSIC COMICS
MOBY DICK
BY HERMAN MELVILLE
CLASSIC COMICS
TREASURE ISLAND
BY ROBERT LOUIS STEVENSON
"PICTURE IT. NINETEENTH-CENTURY MAN WITH HIS HORSES, DOGS, CATS, SLOW MOTION. THEN, IN THE TWENTIETH CENTURY, SPEED UP YOUR CAMERA. CONDENSATIONS. DIGESTS. EVERYTHING BOILS DOWN TO THE SNAP ENDING. CLASSICS CUT TO FILL A TWO-MINUTE BOOK COLUMN."

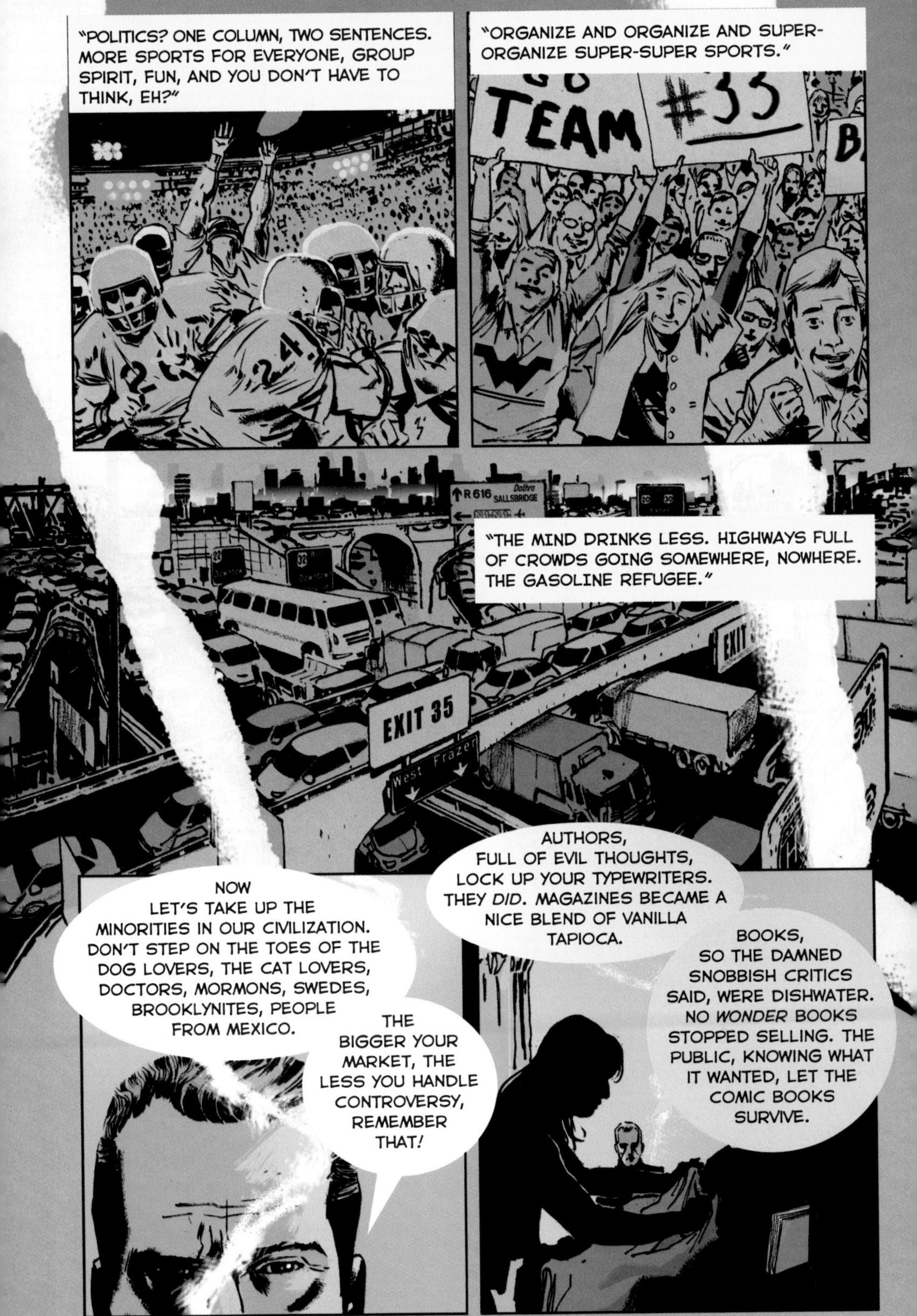
"POLITICS? ONE COLUMN, TWO SENTENCES. MORE SPORTS FOR EVERYONE, GROUP SPIRIT, FUN, AND YOU DON'T HAVE TO THINK, EH?"
"ORGANIZE AND ORGANIZE AND SUPER-ORGANIZE SUPER-SUPER SPORTS."
GO TEAM
#33
R 616
SALLSBRIDGE
"THE MIND DRINKS LESS. HIGHWAYS FULL OF CROWDS GOING SOMEWHERE, NOWHERE. THE GASOLINE REFUGEE."
EXIT
EXIT 35
West Frazer
NOW LET'S TAKE UP THE MINORITIES IN OUR CIVILIZATION. DON'T STEP ON THE TOES OF THE DOG LOVERS, THE CAT LOVERS, DOCTORS, MORMONS, SWEDES, BROOKLYNITES, PEOPLE FROM MEXICO.
THE BIGGER YOUR MARKET, THE LESS YOU HANDLE CONTROVERSY, REMEMBER THAT!
AUTHORS, FULL OF EVIL THOUGHTS, LOCK UP YOUR TYPEWRITERS. THEY *DID*. MAGAZINES BECAME A NICE BLEND OF VANILLA TAPIOCA.
BOOKS, SO THE DAMNED SNOBBISH CRITICS SAID, WERE DISHWATER. NO *WONDER* BOOKS STOPPED SELLING. THE PUBLIC, KNOWING WHAT IT WANTED, LET THE COMIC BOOKS SURVIVE.

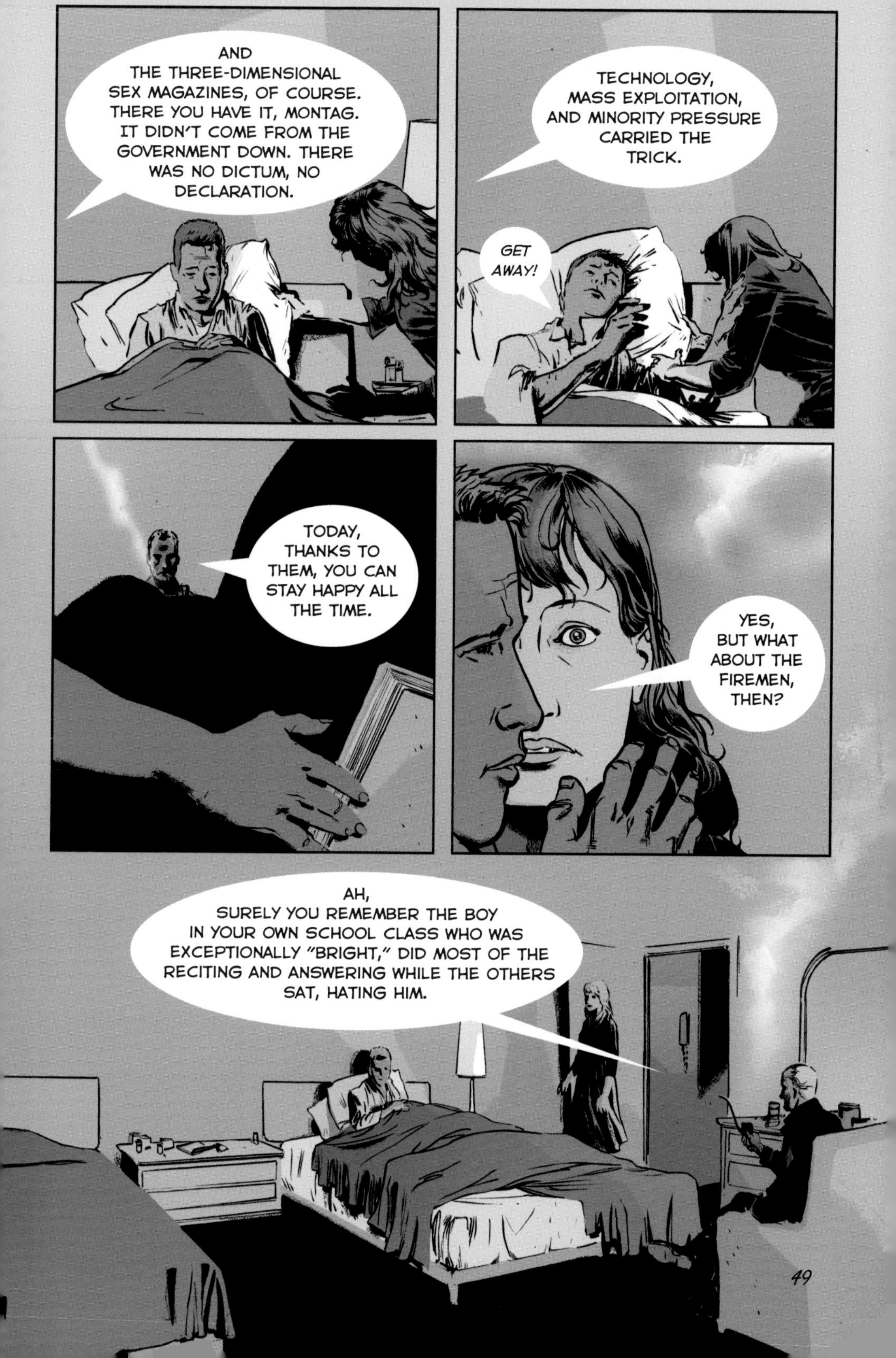
AND THE THREE-DIMENSIONAL SEX MAGAZINES, OF COURSE. THERE YOU HAVE IT, MONTAG. IT DIDN'T COME FROM THE GOVERNMENT DOWN. THERE WAS NO DICTUM, NO DECLARATION.
TECHNOLOGY, MASS EXPLOITATION, AND MINORITY PRESSURE CARRIED THE TRICK.
GET AWAY!
TODAY, THANKS TO THEM, YOU CAN STAY HAPPY ALL THE TIME.
YES, BUT WHAT ABOUT THE FIREMEN, THEN?
AH, SURELY YOU REMEMBER THE BOY IN YOUR OWN SCHOOL CLASS WHO WAS EXCEPTIONALLY "BRIGHT," DID MOST OF THE RECITING AND ANSWERING WHILE THE OTHERS SAT, HATING HIM.

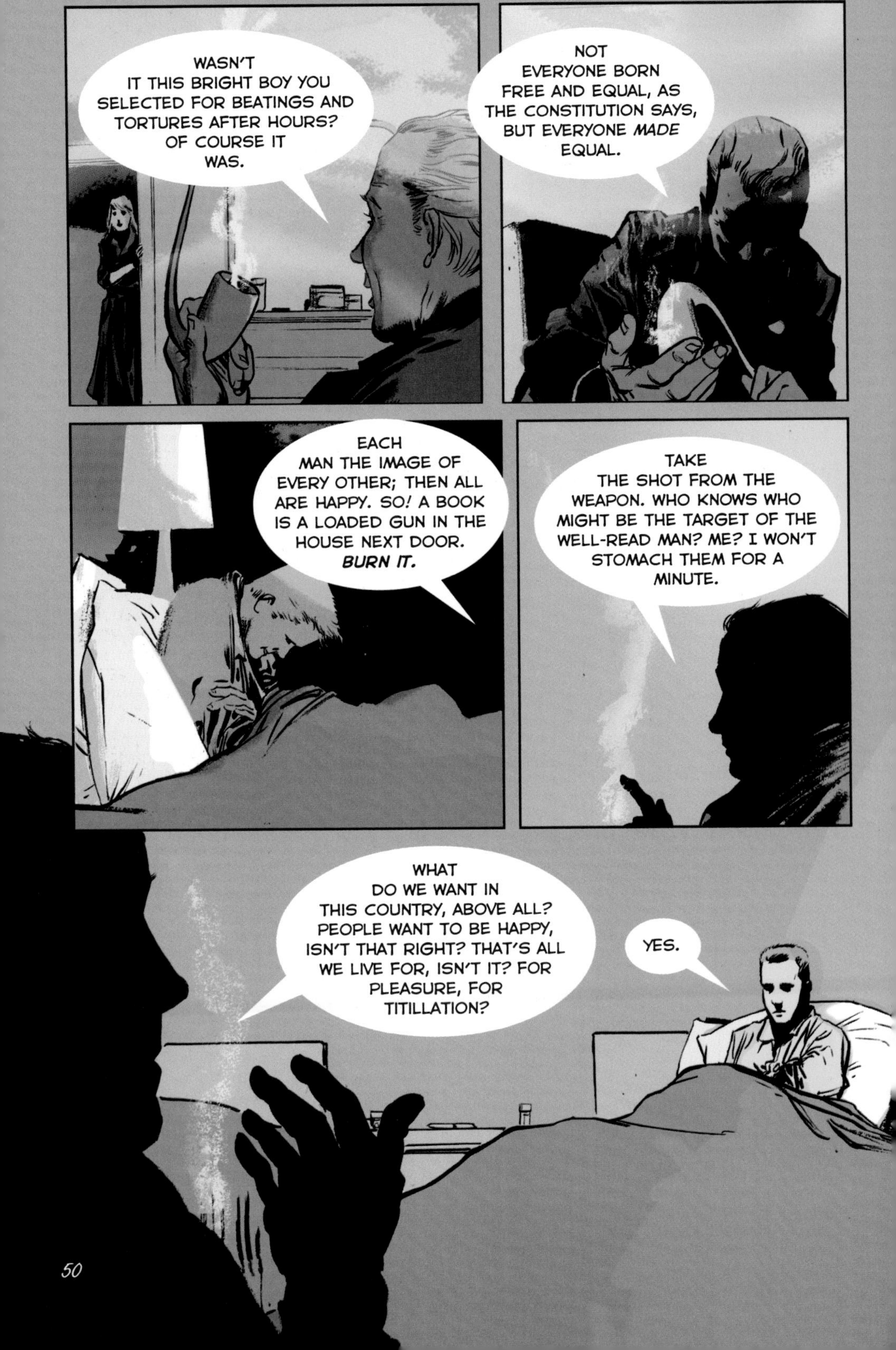
WASN'T IT THIS BRIGHT BOY YOU SELECTED FOR BEATINGS AND TORTURES AFTER HOURS? OF COURSE IT WAS.
NOT EVERYONE BORN FREE AND EQUAL, AS THE CONSTITUTION SAYS, BUT EVERYONE *MADE* EQUAL.
EACH MAN THE IMAGE OF EVERY OTHER; THEN ALL ARE HAPPY. SO! A BOOK IS A LOADED GUN IN THE HOUSE NEXT DOOR. ***BURN IT.***
TAKE THE SHOT FROM THE WEAPON. WHO KNOWS WHO MIGHT BE THE TARGET OF THE WELL-READ MAN? ME? I WON'T STOMACH THEM FOR A MINUTE.
WHAT DO WE WANT IN THIS COUNTRY, ABOVE ALL? PEOPLE WANT TO BE HAPPY, ISN'T THAT RIGHT? THAT'S ALL WE LIVE FOR, ISN'T IT? FOR PLEASURE, FOR TITILLATION?
YES.

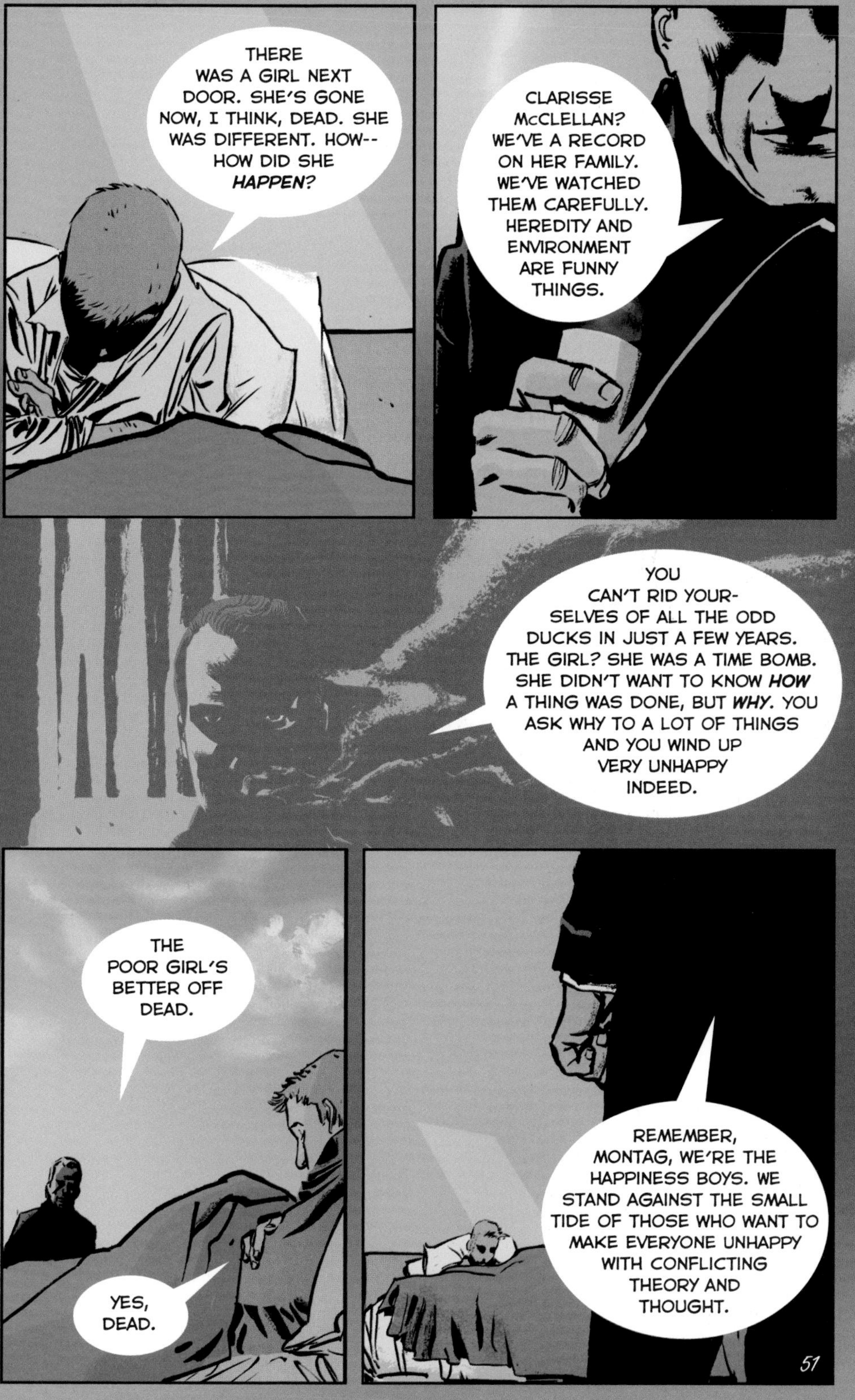
THERE WAS A GIRL NEXT DOOR. SHE'S GONE NOW, I THINK, DEAD. SHE WAS DIFFERENT. HOW-- HOW DID SHE *HAPPEN*?
CLARISSE McCLELLAN? WE'VE A RECORD ON HER FAMILY. WE'VE WATCHED THEM CAREFULLY. HEREDITY AND ENVIRONMENT ARE FUNNY THINGS.
YOU CAN'T RID YOURSELVES OF ALL THE ODD DUCKS IN JUST A FEW YEARS. THE GIRL? SHE WAS A TIME BOMB. SHE DIDN'T WANT TO KNOW *HOW* A THING WAS DONE, BUT *WHY*. YOU ASK WHY TO A LOT OF THINGS AND YOU WIND UP VERY UNHAPPY INDEED.
THE POOR GIRL'S BETTER OFF DEAD.
YES, DEAD.
REMEMBER, MONTAG, WE'RE THE HAPPINESS BOYS. WE STAND AGAINST THE SMALL TIDE OF THOSE WHO WANT TO MAKE EVERYONE UNHAPPY WITH CONFLICTING THEORY AND THOUGHT.

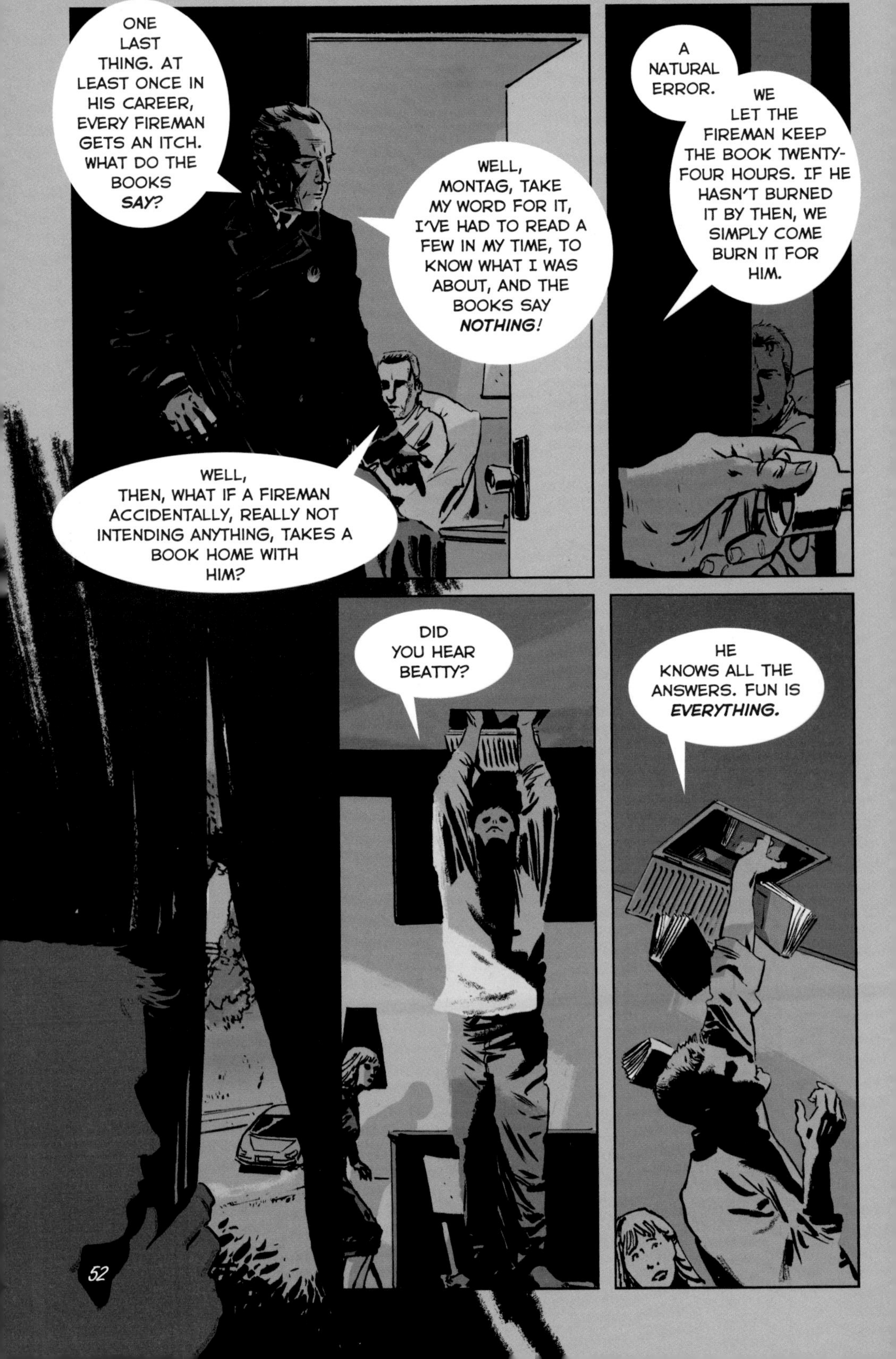

ONE LAST THING. AT LEAST ONCE IN HIS CAREER, EVERY FIREMAN GETS AN ITCH. WHAT DO THE BOOKS SAY?
WELL, MONTAG, TAKE MY WORD FOR IT, I'VE HAD TO READ A FEW IN MY TIME, TO KNOW WHAT I WAS ABOUT, AND THE BOOKS SAY NOTHING!
WELL, THEN, WHAT IF A FIREMAN ACCIDENTALLY, REALLY NOT INTENDING ANYTHING, TAKES A BOOK HOME WITH HIM?
A NATURAL ERROR.
WE LET THE FIREMAN KEEP THE BOOK TWENTY-FOUR HOURS. IF HE HASN'T BURNED IT BY THEN, WE SIMPLY COME BURN IT FOR HIM.
DID YOU HEAR BEATTY?
HE KNOWS ALL THE ANSWERS. FUN IS EVERYTHING.

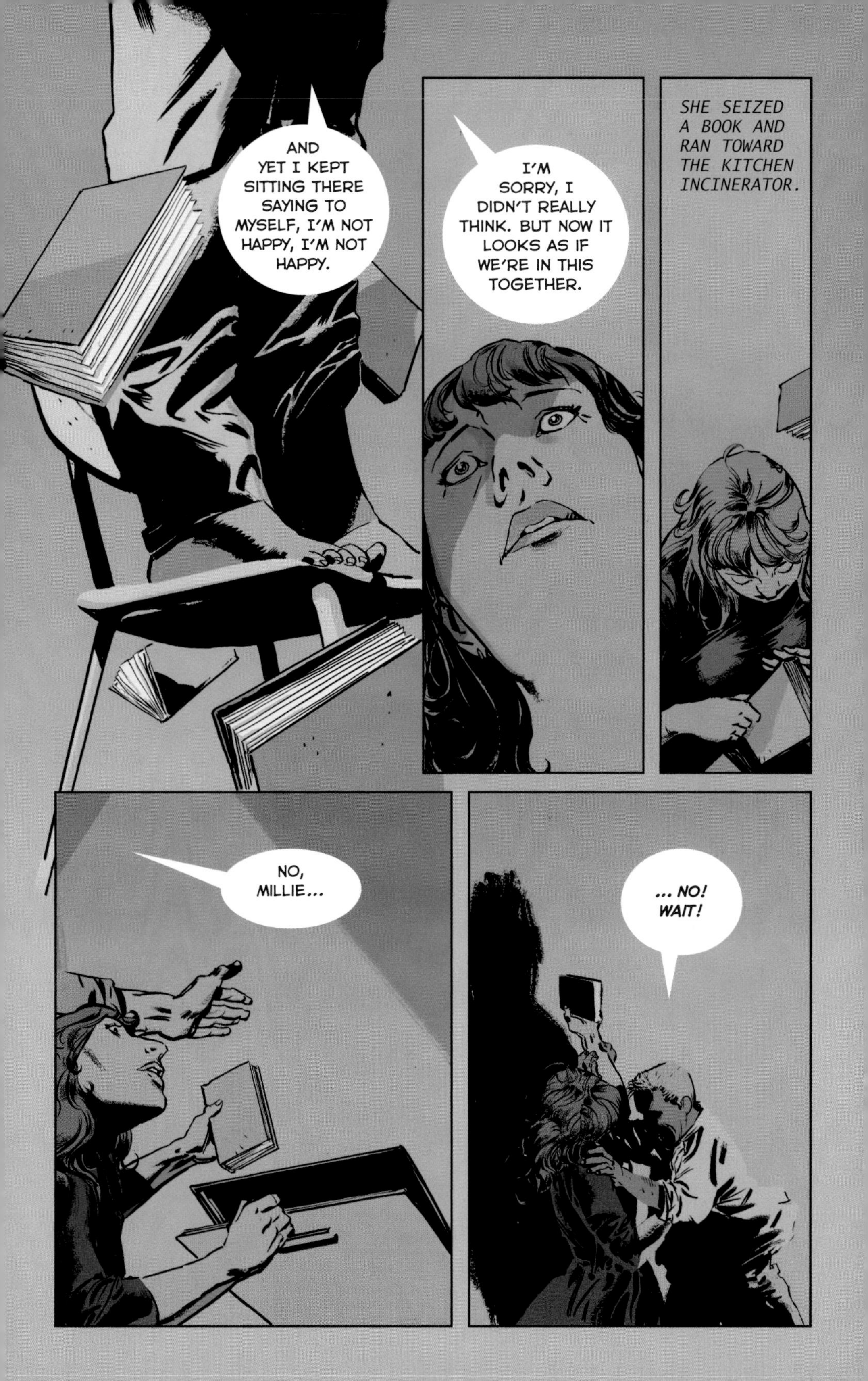
AND YET I KEPT SITTING THERE SAYING TO MYSELF, I'M NOT HAPPY, I'M NOT HAPPY.
I'M SORRY, I DIDN'T REALLY THINK. BUT NOW IT LOOKS AS IF WE'RE IN THIS TOGETHER.
SHE SEIZED A BOOK AND RAN TOWARD THE KITCHEN INCINERATOR.
NO, MILLIE...
... NO! WAIT!

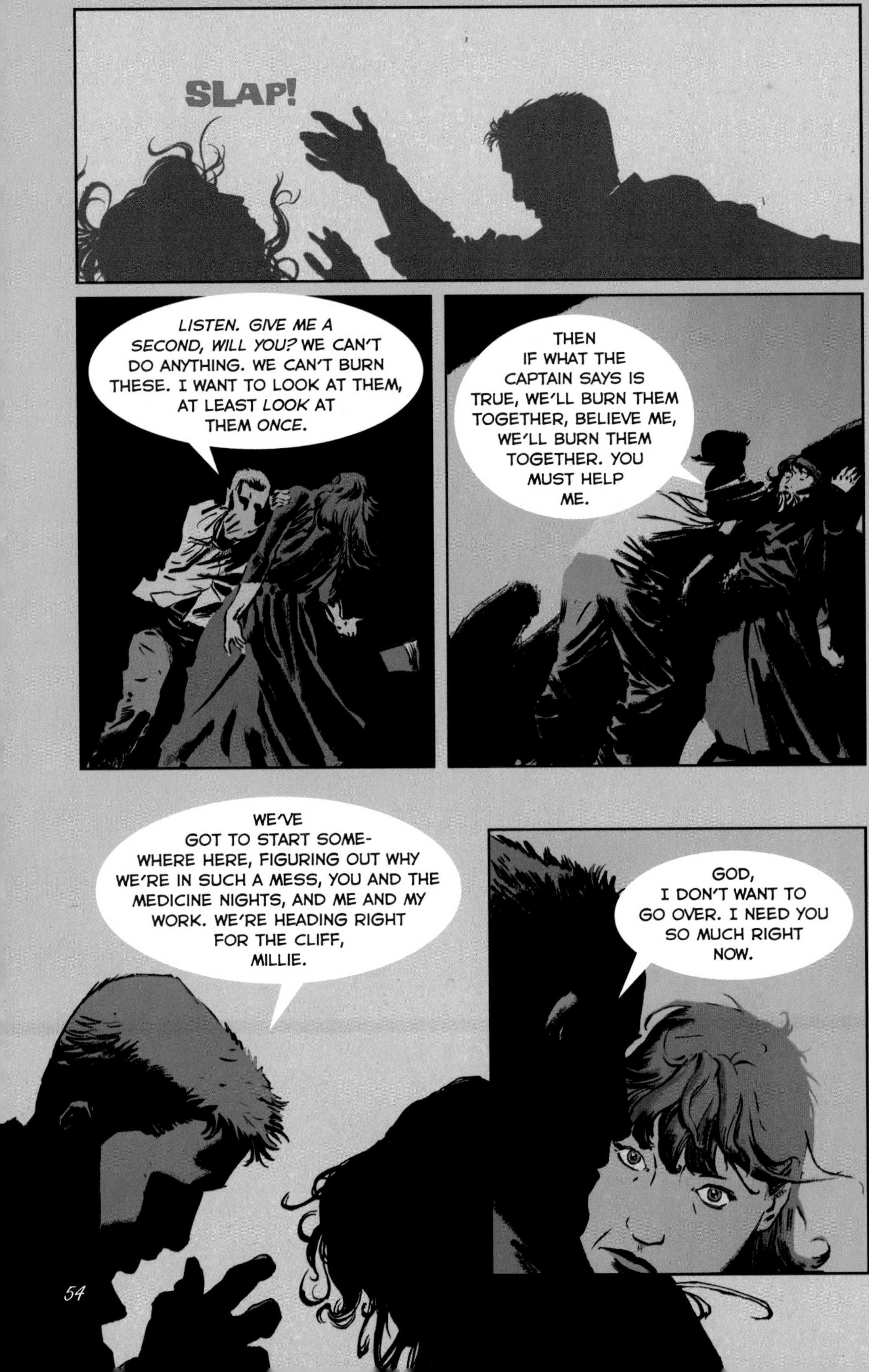
SLAP!
LISTEN. GIVE ME A SECOND, WILL YOU? WE CAN'T DO ANYTHING. WE CAN'T BURN THESE. I WANT TO LOOK AT THEM, AT LEAST LOOK AT THEM ONCE.
THEN IF WHAT THE CAPTAIN SAYS IS TRUE, WE'LL BURN THEM TOGETHER, BELIEVE ME, WE'LL BURN THEM TOGETHER. YOU MUST HELP ME.
WE'VE GOT TO START SOME-WHERE HERE, FIGURING OUT WHY WE'RE IN SUCH A MESS, YOU AND THE MEDICINE NIGHTS, AND ME AND MY WORK. WE'RE HEADING RIGHT FOR THE CLIFF, MILLIE.
GOD, I DON'T WANT TO GO OVER. I NEED YOU SO MUCH RIGHT NOW.

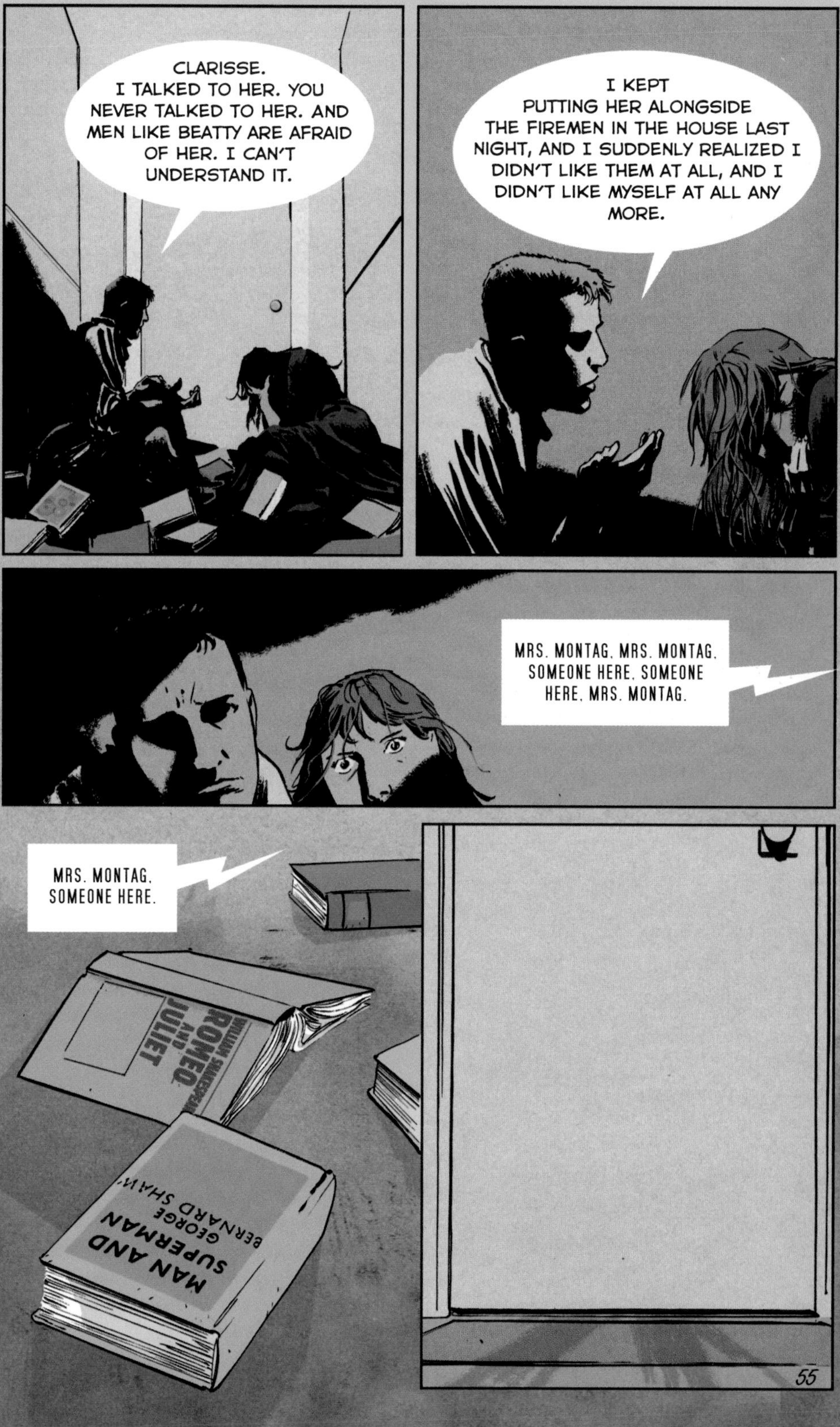
CLARISSE. I TALKED TO HER. YOU NEVER TALKED TO HER. AND MEN LIKE BEATTY ARE AFRAID OF HER. I CAN'T UNDERSTAND IT.
I KEPT PUTTING HER ALONGSIDE THE FIREMEN IN THE HOUSE LAST NIGHT, AND I SUDDENLY REALIZED I DIDN'T LIKE THEM AT ALL, AND I DIDN'T LIKE MYSELF AT ALL ANY MORE.
MRS. MONTAG. MRS. MONTAG. SOMEONE HERE. SOMEONE HERE. MRS. MONTAG.
MRS. MONTAG. SOMEONE HERE.
WILLIAM SHAKESPEARE ROMEO AND JULIET
MAN AND SUPERMAN GEORGE BERNARD SHAW

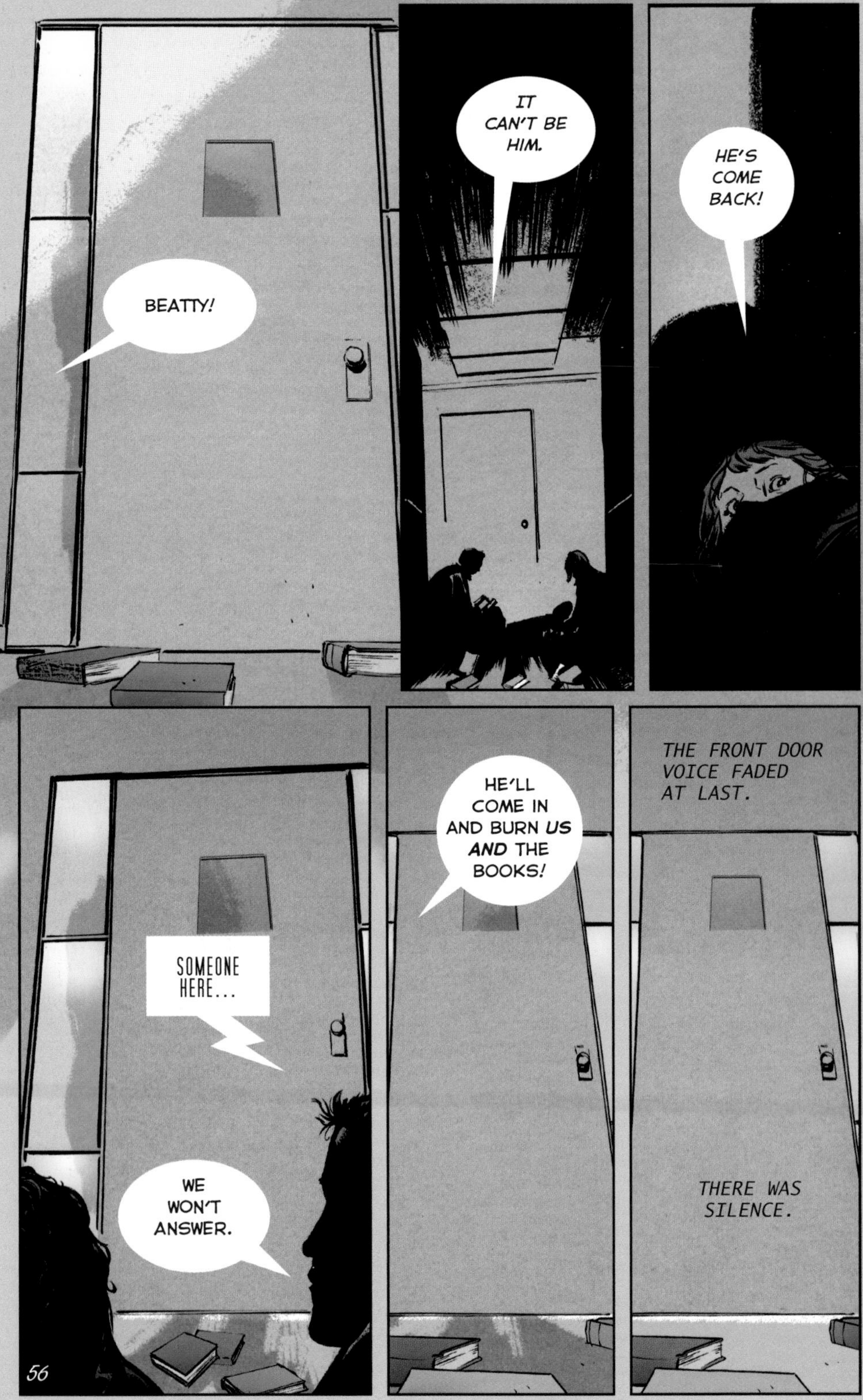
BEATTY!
IT CAN'T BE HIM.
HE'S COME BACK!
SOMEONE HERE...
WE WON'T ANSWER.
HE'LL COME IN AND BURN **US AND** THE BOOKS!
THE FRONT DOOR VOICE FADED AT LAST.
THERE WAS SILENCE.

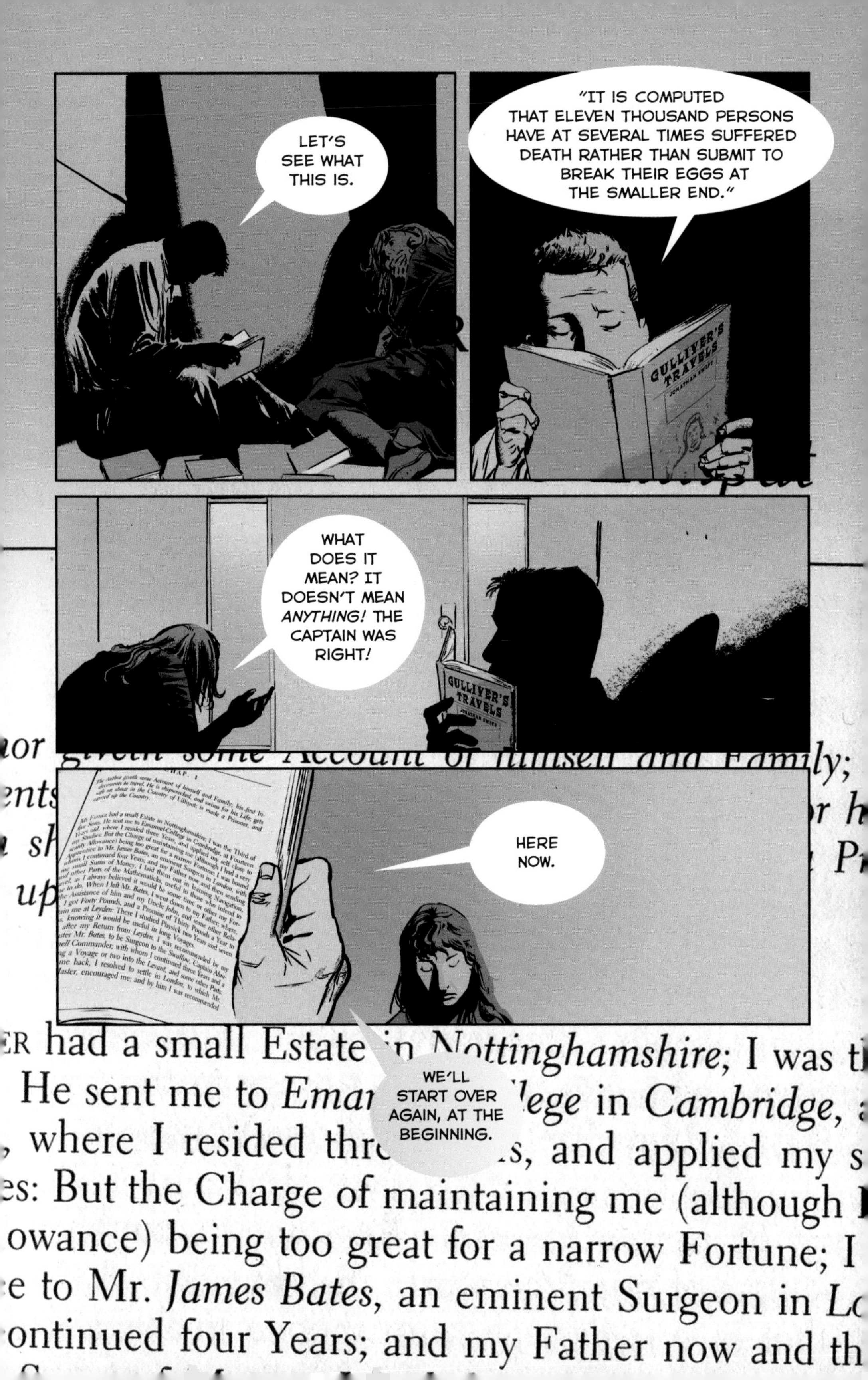
LET'S SEE WHAT THIS IS.
"IT IS COMPUTED THAT ELEVEN THOUSAND PERSONS HAVE AT SEVERAL TIMES SUFFERED DEATH RATHER THAN SUBMIT TO BREAK THEIR EGGS AT THE SMALLER END."
GULLIVER'S TRAVELS
JONATHAN SWIFT
WHAT DOES IT MEAN? IT DOESN'T MEAN *ANYTHING!* THE CAPTAIN WAS RIGHT!
GULLIVER'S TRAVELS
JONATHAN SWIFT
HERE NOW.
WE'LL START OVER AGAIN, AT THE BEGINNING.

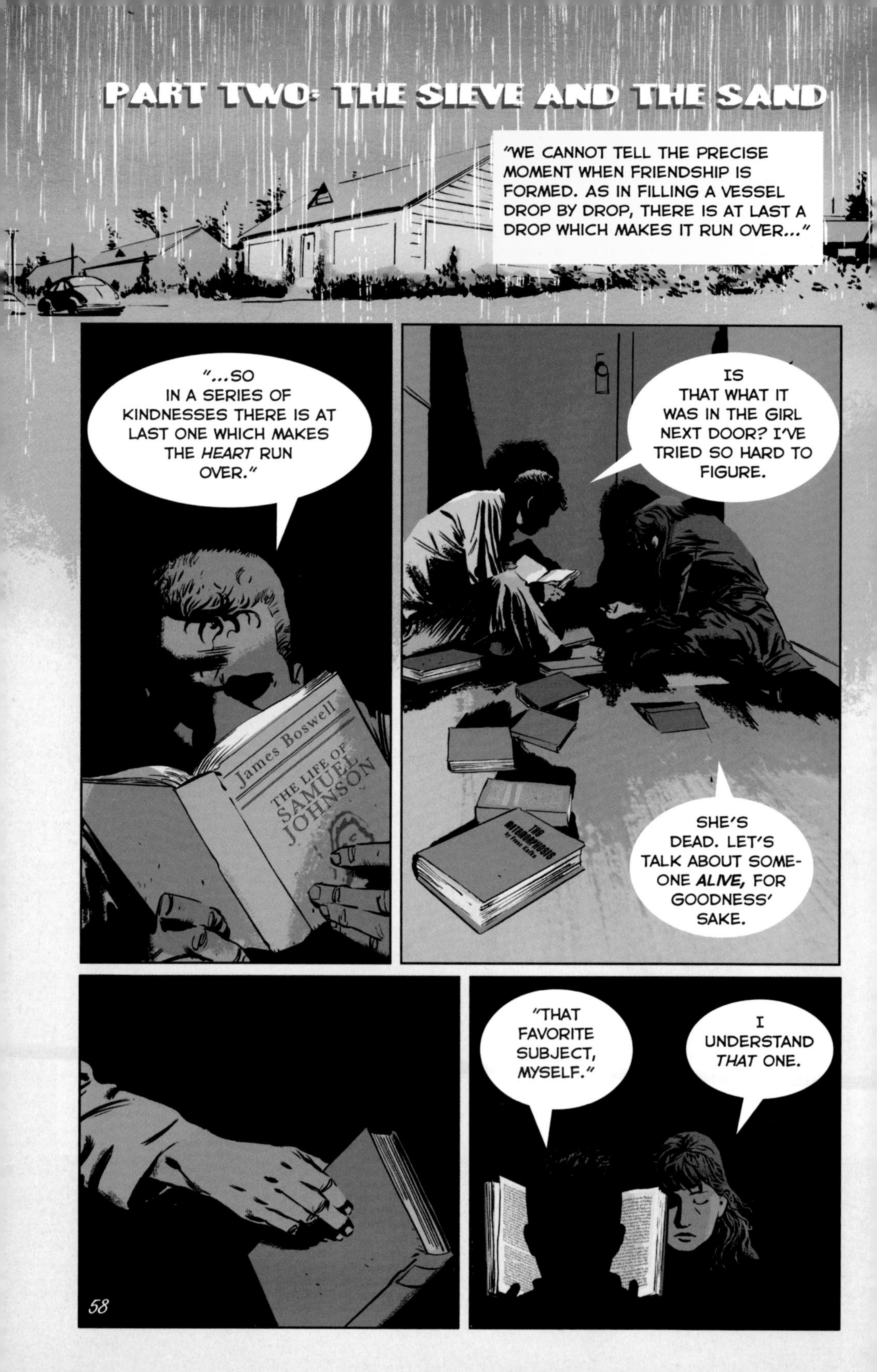
PART TWO: THE SIEVE AND THE SAND
"WE CANNOT TELL THE PRECISE MOMENT WHEN FRIENDSHIP IS FORMED. AS IN FILLING A VESSEL DROP BY DROP, THERE IS AT LAST A DROP WHICH MAKES IT RUN OVER..."
"...SO IN A SERIES OF KINDNESSES THERE IS AT LAST ONE WHICH MAKES THE *HEART* RUN OVER."
James Boswell
THE LIFE OF SAMUEL JOHNSON
IS THAT WHAT IT WAS IN THE GIRL NEXT DOOR? I'VE TRIED SO HARD TO FIGURE.
SHE'S DEAD. LET'S TALK ABOUT SOME-ONE *ALIVE,* FOR GOODNESS' SAKE.
"THAT FAVORITE SUBJECT, MYSELF."
I UNDERSTAND *THAT* ONE.

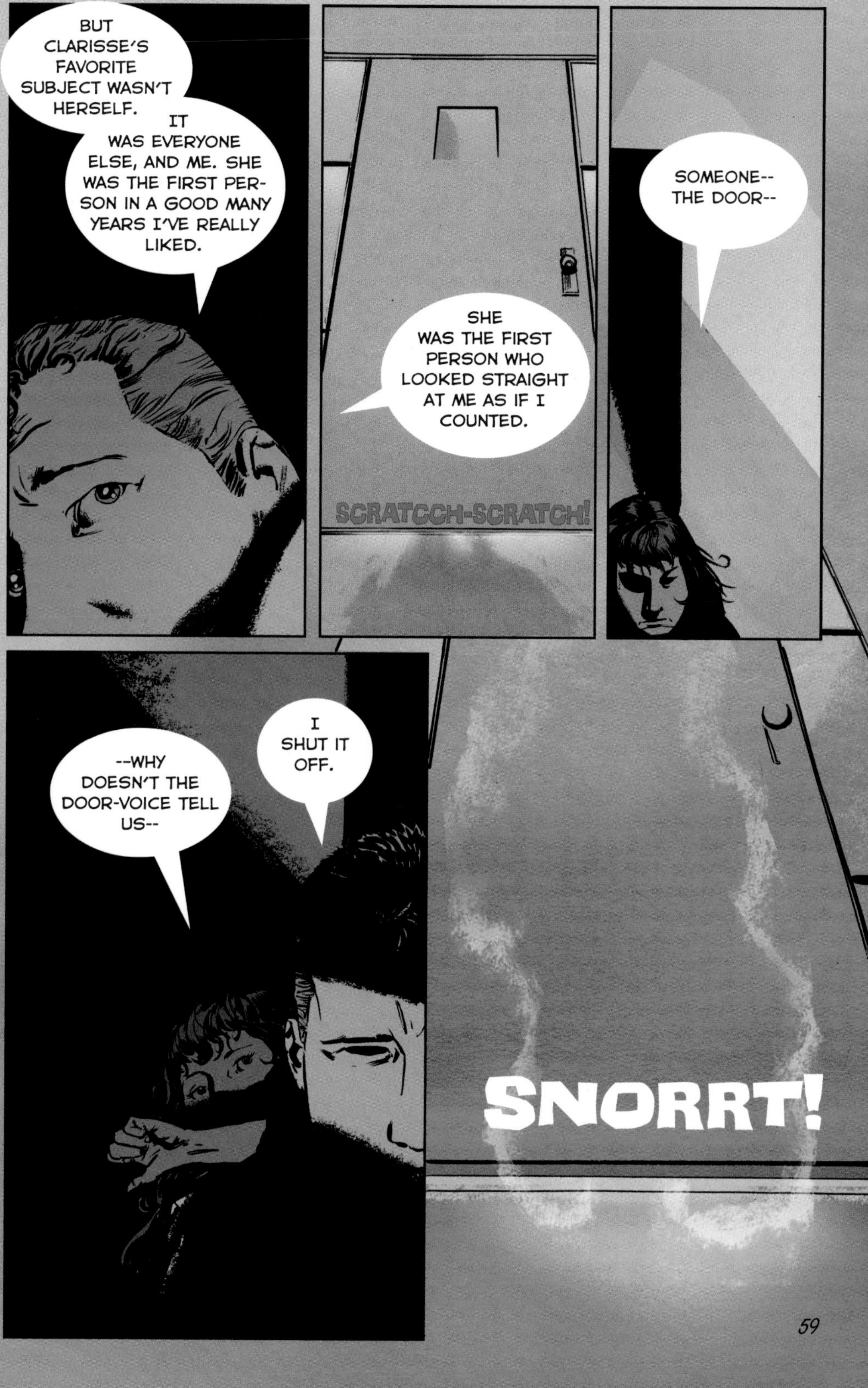
BUT CLARISSE'S FAVORITE SUBJECT WASN'T HERSELF.
IT WAS EVERYONE ELSE, AND ME. SHE WAS THE FIRST PERSON IN A GOOD MANY YEARS I'VE REALLY LIKED.
SHE WAS THE FIRST PERSON WHO LOOKED STRAIGHT AT ME AS IF I COUNTED.
SCRATCCH-SCRATCH!
SOMEONE-- THE DOOR--
--WHY DOESN'T THE DOOR-VOICE TELL US--
I SHUT IT OFF.
SNORRT!

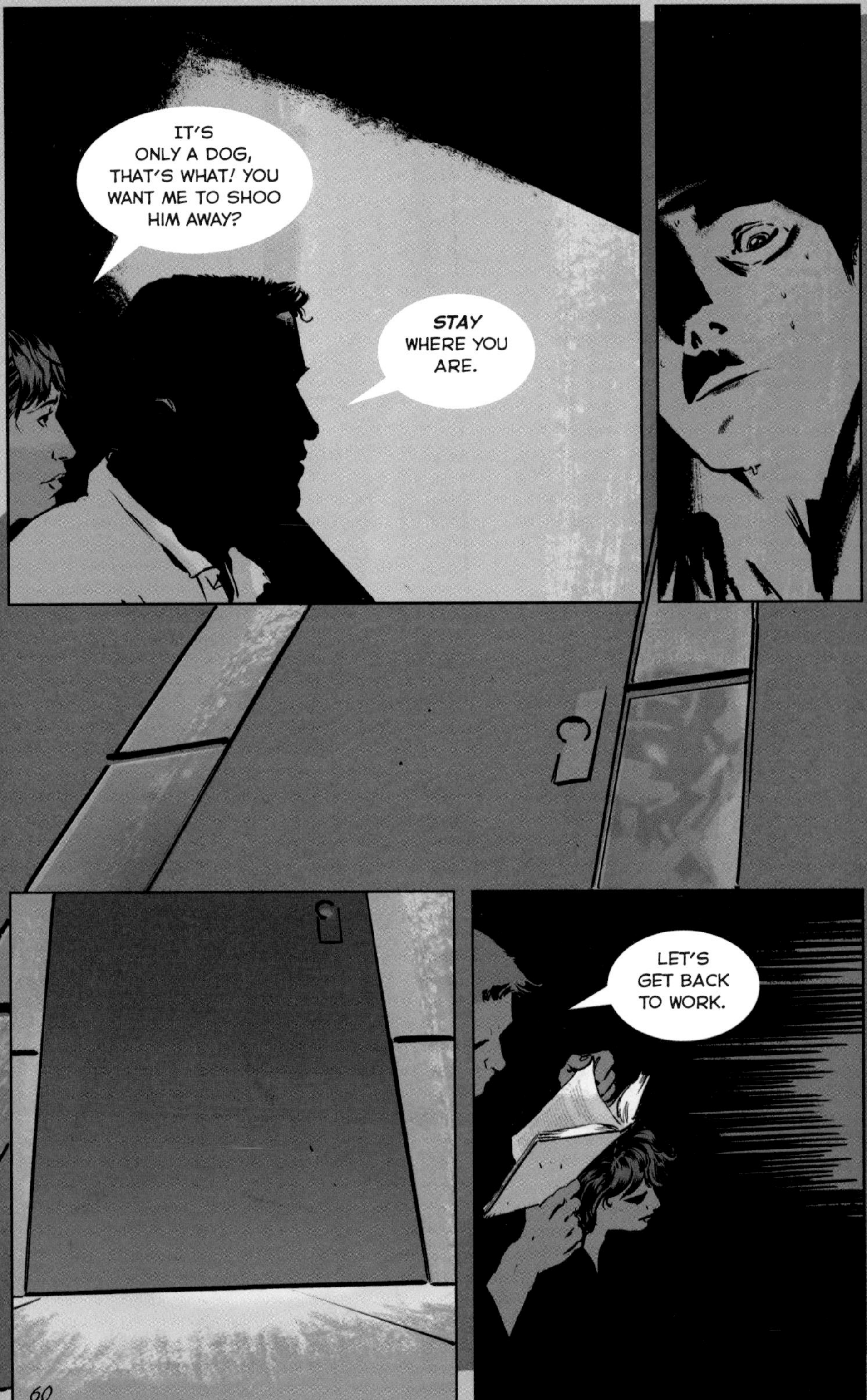
IT'S ONLY A DOG, THAT'S WHAT! YOU WANT ME TO SHOO HIM AWAY?
STAY WHERE YOU ARE.
LET'S GET BACK TO WORK.

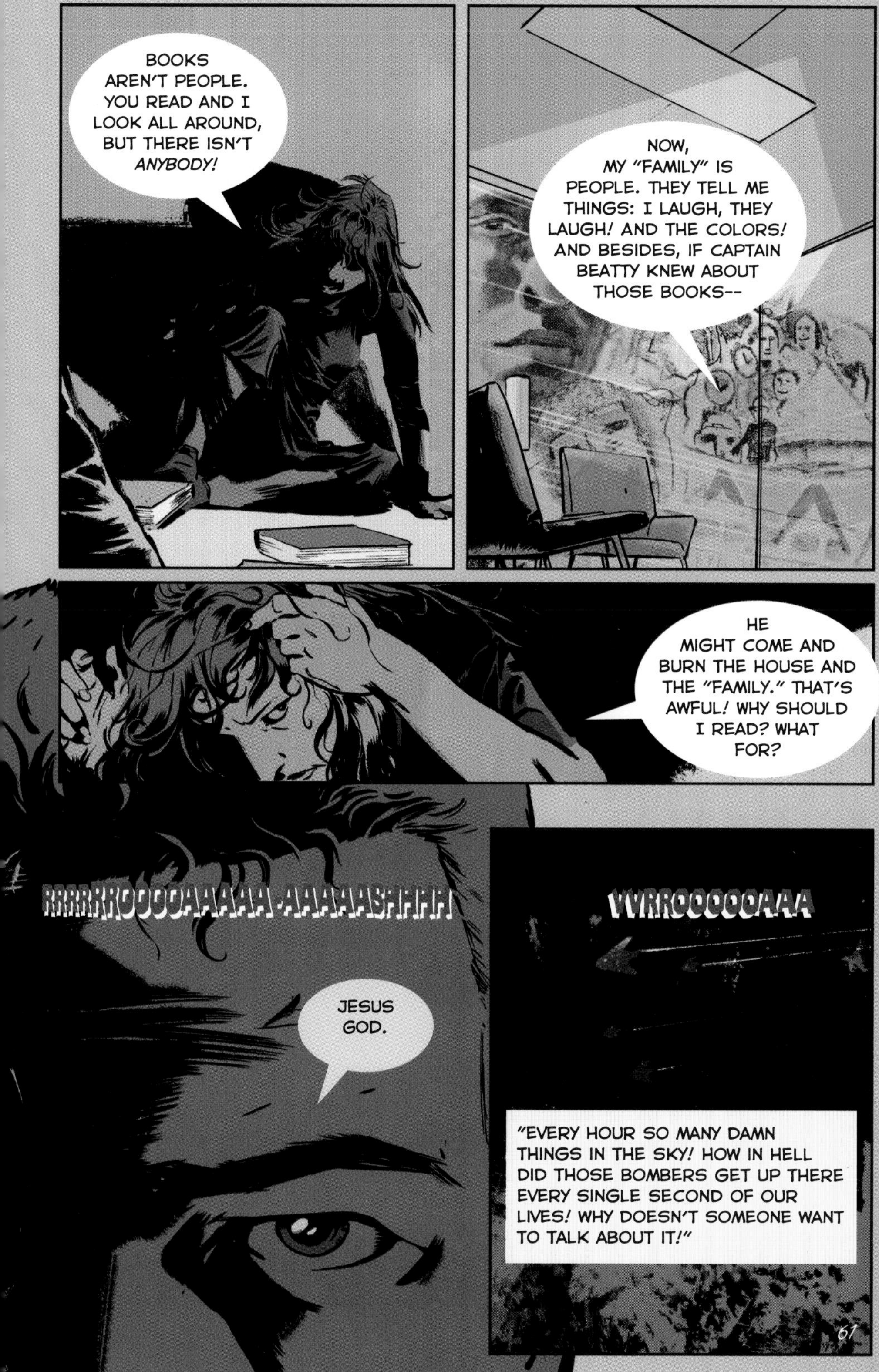
BOOKS AREN'T PEOPLE. YOU READ AND I LOOK ALL AROUND, BUT THERE ISN'T *ANYBODY!*
NOW, MY "FAMILY" IS PEOPLE. THEY TELL ME THINGS: I LAUGH, THEY LAUGH! AND THE COLORS! AND BESIDES, IF CAPTAIN BEATTY KNEW ABOUT THOSE BOOKS--
HE MIGHT COME AND BURN THE HOUSE AND THE "FAMILY." THAT'S AWFUL! WHY SHOULD I READ? WHAT FOR?
RRRRRROOOOOAAAAAA-AAAAASHHHH
JESUS GOD.
VVRROOOOOOAAA
"EVERY HOUR SO MANY DAMN THINGS IN THE SKY! HOW IN HELL DID THOSE BOMBERS GET UP THERE EVERY SINGLE SECOND OF OUR LIVES! WHY DOESN'T SOMEONE WANT TO TALK ABOUT IT!"

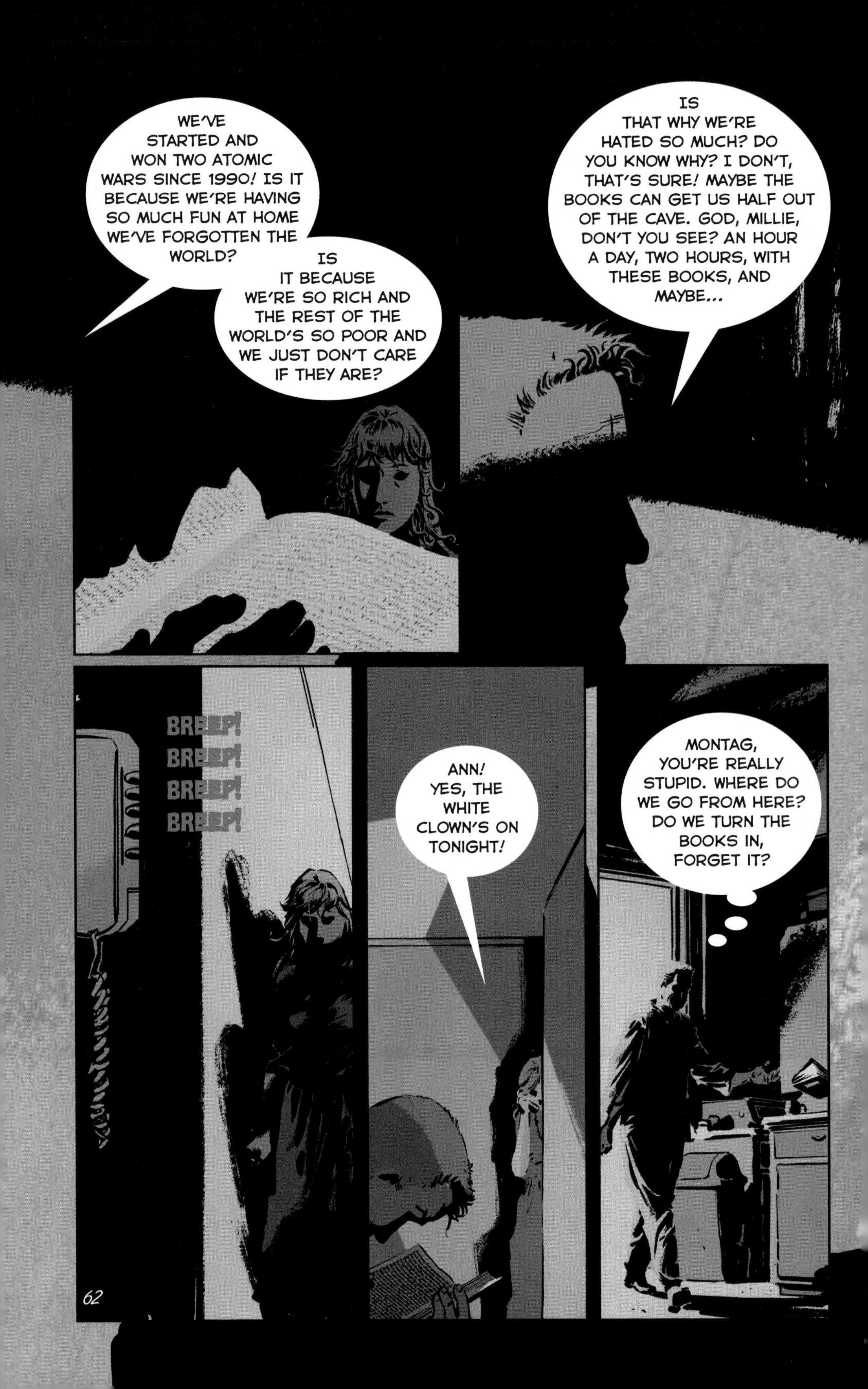
WE'VE STARTED AND WON TWO ATOMIC WARS SINCE 1990! IS IT BECAUSE WE'RE HAVING SO MUCH FUN AT HOME WE'VE FORGOTTEN THE WORLD?
IS IT BECAUSE WE'RE SO RICH AND THE REST OF THE WORLD'S SO POOR AND WE JUST DON'T CARE IF THEY ARE?
IS THAT WHY WE'RE HATED SO MUCH? DO YOU KNOW WHY? I DON'T, THAT'S SURE! MAYBE THE BOOKS CAN GET US HALF OUT OF THE CAVE. GOD, MILLIE, DON'T YOU SEE? AN HOUR A DAY, TWO HOURS, WITH THESE BOOKS, AND MAYBE...
BREEP!
BREEP!
BREEP!
BREEP!
ANN! YES, THE WHITE CLOWN'S ON TONIGHT!
MONTAG, YOU'RE REALLY STUPID. WHERE DO WE GO FROM HERE? DO WE TURN THE BOOKS IN, FORGET IT?

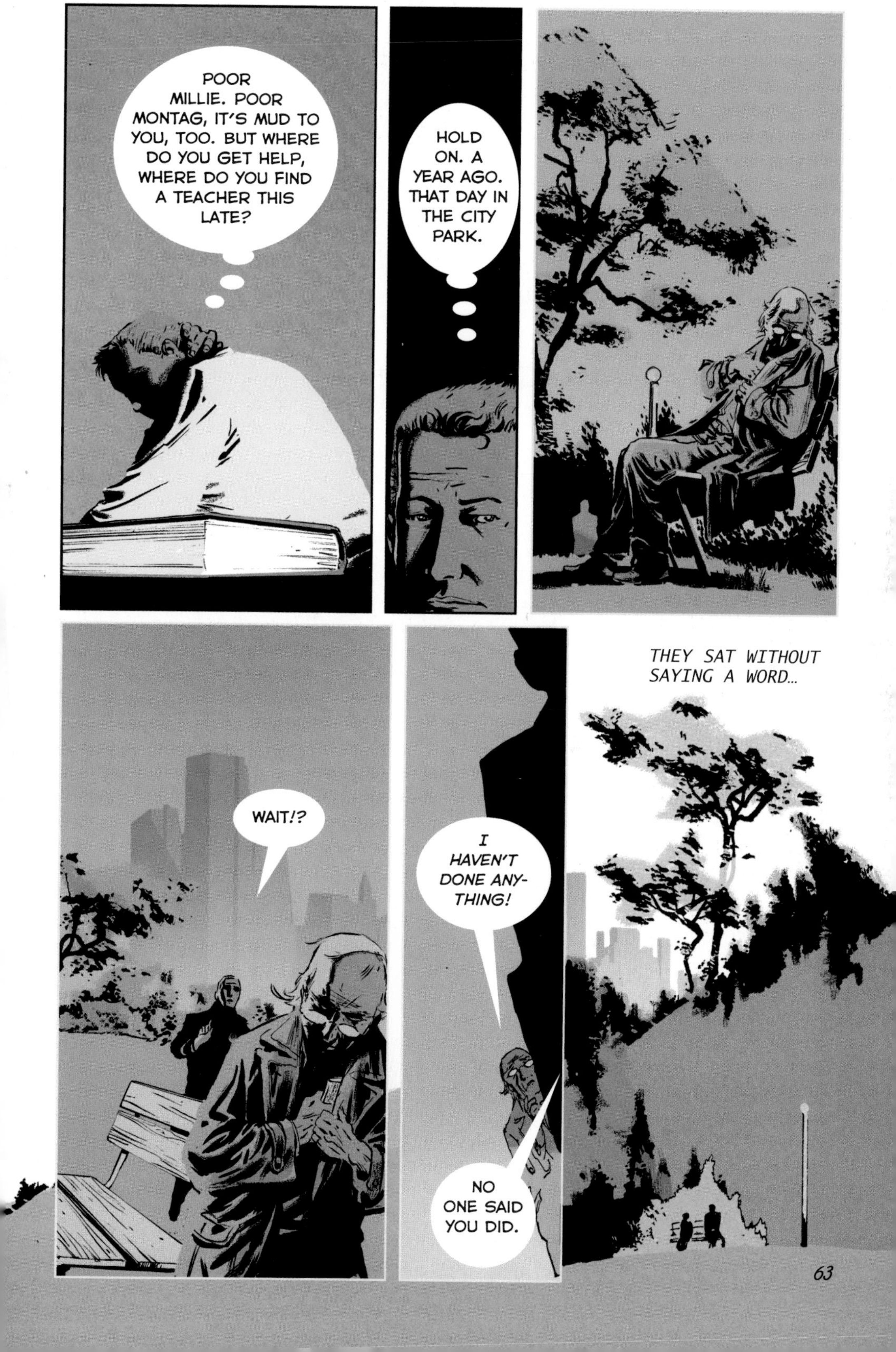
POOR MILLIE. POOR MONTAG, IT'S MUD TO YOU, TOO. BUT WHERE DO YOU GET HELP, WHERE DO YOU FIND A TEACHER THIS LATE?
HOLD ON. A YEAR AGO. THAT DAY IN THE CITY PARK.
WAIT!?
I HAVEN'T DONE ANY-THING!
NO ONE SAID YOU DID.
THEY SAT WITHOUT SAYING A WORD...

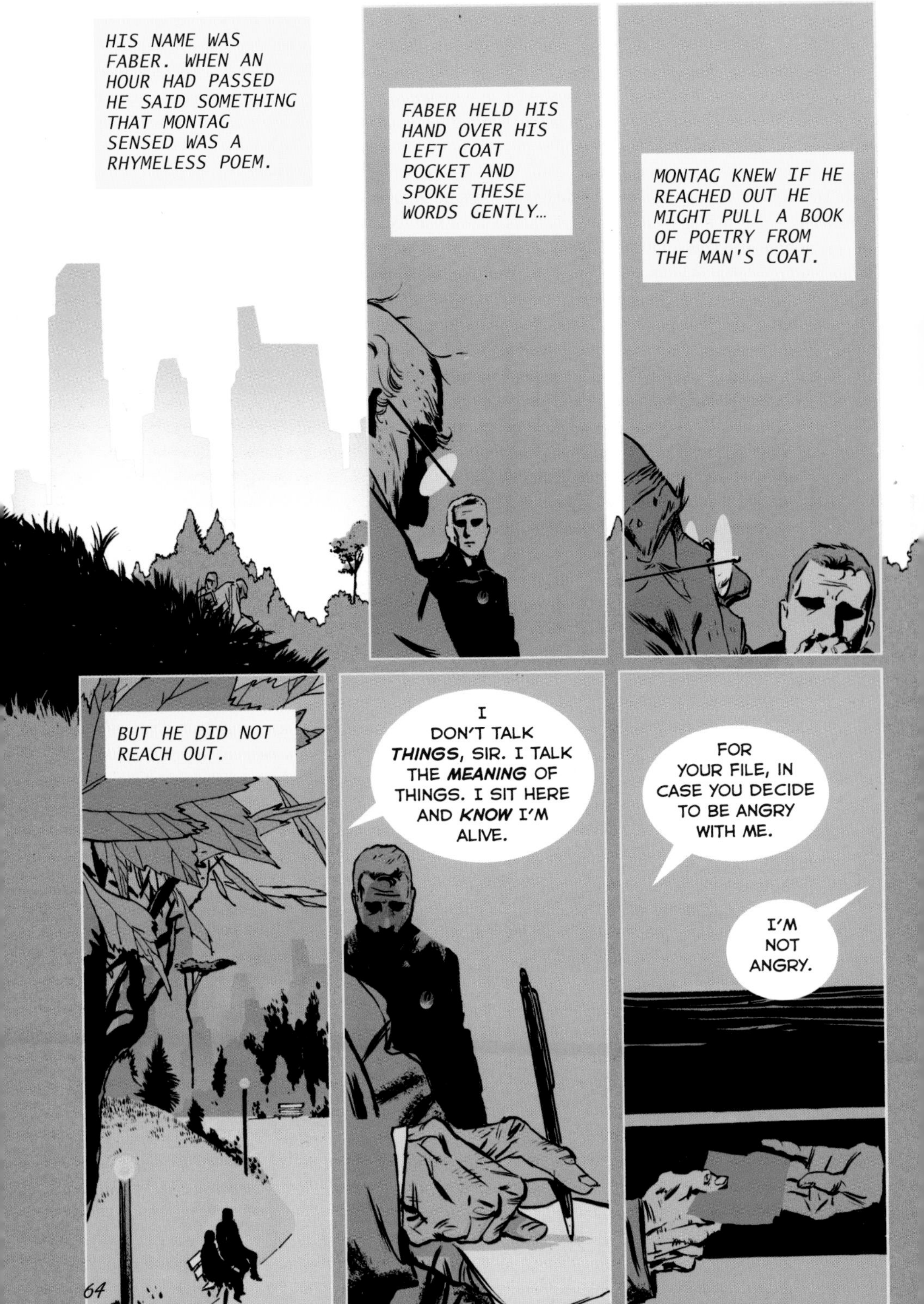
HIS NAME WAS FABER. WHEN AN HOUR HAD PASSED HE SAID SOMETHING THAT MONTAG SENSED WAS A RHYMELESS POEM.
FABER HELD HIS HAND OVER HIS LEFT COAT POCKET AND SPOKE THESE WORDS GENTLY...
MONTAG KNEW IF HE REACHED OUT HE MIGHT PULL A BOOK OF POETRY FROM THE MAN'S COAT.
BUT HE DID NOT REACH OUT.
I DON'T TALK THINGS, SIR. I TALK THE MEANING OF THINGS. I SIT HERE AND KNOW I'M ALIVE.
FOR YOUR FILE, IN CASE YOU DECIDE TO BE ANGRY WITH ME.
I'M NOT ANGRY.

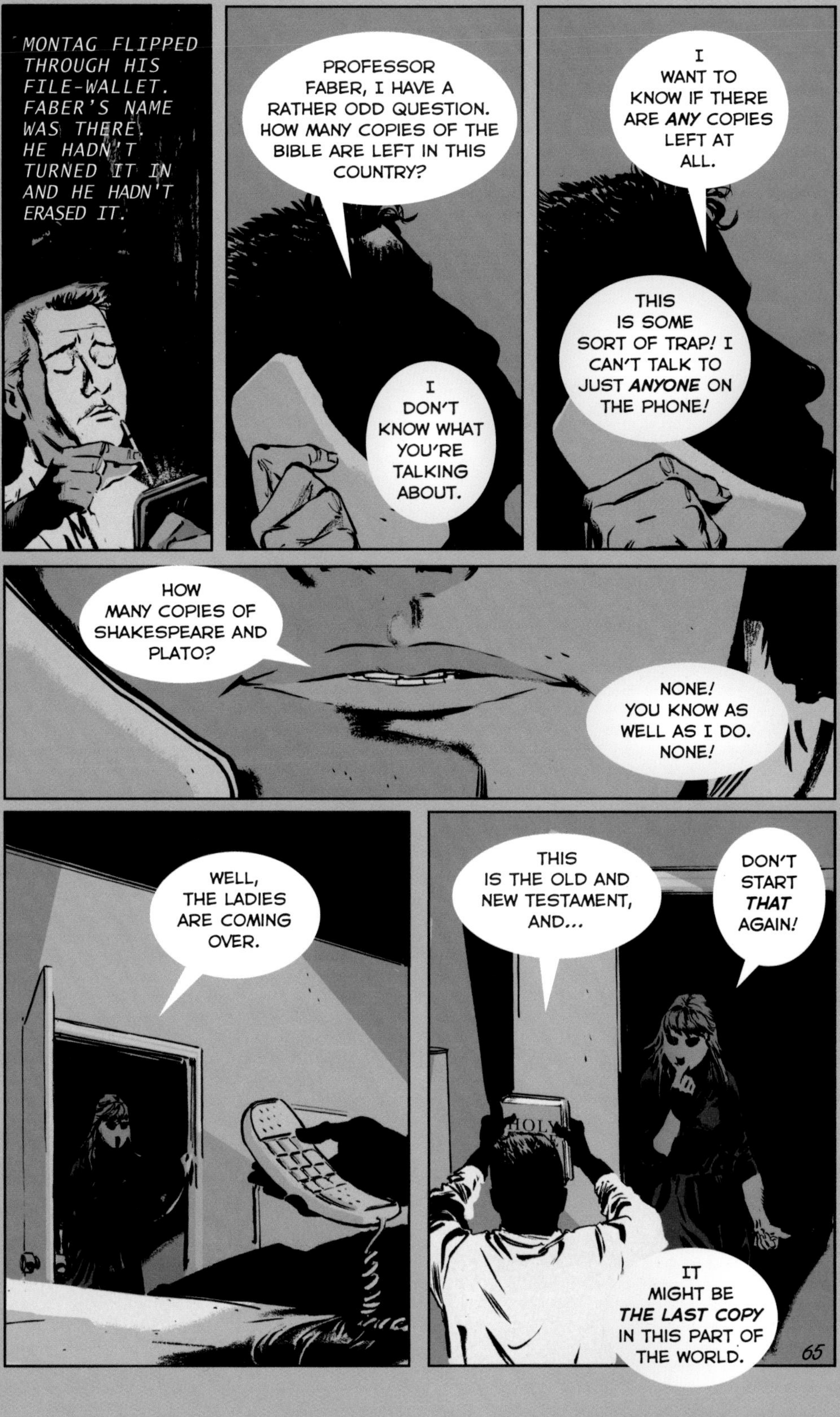
MONTAG FLIPPED THROUGH HIS FILE-WALLET. FABER'S NAME WAS THERE. HE HADN'T TURNED IT IN AND HE HADN'T ERASED IT.
PROFESSOR FABER, I HAVE A RATHER ODD QUESTION. HOW MANY COPIES OF THE BIBLE ARE LEFT IN THIS COUNTRY?
I DON'T KNOW WHAT YOU'RE TALKING ABOUT.
I WANT TO KNOW IF THERE ARE ANY COPIES LEFT AT ALL.
THIS IS SOME SORT OF TRAP! I CAN'T TALK TO JUST ANYONE ON THE PHONE!
HOW MANY COPIES OF SHAKESPEARE AND PLATO?
NONE! YOU KNOW AS WELL AS I DO. NONE!
WELL, THE LADIES ARE COMING OVER.
THIS IS THE OLD AND NEW TESTAMENT, AND...
DON'T START THAT AGAIN!
IT MIGHT BE THE LAST COPY IN THIS PART OF THE WORLD.

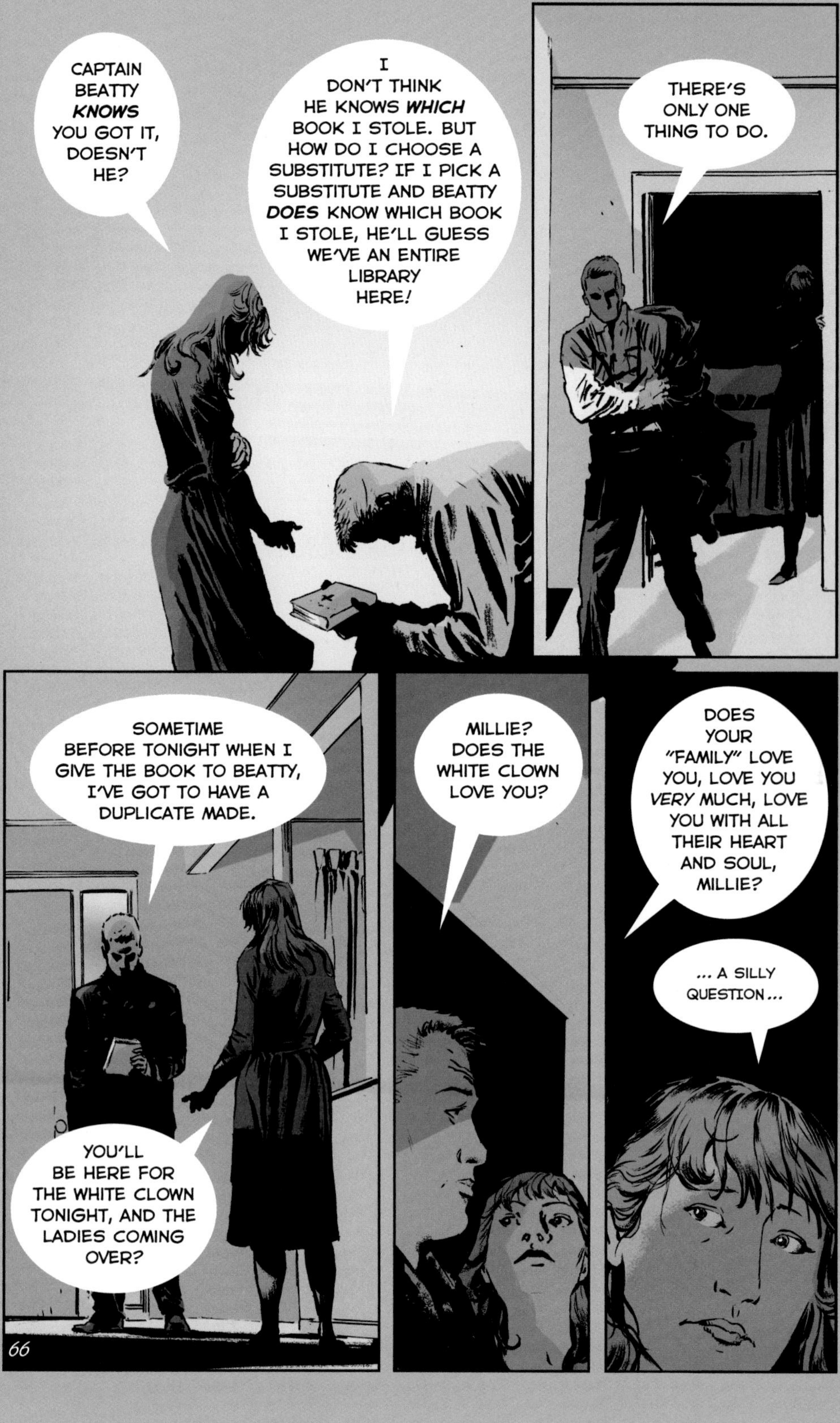
CAPTAIN BEATTY KNOWS YOU GOT IT, DOESN'T HE?
I DON'T THINK HE KNOWS WHICH BOOK I STOLE. BUT HOW DO I CHOOSE A SUBSTITUTE? IF I PICK A SUBSTITUTE AND BEATTY DOES KNOW WHICH BOOK I STOLE, HE'LL GUESS WE'VE AN ENTIRE LIBRARY HERE!
THERE'S ONLY ONE THING TO DO.
SOMETIME BEFORE TONIGHT WHEN I GIVE THE BOOK TO BEATTY, I'VE GOT TO HAVE A DUPLICATE MADE.
YOU'LL BE HERE FOR THE WHITE CLOWN TONIGHT, AND THE LADIES COMING OVER?
MILLIE? DOES THE WHITE CLOWN LOVE YOU?
DOES YOUR "FAMILY" LOVE YOU, LOVE YOU VERY MUCH, LOVE YOU WITH ALL THEIR HEART AND SOUL, MILLIE?
... A SILLY QUESTION ...

IF YOU SEE THAT DOG OUTSIDE, GIVE HIM A KICK FOR ME.

I'M NUMB. WHEN DID THE NUMBNESS REALLY BEGIN IN MY FACE?

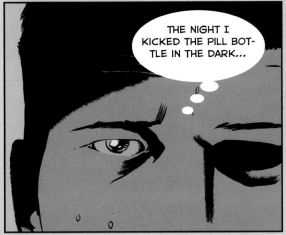

THE NIGHT I KICKED THE PILL BOTTLE IN THE DARK...

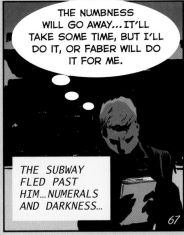

THE NUMBNESS WILL GO AWAY... IT'LL TAKE SOME TIME, BUT I'LL DO IT, OR FABER WILL DO IT FOR ME.

THE SUBWAY FLED PAST HIM... NUMERALS AND DARKNESS...

67

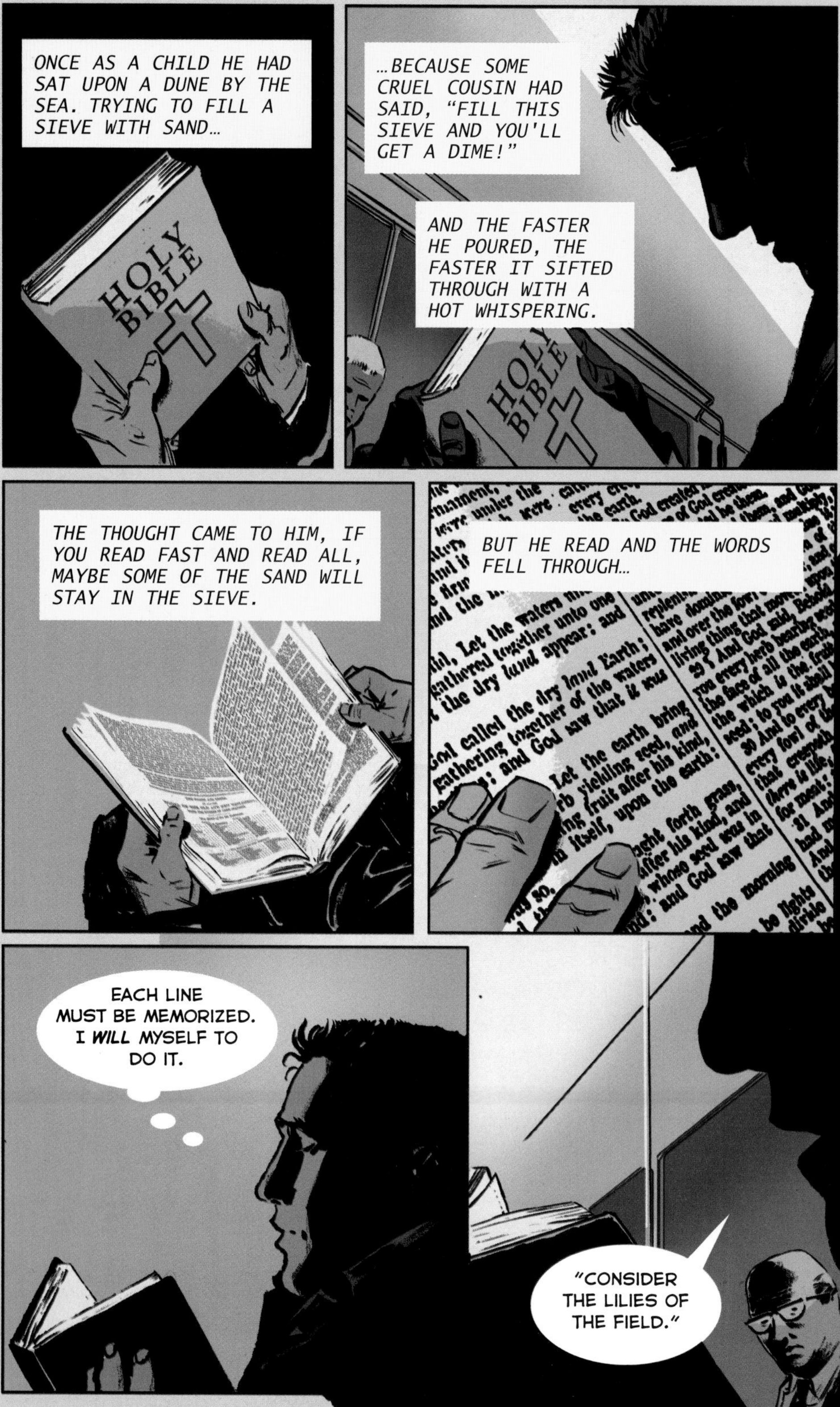
ONCE AS A CHILD HE HAD SAT UPON A DUNE BY THE SEA. TRYING TO FILL A SIEVE WITH SAND...
HOLY BIBLE
...BECAUSE SOME CRUEL COUSIN HAD SAID, "FILL THIS SIEVE AND YOU'LL GET A DIME!"
AND THE FASTER HE POURED, THE FASTER IT SIFTED THROUGH WITH A HOT WHISPERING.
HOLY BIBLE
THE THOUGHT CAME TO HIM, IF YOU READ FAST AND READ ALL, MAYBE SOME OF THE SAND WILL STAY IN THE SIEVE.
BUT HE READ AND THE WORDS FELL THROUGH...
EACH LINE MUST BE MEMORIZED. I *WILL* MYSELF TO DO IT.
"CONSIDER THE LILIES OF THE FIELD."

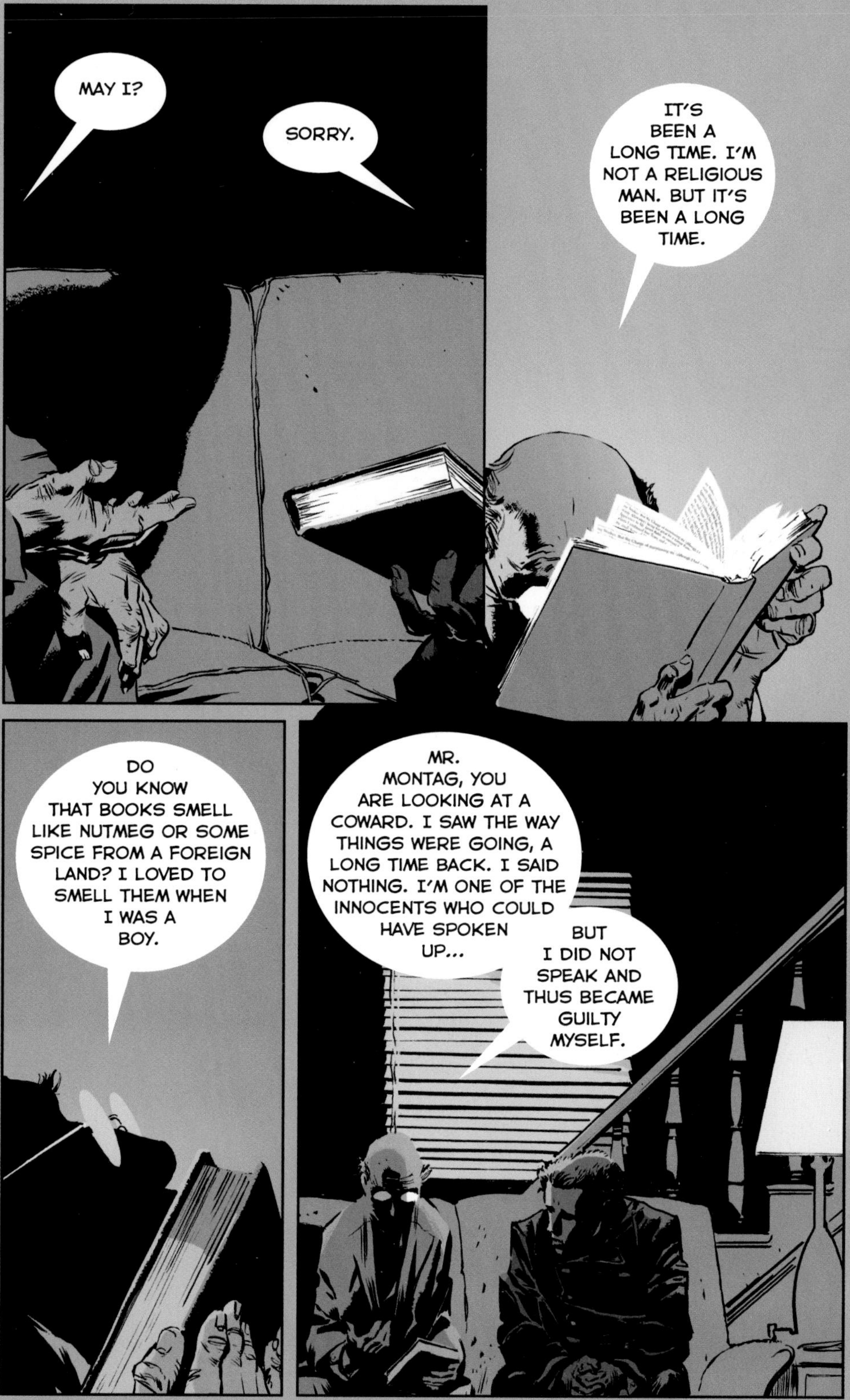
MAY I?
SORRY.
IT'S BEEN A LONG TIME. I'M NOT A RELIGIOUS MAN. BUT IT'S BEEN A LONG TIME.
DO YOU KNOW THAT BOOKS SMELL LIKE NUTMEG OR SOME SPICE FROM A FOREIGN LAND? I LOVED TO SMELL THEM WHEN I WAS A BOY.
MR. MONTAG, YOU ARE LOOKING AT A COWARD. I SAW THE WAY THINGS WERE GOING, A LONG TIME BACK. I SAID NOTHING. I'M ONE OF THE INNOCENTS WHO COULD HAVE SPOKEN UP...
BUT I DID NOT SPEAK AND THUS BECAME GUILTY MYSELF.

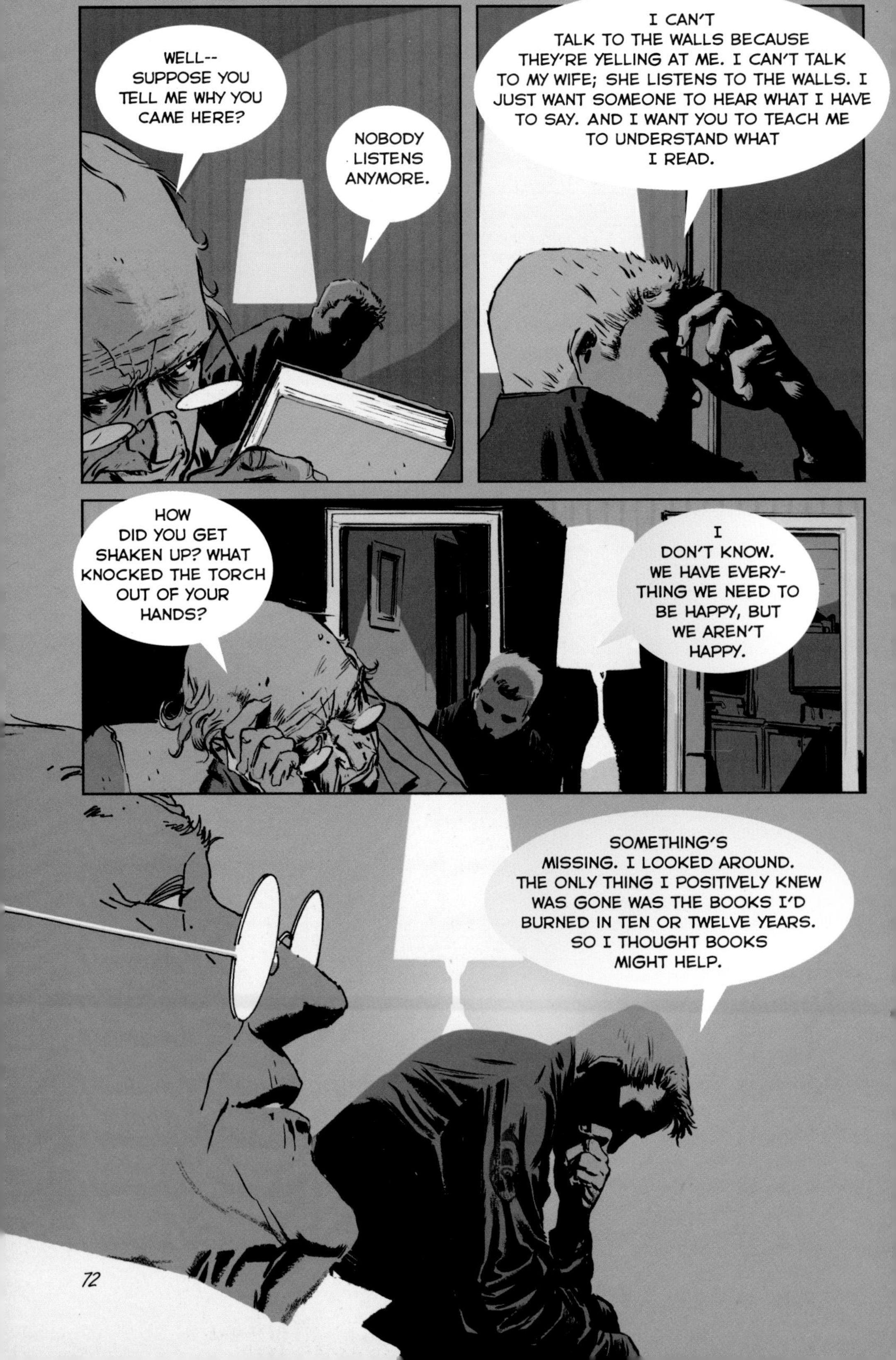
WELL-- SUPPOSE YOU TELL ME WHY YOU CAME HERE?
NOBODY LISTENS ANYMORE.
I CAN'T TALK TO THE WALLS BECAUSE THEY'RE YELLING AT ME. I CAN'T TALK TO MY WIFE; SHE LISTENS TO THE WALLS. I JUST WANT SOMEONE TO HEAR WHAT I HAVE TO SAY. AND I WANT YOU TO TEACH ME TO UNDERSTAND WHAT I READ.
HOW DID YOU GET SHAKEN UP? WHAT KNOCKED THE TORCH OUT OF YOUR HANDS?
I DON'T KNOW. WE HAVE EVERY-THING WE NEED TO BE HAPPY, BUT WE AREN'T HAPPY.
SOMETHING'S MISSING. I LOOKED AROUND. THE ONLY THING I POSITIVELY KNEW WAS GONE WAS THE BOOKS I'D BURNED IN TEN OR TWELVE YEARS. SO I THOUGHT BOOKS MIGHT HELP.

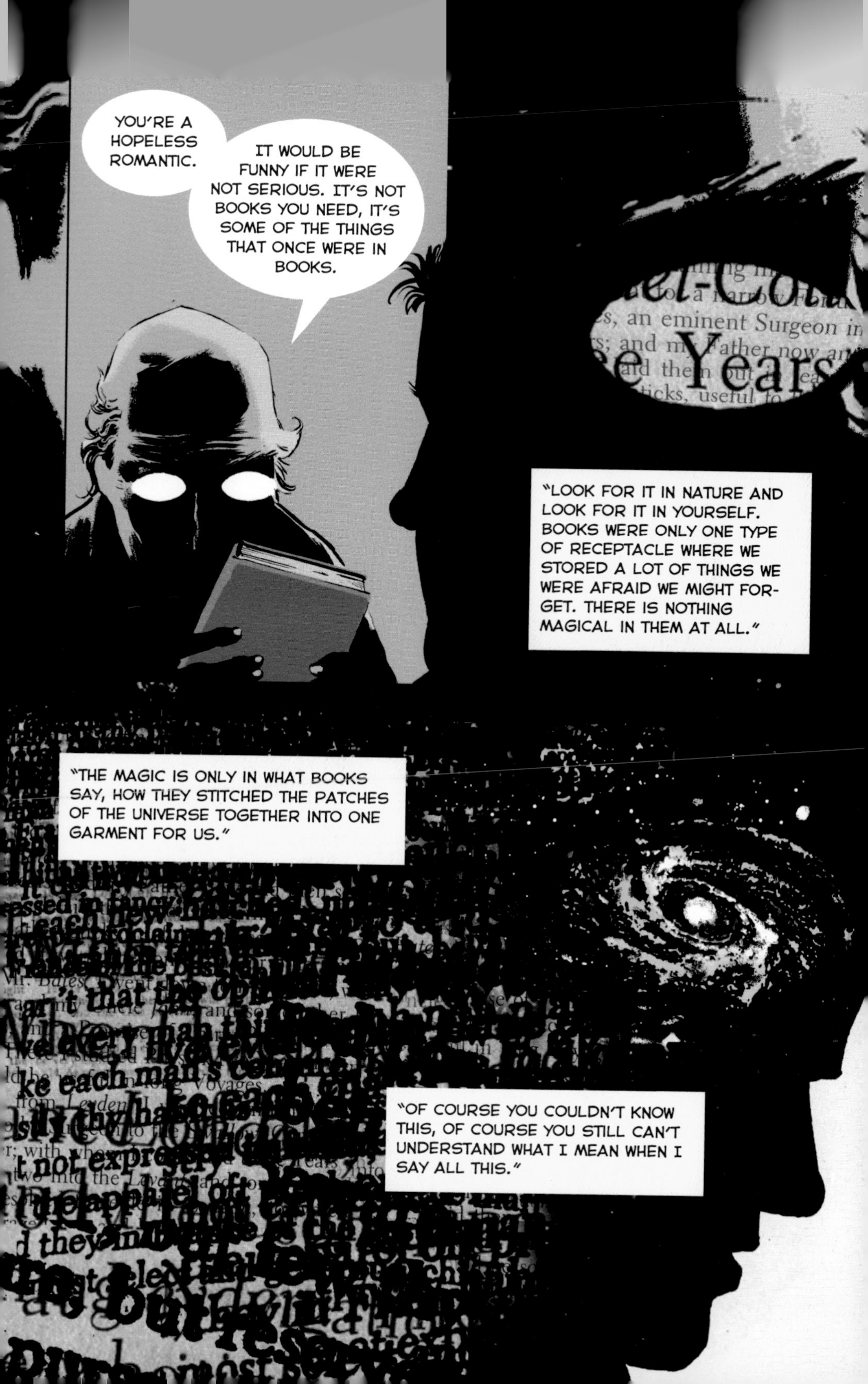
YOU'RE A HOPELESS ROMANTIC.
IT WOULD BE FUNNY IF IT WERE NOT SERIOUS. IT'S NOT BOOKS YOU NEED, IT'S SOME OF THE THINGS THAT ONCE WERE IN BOOKS.
"LOOK FOR IT IN NATURE AND LOOK FOR IT IN YOURSELF. BOOKS WERE ONLY ONE TYPE OF RECEPTACLE WHERE WE STORED A LOT OF THINGS WE WERE AFRAID WE MIGHT FORGET. THERE IS NOTHING MAGICAL IN THEM AT ALL."
"THE MAGIC IS ONLY IN WHAT BOOKS SAY, HOW THEY STITCHED THE PATCHES OF THE UNIVERSE TOGETHER INTO ONE GARMENT FOR US."
"OF COURSE YOU COULDN'T KNOW THIS, OF COURSE YOU STILL CAN'T UNDERSTAND WHAT I MEAN WHEN I SAY ALL THIS."

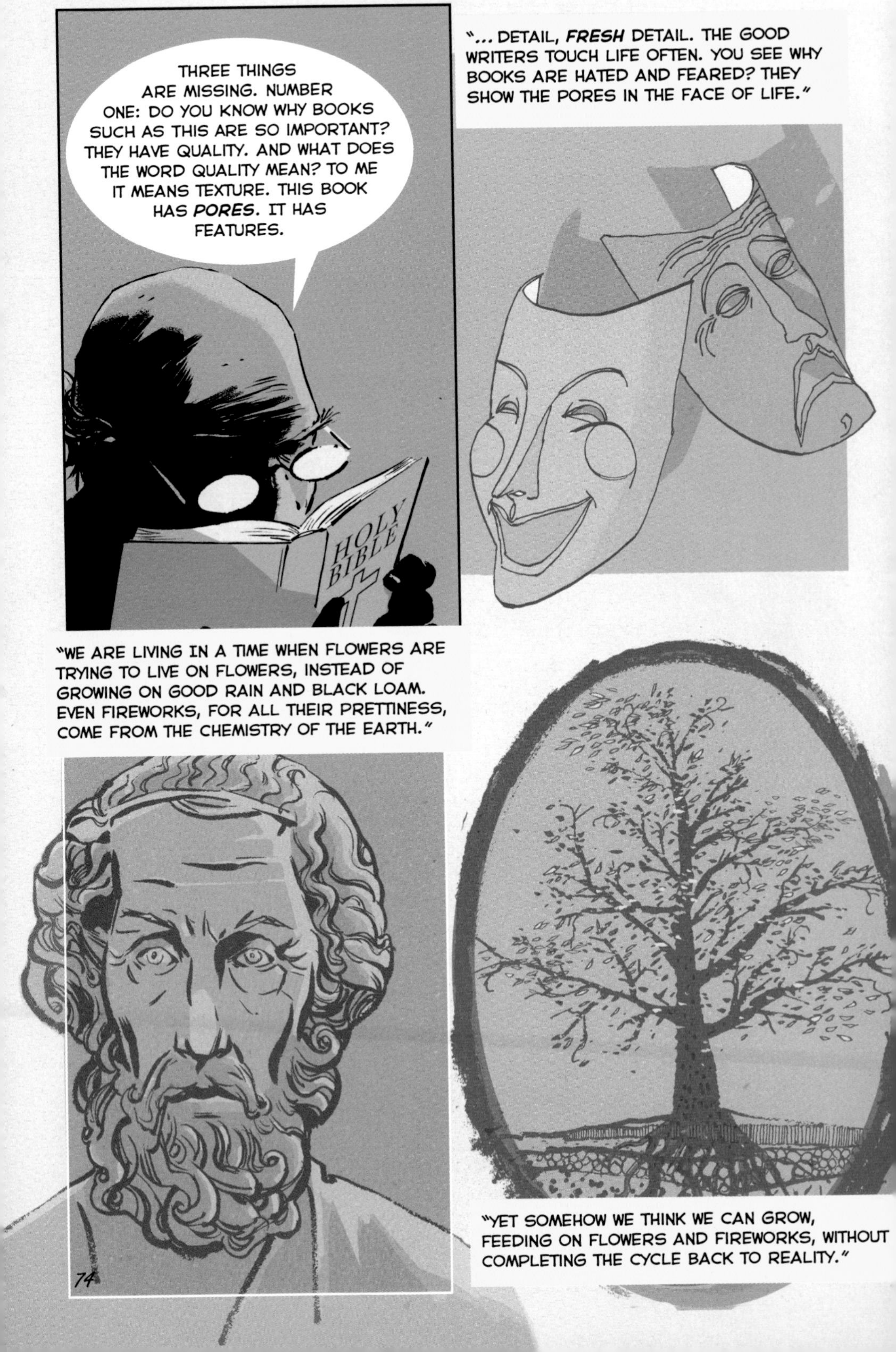
THREE THINGS ARE MISSING. NUMBER ONE: DO YOU KNOW WHY BOOKS SUCH AS THIS ARE SO IMPORTANT? THEY HAVE QUALITY. AND WHAT DOES THE WORD QUALITY MEAN? TO ME IT MEANS TEXTURE. THIS BOOK HAS ***PORES***. IT HAS FEATURES.
HOLY BIBLE
"... DETAIL, ***FRESH*** DETAIL. THE GOOD WRITERS TOUCH LIFE OFTEN. YOU SEE WHY BOOKS ARE HATED AND FEARED? THEY SHOW THE PORES IN THE FACE OF LIFE."
"WE ARE LIVING IN A TIME WHEN FLOWERS ARE TRYING TO LIVE ON FLOWERS, INSTEAD OF GROWING ON GOOD RAIN AND BLACK LOAM. EVEN FIREWORKS, FOR ALL THEIR PRETTINESS, COME FROM THE CHEMISTRY OF THE EARTH."
"YET SOMEHOW WE THINK WE CAN GROW, FEEDING ON FLOWERS AND FIREWORKS, WITHOUT COMPLETING THE CYCLE BACK TO REALITY."

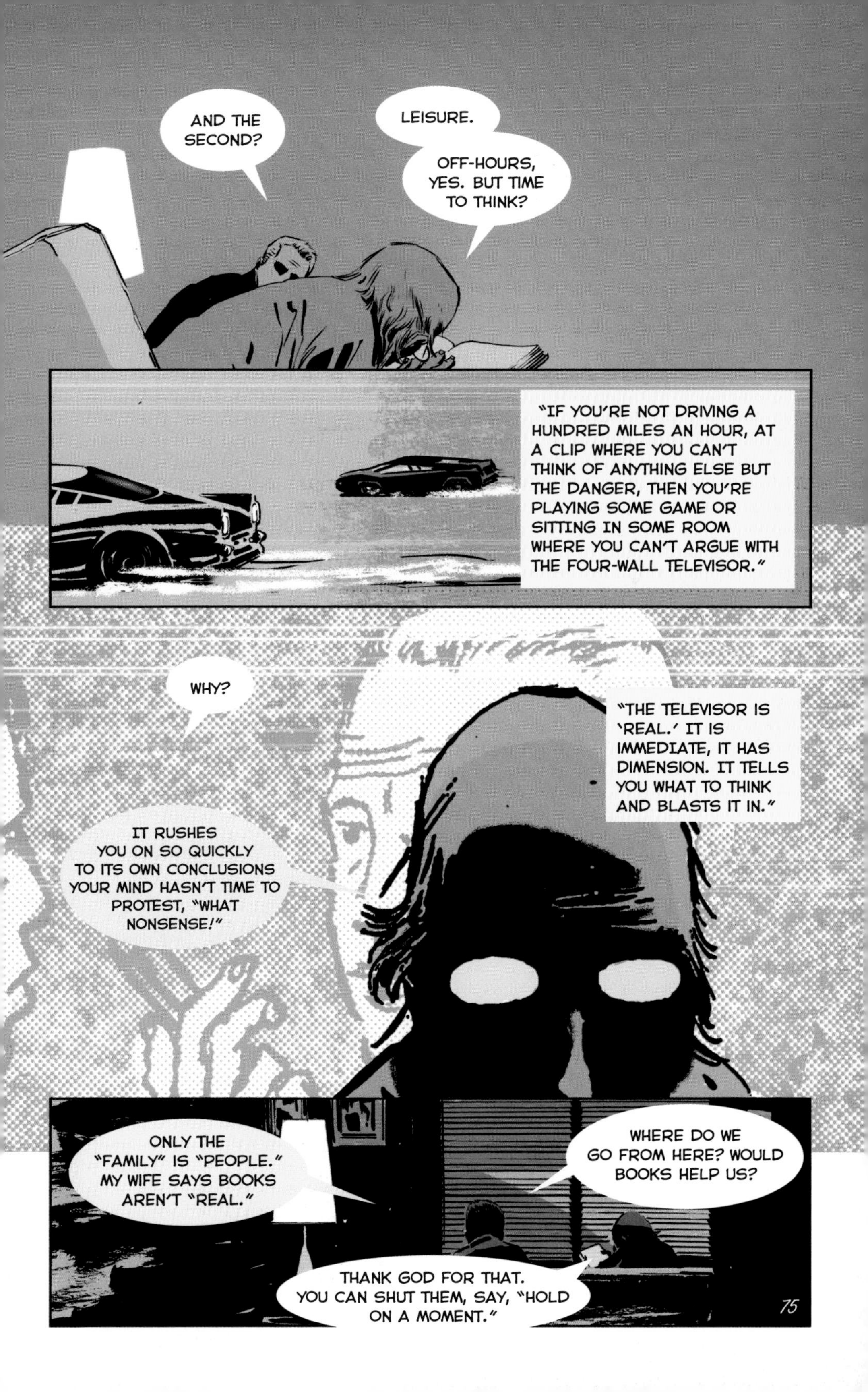
AND THE SECOND?
LEISURE.
OFF-HOURS, YES. BUT TIME TO THINK?
"IF YOU'RE NOT DRIVING A HUNDRED MILES AN HOUR, AT A CLIP WHERE YOU CAN'T THINK OF ANYTHING ELSE BUT THE DANGER, THEN YOU'RE PLAYING SOME GAME OR SITTING IN SOME ROOM WHERE YOU CAN'T ARGUE WITH THE FOUR-WALL TELEVISOR."
WHY?
"THE TELEVISOR IS 'REAL.' IT IS IMMEDIATE, IT HAS DIMENSION. IT TELLS YOU WHAT TO THINK AND BLASTS IT IN."
IT RUSHES YOU ON SO QUICKLY TO ITS OWN CONCLUSIONS YOUR MIND HASN'T TIME TO PROTEST, "WHAT NONSENSE!"
ONLY THE "FAMILY" IS "PEOPLE." MY WIFE SAYS BOOKS AREN'T "REAL."
WHERE DO WE GO FROM HERE? WOULD BOOKS HELP US?
THANK GOD FOR THAT. YOU CAN SHUT THEM, SAY, "HOLD ON A MOMENT."

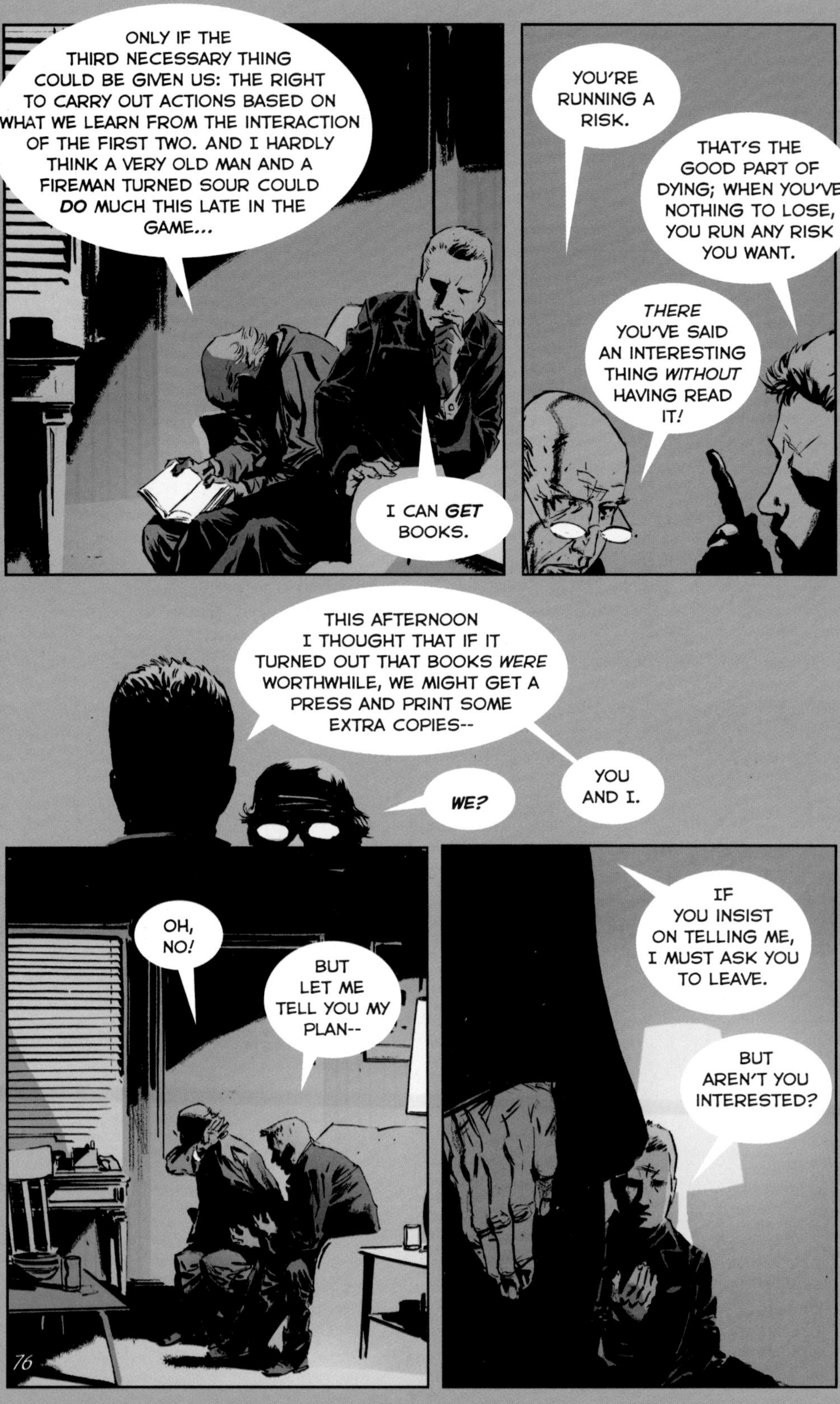
ONLY IF THE THIRD NECESSARY THING COULD BE GIVEN US: THE RIGHT TO CARRY OUT ACTIONS BASED ON WHAT WE LEARN FROM THE INTERACTION OF THE FIRST TWO. AND I HARDLY THINK A VERY OLD MAN AND A FIREMAN TURNED SOUR COULD *DO* MUCH THIS LATE IN THE GAME...
I CAN ***GET*** BOOKS.
YOU'RE RUNNING A RISK.
THAT'S THE GOOD PART OF DYING; WHEN YOU'VE NOTHING TO LOSE, YOU RUN ANY RISK YOU WANT.
THERE YOU'VE SAID AN INTERESTING THING *WITHOUT* HAVING READ IT*!*
THIS AFTERNOON I THOUGHT THAT IF IT TURNED OUT THAT BOOKS *WERE* WORTHWHILE, WE MIGHT GET A PRESS AND PRINT SOME EXTRA COPIES--
WE?
YOU AND I.
OH, NO*!*
BUT LET ME TELL YOU MY PLAN--
IF YOU INSIST ON TELLING ME, I MUST ASK YOU TO LEAVE.
BUT AREN'T YOU INTERESTED?

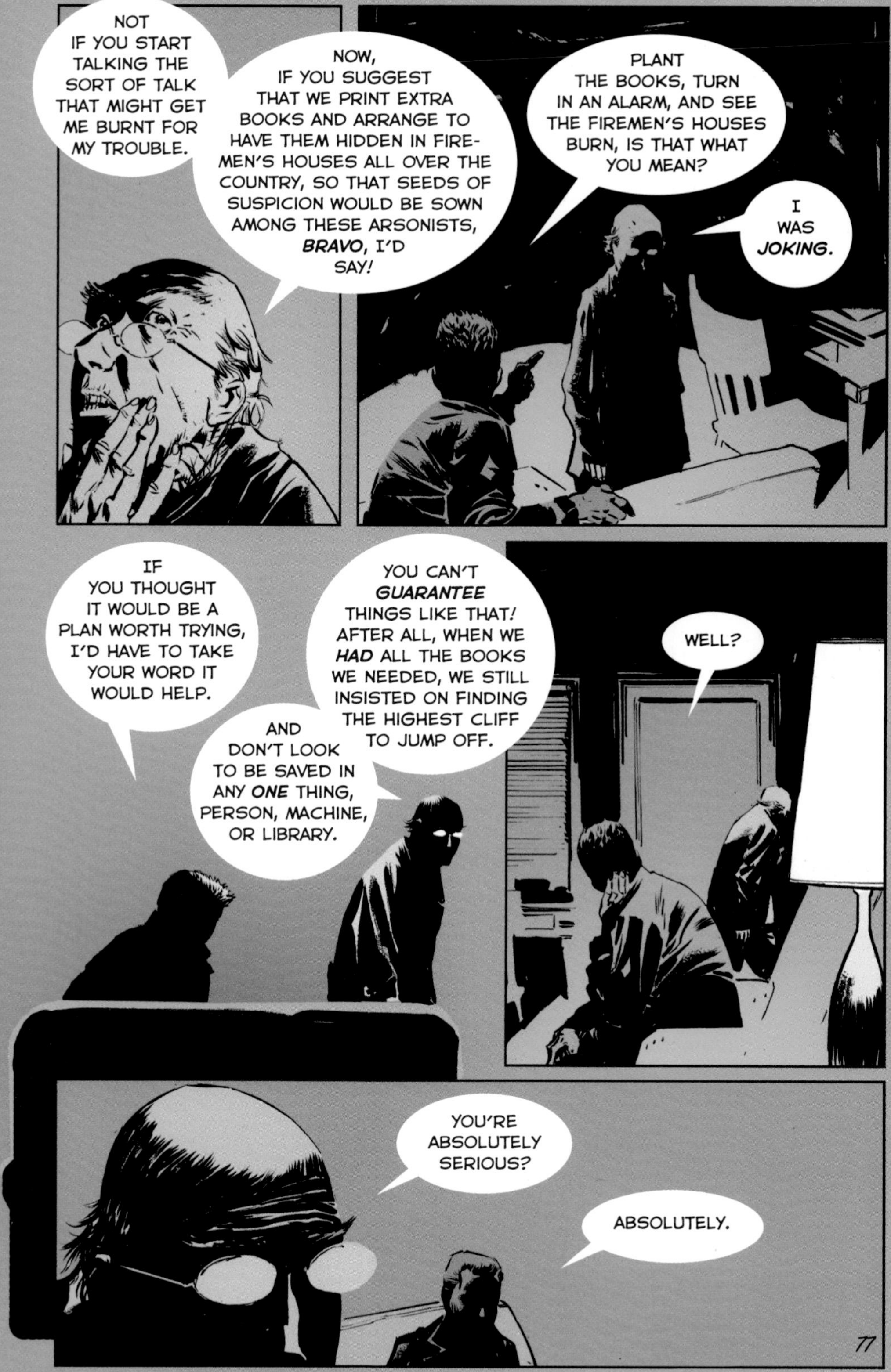
NOT IF YOU START TALKING THE SORT OF TALK THAT MIGHT GET ME BURNT FOR MY TROUBLE.
NOW, IF YOU SUGGEST THAT WE PRINT EXTRA BOOKS AND ARRANGE TO HAVE THEM HIDDEN IN FIRE-MEN'S HOUSES ALL OVER THE COUNTRY, SO THAT SEEDS OF SUSPICION WOULD BE SOWN AMONG THESE ARSONISTS, BRAVO, I'D SAY!
PLANT THE BOOKS, TURN IN AN ALARM, AND SEE THE FIREMEN'S HOUSES BURN, IS THAT WHAT YOU MEAN?
I WAS JOKING.
IF YOU THOUGHT IT WOULD BE A PLAN WORTH TRYING, I'D HAVE TO TAKE YOUR WORD IT WOULD HELP.
YOU CAN'T GUARANTEE THINGS LIKE THAT! AFTER ALL, WHEN WE HAD ALL THE BOOKS WE NEEDED, WE STILL INSISTED ON FINDING THE HIGHEST CLIFF TO JUMP OFF.
AND DON'T LOOK TO BE SAVED IN ANY ONE THING, PERSON, MACHINE, OR LIBRARY.
WELL?
YOU'RE ABSOLUTELY SERIOUS?
ABSOLUTELY.

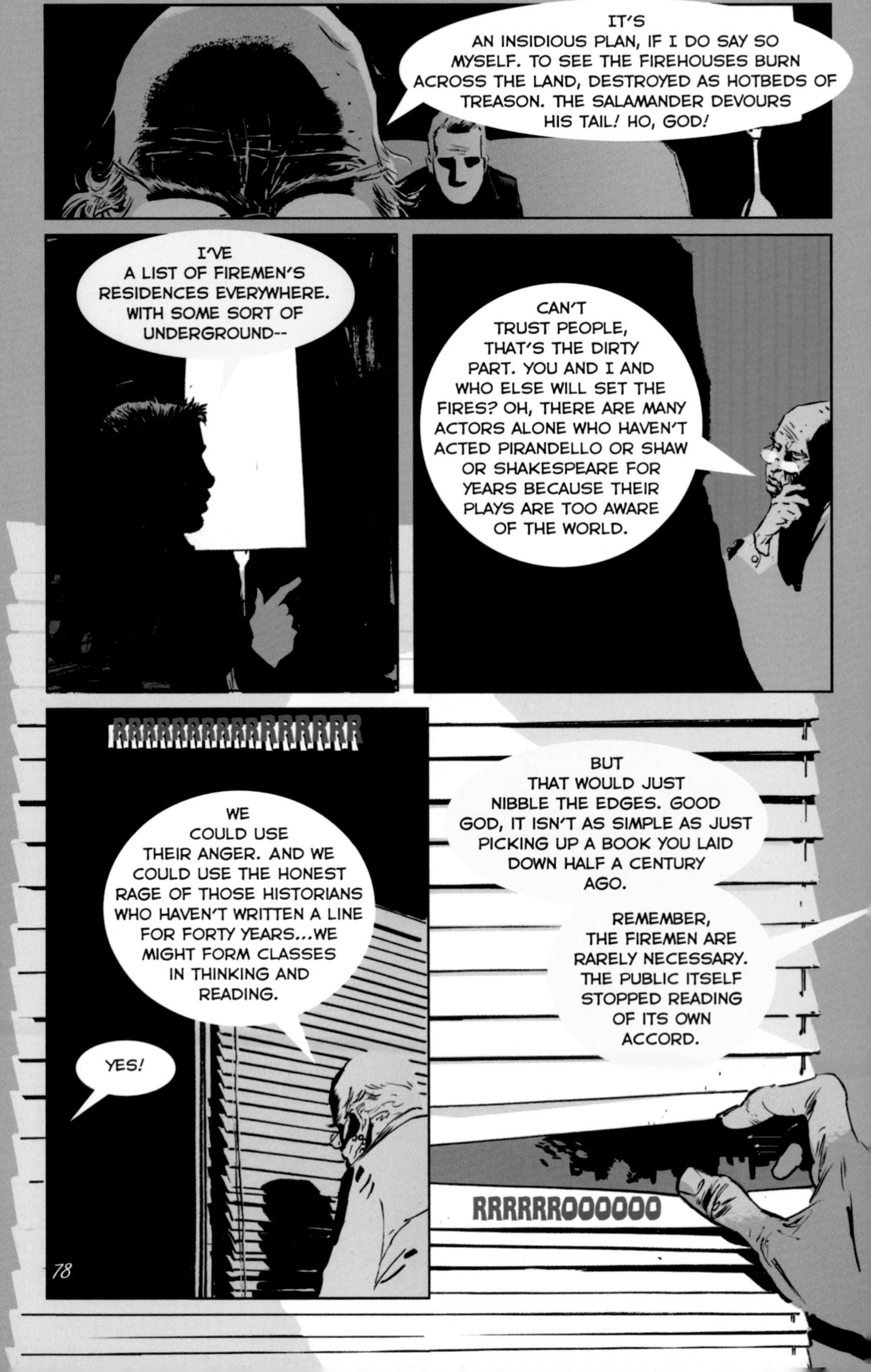

IT'S AN INSIDIOUS PLAN, IF I DO SAY SO MYSELF. TO SEE THE FIREHOUSES BURN ACROSS THE LAND, DESTROYED AS HOTBEDS OF TREASON. THE SALAMANDER DEVOURS HIS TAIL! HO, GOD!
I'VE A LIST OF FIREMEN'S RESIDENCES EVERYWHERE. WITH SOME SORT OF UNDERGROUND--
CAN'T TRUST PEOPLE, THAT'S THE DIRTY PART. YOU AND I AND WHO ELSE WILL SET THE FIRES? OH, THERE ARE MANY ACTORS ALONE WHO HAVEN'T ACTED PIRANDELLO OR SHAW OR SHAKESPEARE FOR YEARS BECAUSE THEIR PLAYS ARE TOO AWARE OF THE WORLD.
RRRRRRRRRRRRRRRR
WE COULD USE THEIR ANGER. AND WE COULD USE THE HONEST RAGE OF THOSE HISTORIANS WHO HAVEN'T WRITTEN A LINE FOR FORTY YEARS...WE MIGHT FORM CLASSES IN THINKING AND READING.
YES!
BUT THAT WOULD JUST NIBBLE THE EDGES. GOOD GOD, IT ISN'T AS SIMPLE AS JUST PICKING UP A BOOK YOU LAID DOWN HALF A CENTURY AGO.
REMEMBER, THE FIREMEN ARE RARELY NECESSARY. THE PUBLIC ITSELF STOPPED READING OF ITS OWN ACCORD.
RRRRRROOOOOO

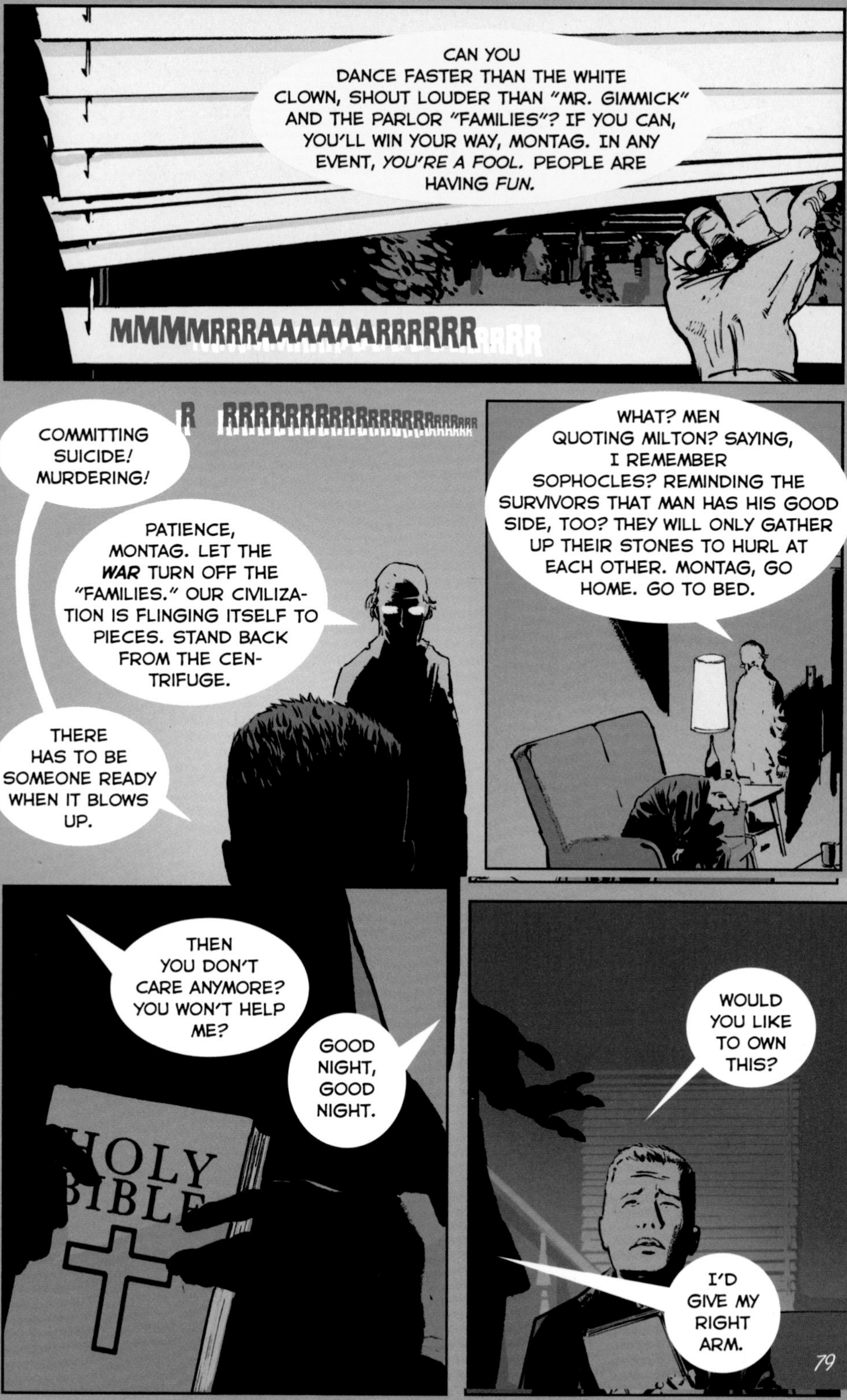
CAN YOU DANCE FASTER THAN THE WHITE CLOWN, SHOUT LOUDER THAN "MR. GIMMICK" AND THE PARLOR "FAMILIES"? IF YOU CAN, YOU'LL WIN YOUR WAY, MONTAG. IN ANY EVENT, YOU'RE A FOOL. PEOPLE ARE HAVING FUN.
MMMMRRRAAAAAAARRRRRRRRRR
R RRRRRRRRRRRRRRRRRRRRRR
COMMITTING SUICIDE! MURDERING!
PATIENCE, MONTAG. LET THE WAR TURN OFF THE "FAMILIES." OUR CIVILIZATION IS FLINGING ITSELF TO PIECES. STAND BACK FROM THE CENTRIFUGE.
THERE HAS TO BE SOMEONE READY WHEN IT BLOWS UP.
WHAT? MEN QUOTING MILTON? SAYING, I REMEMBER SOPHOCLES? REMINDING THE SURVIVORS THAT MAN HAS HIS GOOD SIDE, TOO? THEY WILL ONLY GATHER UP THEIR STONES TO HURL AT EACH OTHER. MONTAG, GO HOME. GO TO BED.
THEN YOU DON'T CARE ANYMORE? YOU WON'T HELP ME?
GOOD NIGHT, GOOD NIGHT.
HOLY BIBLE
WOULD YOU LIKE TO OWN THIS?
I'D GIVE MY RIGHT ARM.

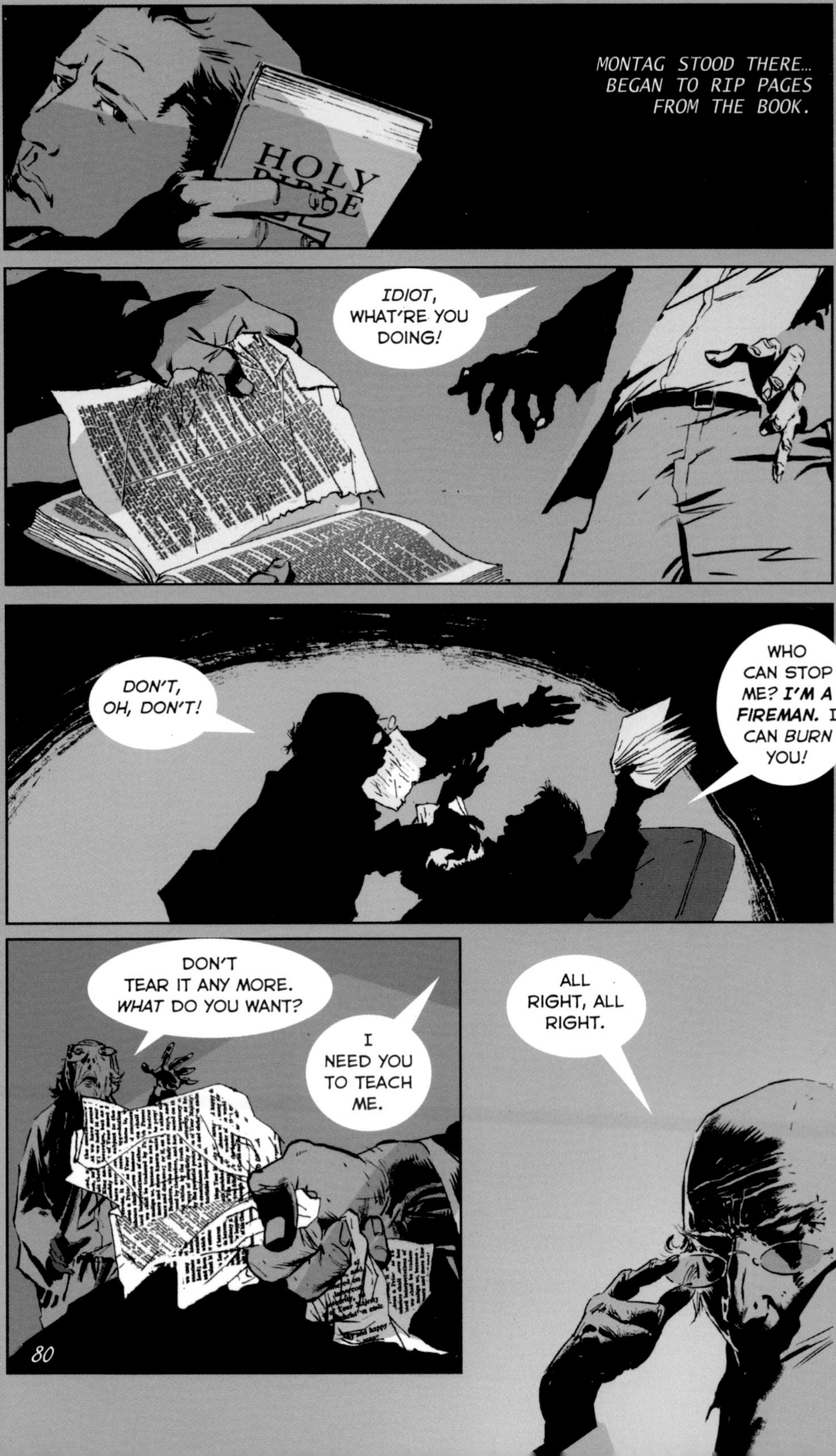
MONTAG STOOD THERE... BEGAN TO RIP PAGES FROM THE BOOK.
HOLY BIBLE
IDIOT, WHAT'RE YOU DOING!
DON'T, OH, DON'T!
WHO CAN STOP ME? I'M A FIREMAN. I CAN BURN YOU!
DON'T TEAR IT ANY MORE. WHAT DO YOU WANT?
I NEED YOU TO TEACH ME.
ALL RIGHT, ALL RIGHT.

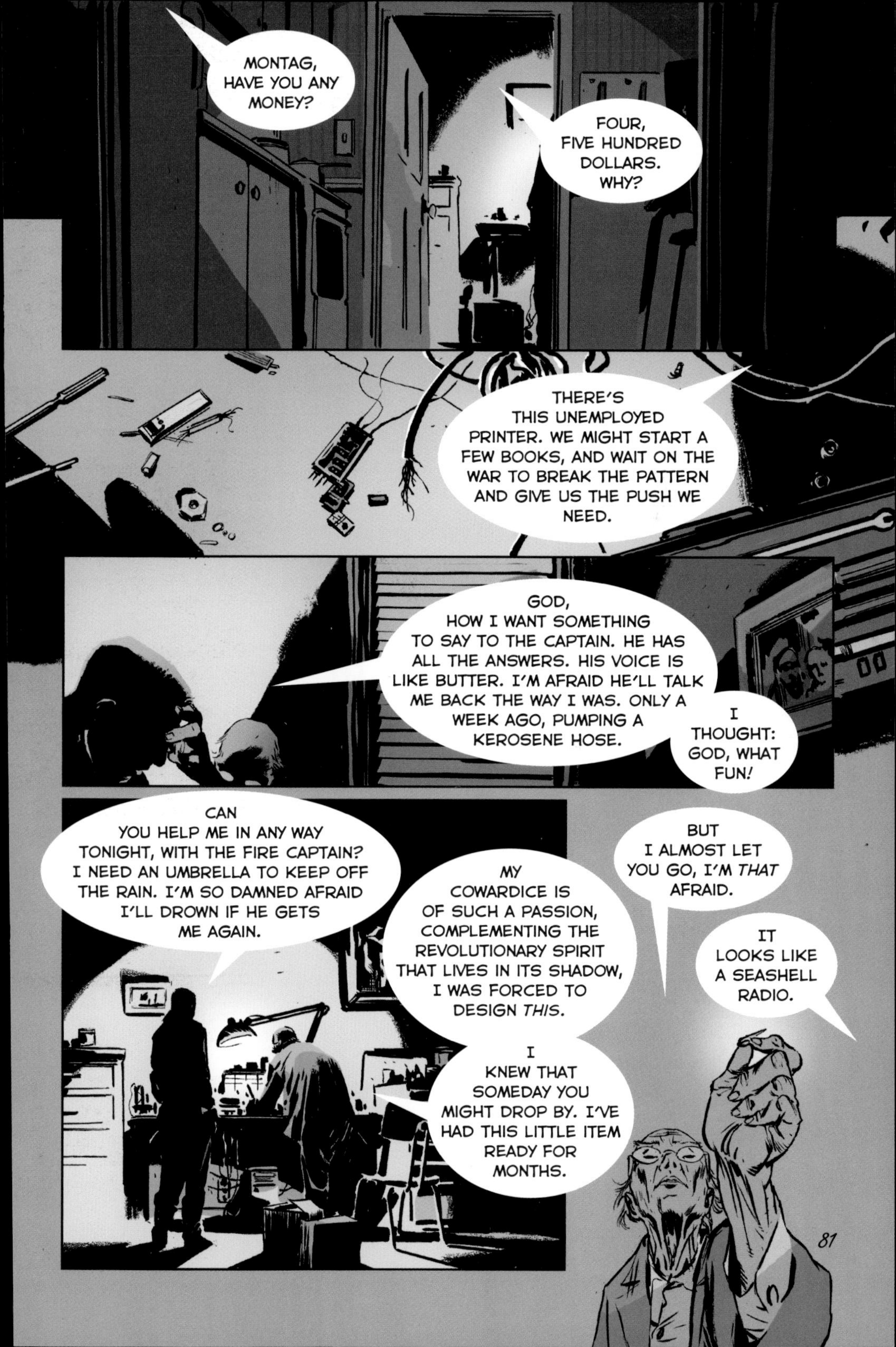
MONTAG, HAVE YOU ANY MONEY?
FOUR, FIVE HUNDRED DOLLARS. WHY?
THERE'S THIS UNEMPLOYED PRINTER. WE MIGHT START A FEW BOOKS, AND WAIT ON THE WAR TO BREAK THE PATTERN AND GIVE US THE PUSH WE NEED.
GOD, HOW I WANT SOMETHING TO SAY TO THE CAPTAIN. HE HAS ALL THE ANSWERS. HIS VOICE IS LIKE BUTTER. I'M AFRAID HE'LL TALK ME BACK THE WAY I WAS. ONLY A WEEK AGO, PUMPING A KEROSENE HOSE.
I THOUGHT: GOD, WHAT FUN!
CAN YOU HELP ME IN ANY WAY TONIGHT, WITH THE FIRE CAPTAIN? I NEED AN UMBRELLA TO KEEP OFF THE RAIN. I'M SO DAMNED AFRAID I'LL DROWN IF HE GETS ME AGAIN.
MY COWARDICE IS OF SUCH A PASSION, COMPLEMENTING THE REVOLUTIONARY SPIRIT THAT LIVES IN ITS SHADOW, I WAS FORCED TO DESIGN *THIS*.
I KNEW THAT SOMEDAY YOU MIGHT DROP BY. I'VE HAD THIS LITTLE ITEM READY FOR MONTHS.
BUT I ALMOST LET YOU GO, I'M *THAT* AFRAID.
IT LOOKS LIKE A SEASHELL RADIO.
81

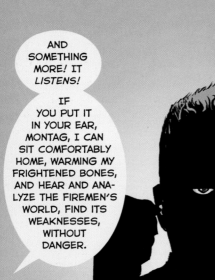

AND SOMETHING MORE! IT LISTENS!

IF YOU PUT IT IN YOUR EAR, MONTAG, I CAN SIT COMFORTABLY HOME, WARMING MY FRIGHTENED BONES, AND HEAR AND ANALYZE THE FIREMEN'S WORLD, FIND ITS WEAKNESSES, WITHOUT DANGER.

GO TO THE FIRE-HOUSE WHEN IT'S TIME. I'LL BE WITH YOU. LET'S LISTEN TO THIS CAPTAIN BEATTY TOGETHER. I'LL GIVE YOU THINGS TO SAY.

HERE. I'LL CHANCE TURNING IN A SUBSTITUTE.

GOOD NIGHT, PRO-FESSOR.

NOT GOOD NIGHT. I'LL BE WITH YOU THE REST OF THE NIGHT, A VINEGAR GNAT TICKLING YOUR EAR WHEN YOU NEED ME. GOOD LUCK.

FABER?

YES.

I'M NOT THINKING. I'M JUST DOING LIKE I'M TOLD, LIKE ALWAYS. WHEN DO I START WORKING THINGS OUT ON MY OWN?

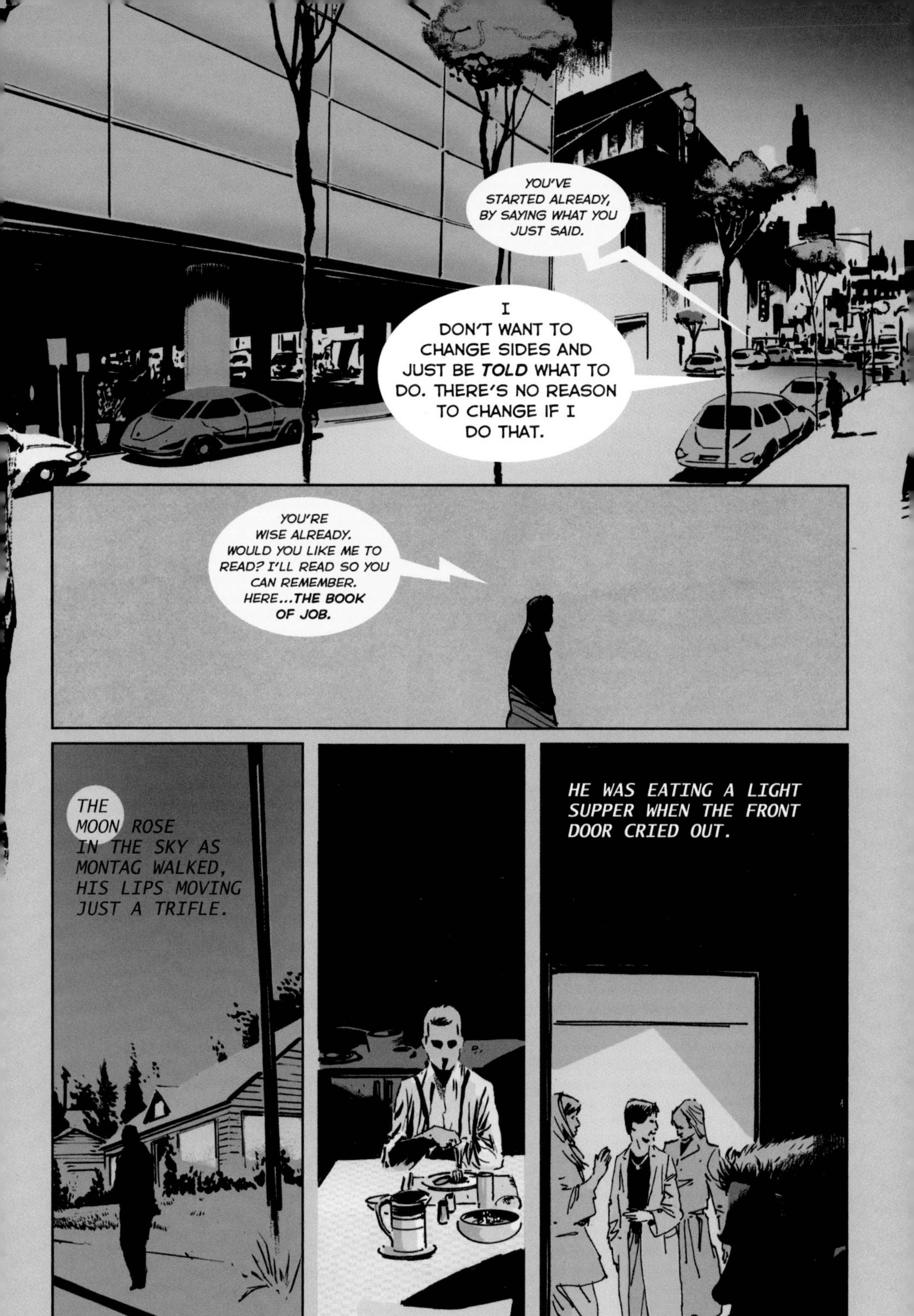
YOU'VE STARTED ALREADY, BY SAYING WHAT YOU JUST SAID.
I DON'T WANT TO CHANGE SIDES AND JUST BE TOLD WHAT TO DO. THERE'S NO REASON TO CHANGE IF I DO THAT.
YOU'RE WISE ALREADY. WOULD YOU LIKE ME TO READ? I'LL READ SO YOU CAN REMEMBER. HERE...THE BOOK OF JOB.
THE MOON ROSE IN THE SKY AS MONTAG WALKED, HIS LIPS MOVING JUST A TRIFLE.
HE WAS EATING A LIGHT SUPPER WHEN THE FRONT DOOR CRIED OUT.

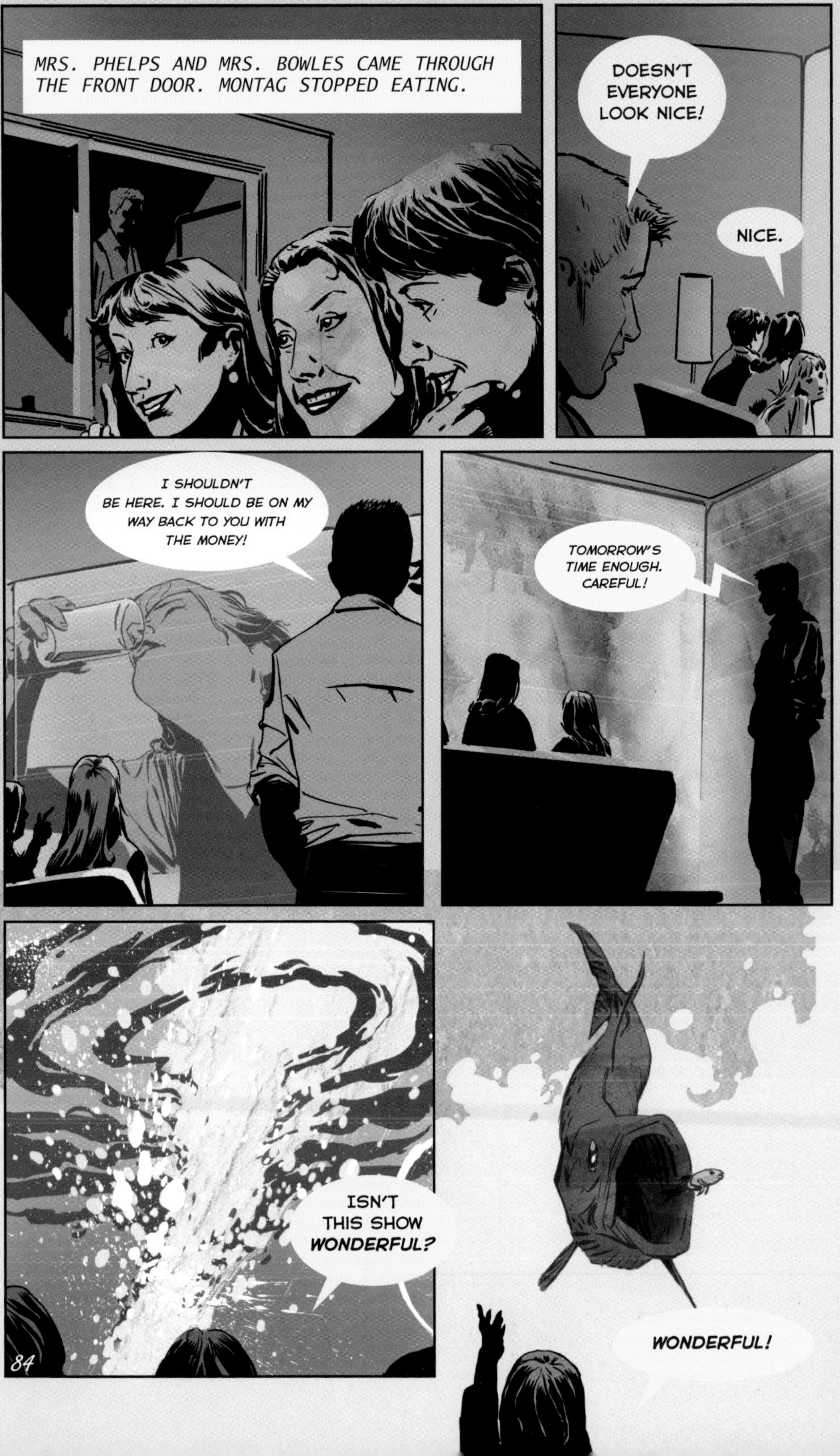
MRS. PHELPS AND MRS. BOWLES CAME THROUGH THE FRONT DOOR. MONTAG STOPPED EATING.
DOESN'T EVERYONE LOOK NICE!
NICE.
I SHOULDN'T BE HERE. I SHOULD BE ON MY WAY BACK TO YOU WITH THE MONEY!
TOMORROW'S TIME ENOUGH. CAREFUL!
ISN'T THIS SHOW WONDERFUL?
WONDERFUL!

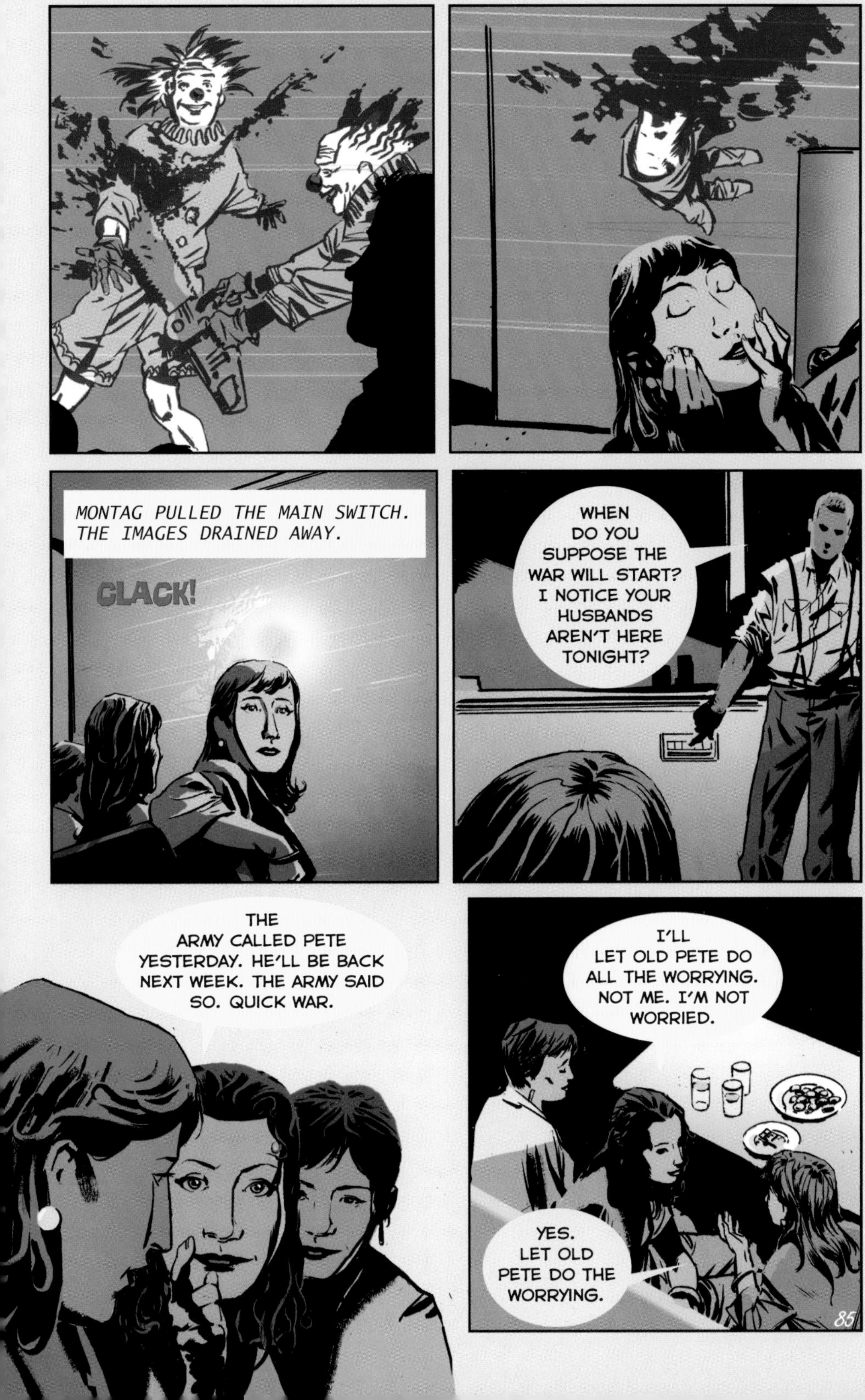
MONTAG PULLED THE MAIN SWITCH. THE IMAGES DRAINED AWAY.
CLACK!
WHEN DO YOU SUPPOSE THE WAR WILL START? I NOTICE YOUR HUSBANDS AREN'T HERE TONIGHT?
THE ARMY CALLED PETE YESTERDAY. HE'LL BE BACK NEXT WEEK. THE ARMY SAID SO. QUICK WAR.
I'LL LET OLD PETE DO ALL THE WORRYING. NOT ME. I'M NOT WORRIED.
YES. LET OLD PETE DO THE WORRYING.

HE SAID, IF I GET KILLED OFF, YOU JUST GO RIGHT AHEAD AND DON'T CRY, BUT GET MARRIED AGAIN, AND DON'T THINK OF ME.

...ROMANCE LAST NIGHT IN YOUR WALL? WELL, IT WAS ALL ABOUT THIS WOMAN WHO--

THAT REMINDS ME. DID YOU SEE THAT CLARA DOVE FIVE-MINUTE...

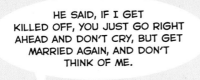

MONTAG SAID NOTHING...THE WOMEN'S FACES GREW HAUNTED WITH SILENCE.

LET'S TALK.

LET'S TALK POLITICS, TO PLEASE GUY!

THE THREE EMPTY WALLS OF THE ROOM WERE LIKE THE PALE BROWS OF SLEEPING GIANTS...

SOUNDS FINE. I VOTED LAST ELECTION, SAME AS EVERYONE, AND I LAID IT ON THE LINE FOR PRESIDENT NOBLE. I THINK HE'S ONE OF THE NICEST-LOOKING MEN EVER BECAME PRESIDENT.

OH, BUT THE MAN THEY RAN AGAINST HIM!

HE WASN'T MUCH, WAS HE? KIND OF SMALL AND HOMELY AND HE DIDN'T SHAVE TOO CLOSE OR COMB HIS HAIR VERY WELL.

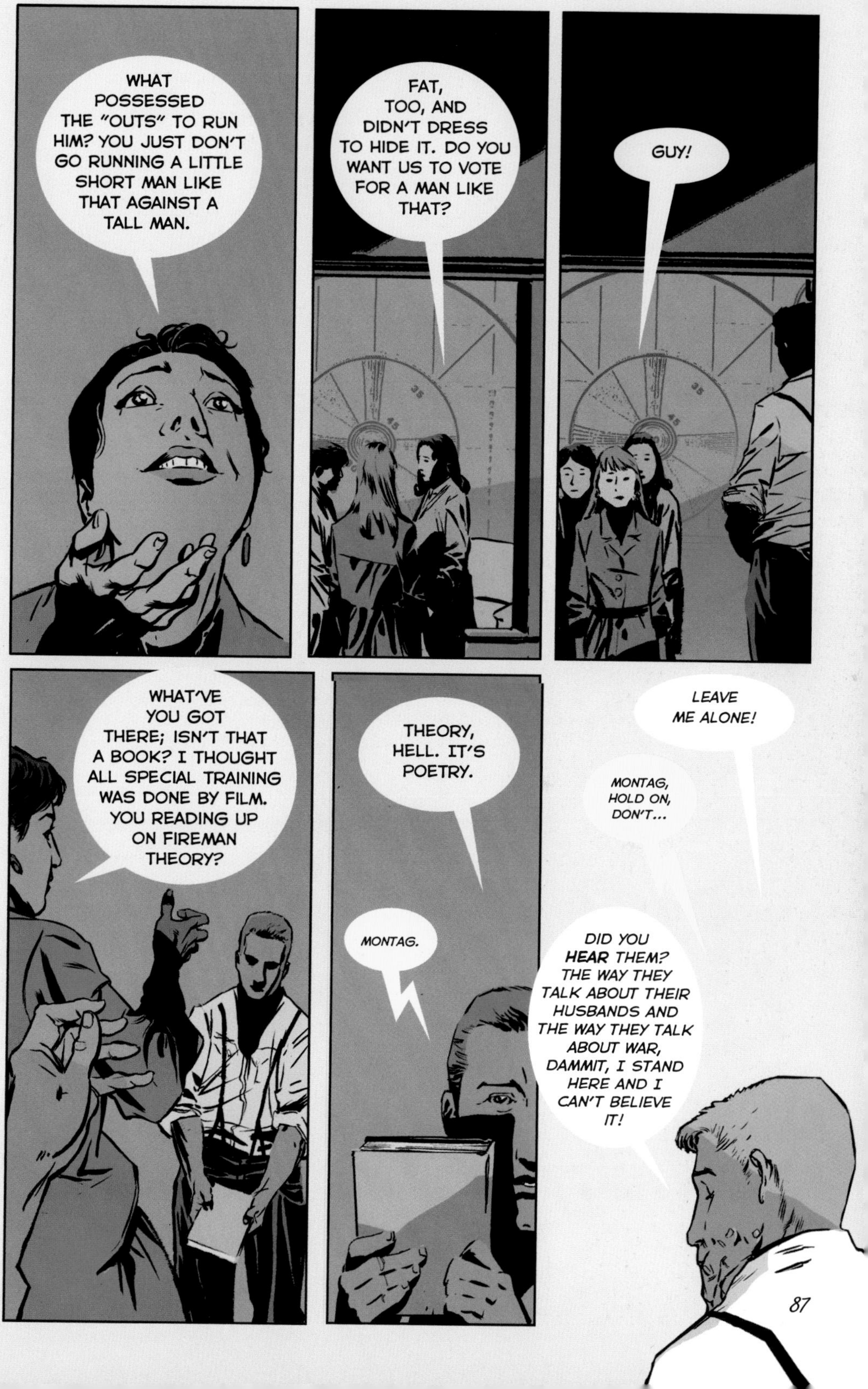
WHAT POSSESSED THE "OUTS" TO RUN HIM? YOU JUST DON'T GO RUNNING A LITTLE SHORT MAN LIKE THAT AGAINST A TALL MAN.
FAT, TOO, AND DIDN'T DRESS TO HIDE IT. DO YOU WANT US TO VOTE FOR A MAN LIKE THAT?
GUY!
WHAT'VE YOU GOT THERE; ISN'T THAT A BOOK? I THOUGHT ALL SPECIAL TRAINING WAS DONE BY FILM. YOU READING UP ON FIREMAN THEORY?
THEORY, HELL. IT'S POETRY.
MONTAG.
LEAVE ME ALONE!
MONTAG, HOLD ON, DON'T...
DID YOU **HEAR** THEM? THE WAY THEY TALK ABOUT THEIR HUSBANDS AND THE WAY THEY TALK ABOUT WAR, DAMMIT, I STAND HERE AND I CAN'T BELIEVE IT!

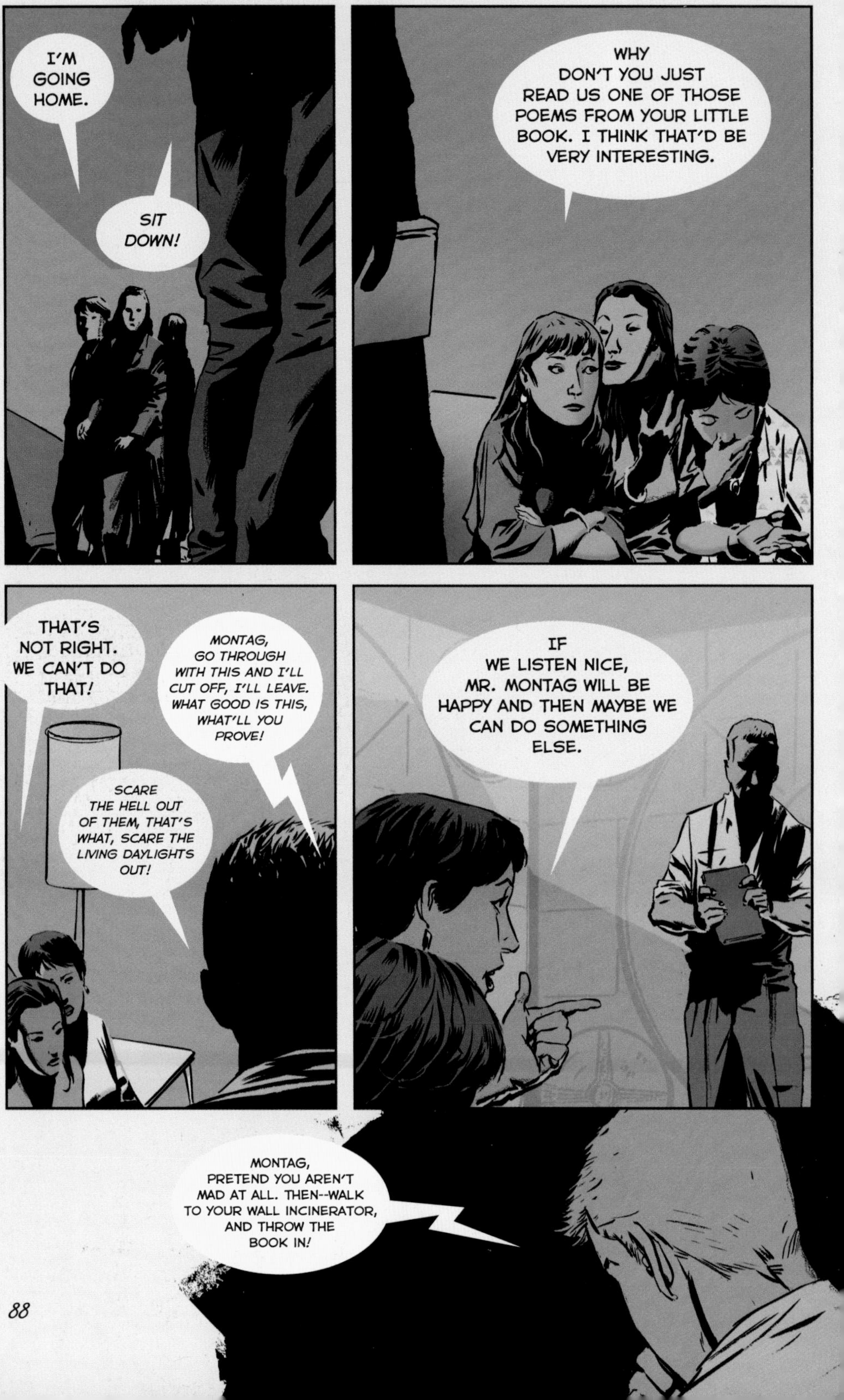

I'M GOING HOME.
SIT DOWN!
WHY DON'T YOU JUST READ US ONE OF THOSE POEMS FROM YOUR LITTLE BOOK. I THINK THAT'D BE VERY INTERESTING.
THAT'S NOT RIGHT. WE CAN'T DO THAT!
MONTAG, GO THROUGH WITH THIS AND I'LL CUT OFF, I'LL LEAVE. WHAT GOOD IS THIS, WHAT'LL YOU PROVE!
SCARE THE HELL OUT OF THEM, THAT'S WHAT, SCARE THE LIVING DAYLIGHTS OUT!
IF WE LISTEN NICE, MR. MONTAG WILL BE HAPPY AND THEN MAYBE WE CAN DO SOMETHING ELSE.
MONTAG, PRETEND YOU AREN'T MAD AT ALL. THEN--WALK TO YOUR WALL INCINERATOR, AND THROW THE BOOK IN!

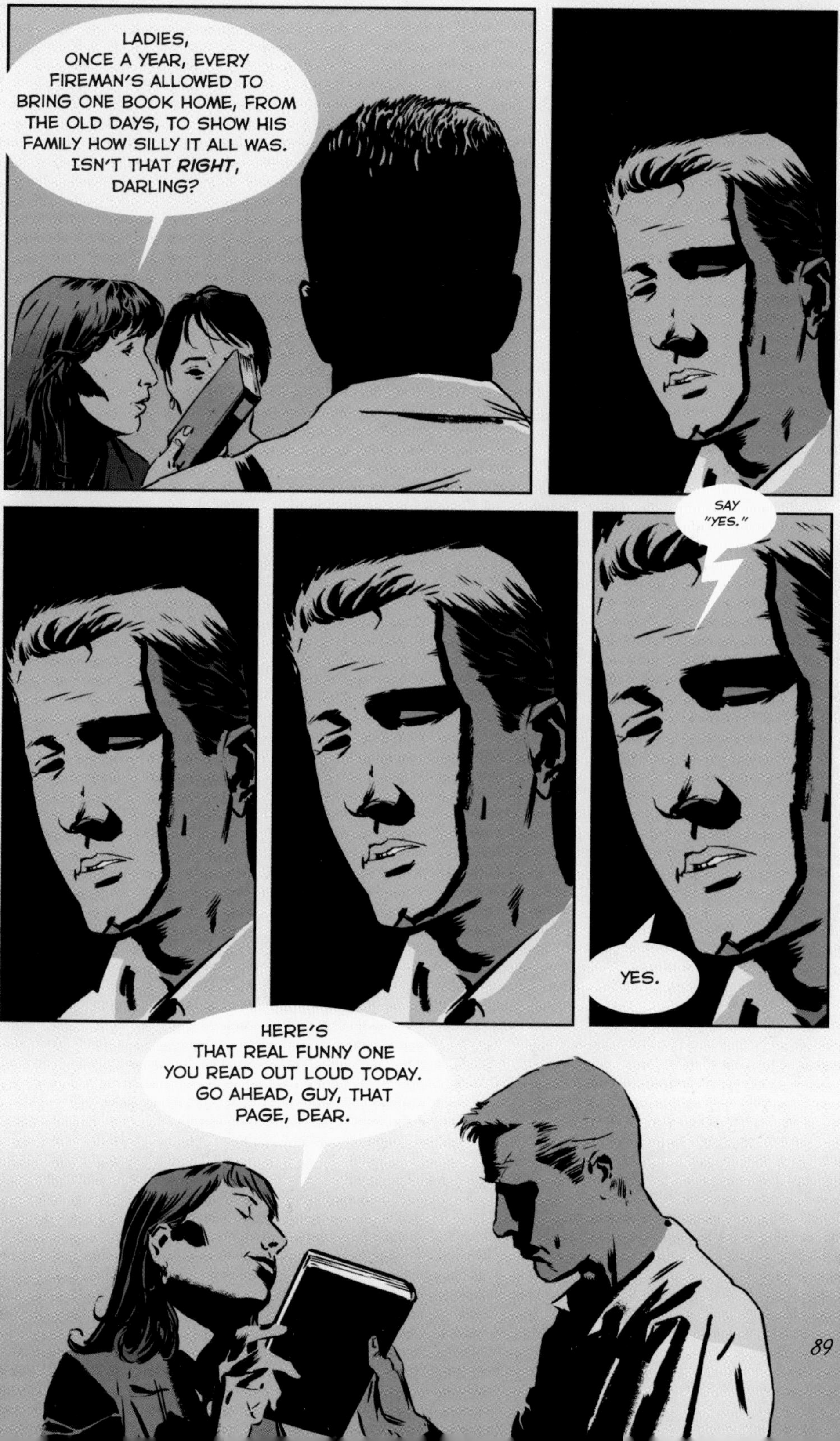
LADIES, ONCE A YEAR, EVERY FIREMAN'S ALLOWED TO BRING ONE BOOK HOME, FROM THE OLD DAYS, TO SHOW HIS FAMILY HOW SILLY IT ALL WAS. ISN'T THAT *RIGHT*, DARLING?
SAY "YES."
YES.
HERE'S THAT REAL FUNNY ONE YOU READ OUT LOUD TODAY. GO AHEAD, GUY, THAT PAGE, DEAR.

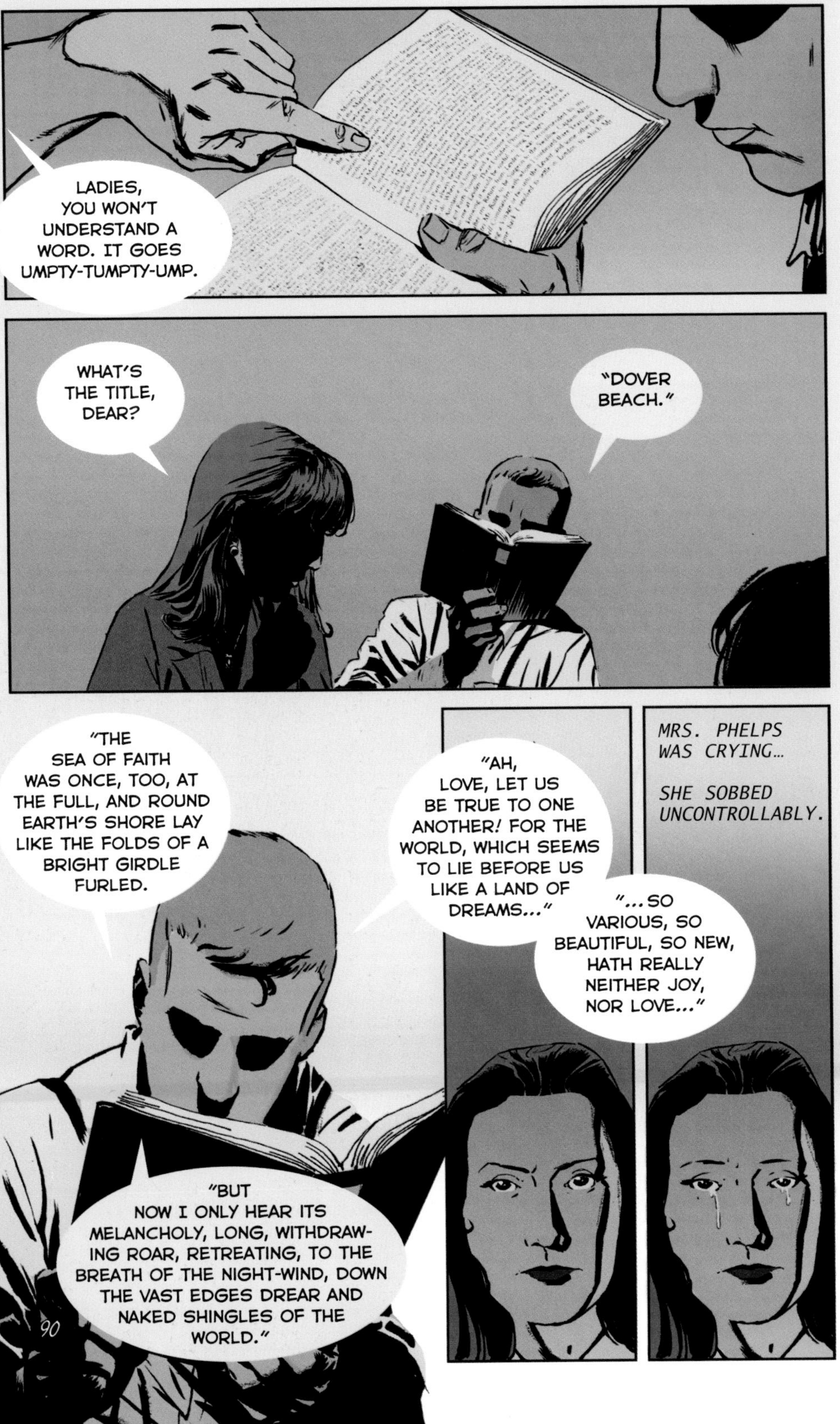
LADIES, YOU WON'T UNDERSTAND A WORD. IT GOES UMPTY-TUMPTY-UMP.
WHAT'S THE TITLE, DEAR?
"DOVER BEACH."
"THE SEA OF FAITH WAS ONCE, TOO, AT THE FULL, AND ROUND EARTH'S SHORE LAY LIKE THE FOLDS OF A BRIGHT GIRDLE FURLED.
"BUT NOW I ONLY HEAR ITS MELANCHOLY, LONG, WITHDRAW-ING ROAR, RETREATING, TO THE BREATH OF THE NIGHT-WIND, DOWN THE VAST EDGES DREAR AND NAKED SHINGLES OF THE WORLD."
"AH, LOVE, LET US BE TRUE TO ONE ANOTHER! FOR THE WORLD, WHICH SEEMS TO LIE BEFORE US LIKE A LAND OF DREAMS..."
"...SO VARIOUS, SO BEAUTIFUL, SO NEW, HATH REALLY NEITHER JOY, NOR LOVE..."
MRS. PHELPS WAS CRYING...
SHE SOBBED UNCONTROLLABLY.

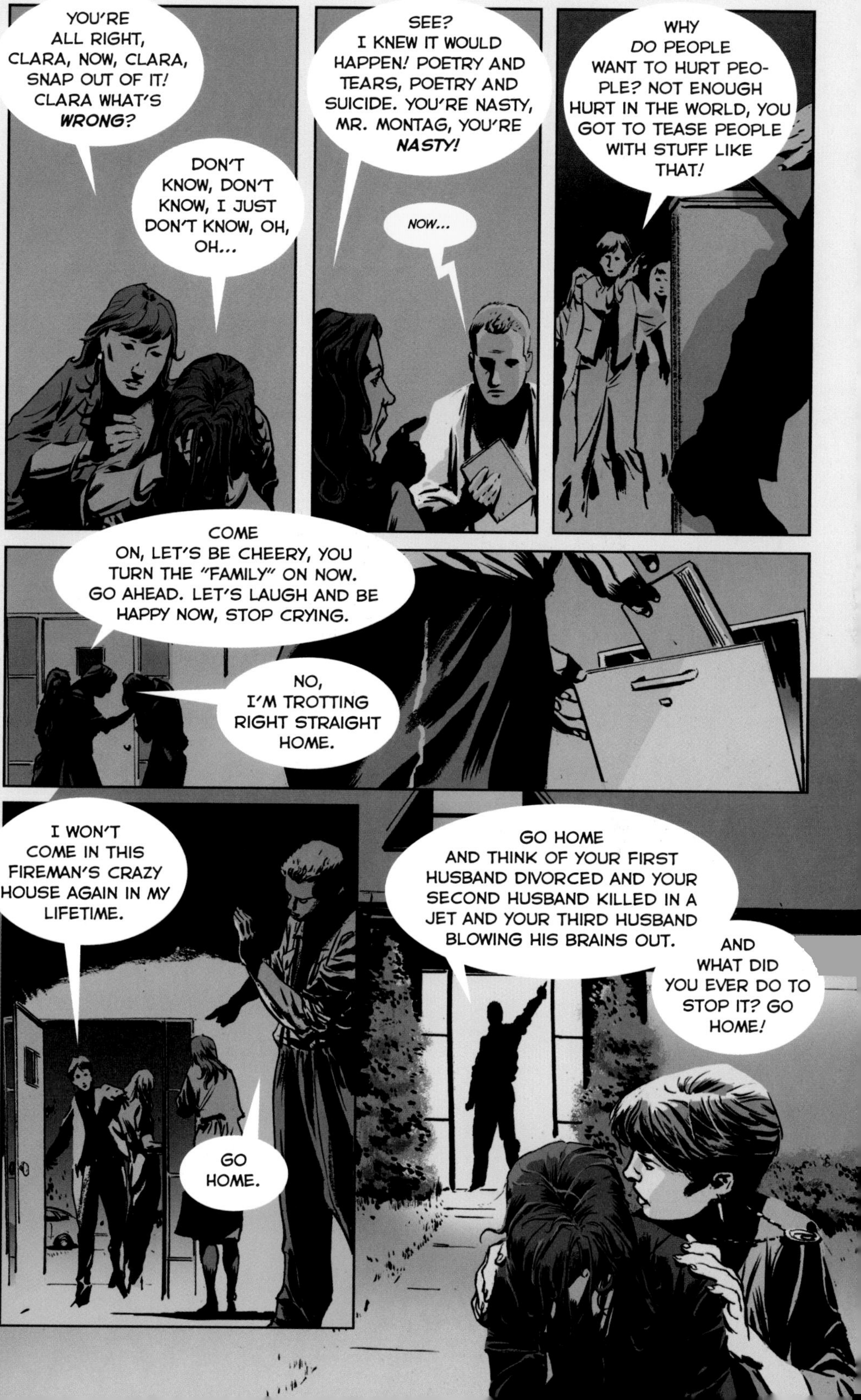
YOU'RE ALL RIGHT, CLARA, NOW, CLARA, SNAP OUT OF IT! CLARA WHAT'S WRONG?
DON'T KNOW, DON'T KNOW, I JUST DON'T KNOW, OH, OH...
SEE? I KNEW IT WOULD HAPPEN! POETRY AND TEARS, POETRY AND SUICIDE. YOU'RE NASTY, MR. MONTAG, YOU'RE NASTY!
NOW...
WHY DO PEOPLE WANT TO HURT PEOPLE? NOT ENOUGH HURT IN THE WORLD, YOU GOT TO TEASE PEOPLE WITH STUFF LIKE THAT!
COME ON, LET'S BE CHEERY, YOU TURN THE "FAMILY" ON NOW. GO AHEAD. LET'S LAUGH AND BE HAPPY NOW, STOP CRYING.
NO, I'M TROTTING RIGHT STRAIGHT HOME.
I WON'T COME IN THIS FIREMAN'S CRAZY HOUSE AGAIN IN MY LIFETIME.
GO HOME.
GO HOME AND THINK OF YOUR FIRST HUSBAND DIVORCED AND YOUR SECOND HUSBAND KILLED IN A JET AND YOUR THIRD HUSBAND BLOWING HIS BRAINS OUT.
AND WHAT DID YOU EVER DO TO STOP IT? GO HOME!

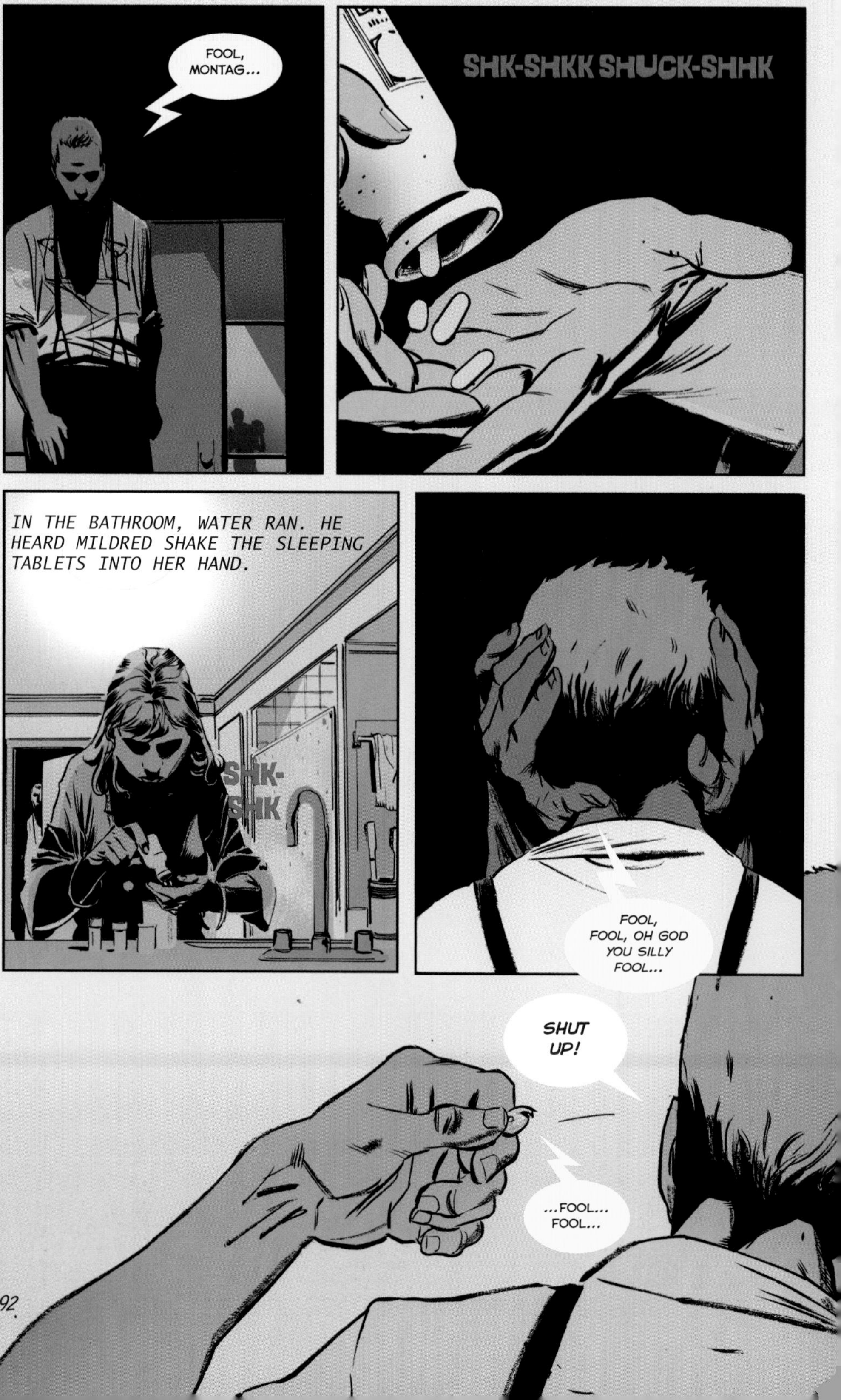

FOOL, MONTAG...
SHK-SHKK SHUCK-SHHK
IN THE BATHROOM, WATER RAN. HE HEARD MILDRED SHAKE THE SLEEPING TABLETS INTO HER HAND.
SHK-SHK
FOOL, FOOL, OH GOD YOU SILLY FOOL...
SHUT UP!
...FOOL... FOOL...

HE SEARCHED THE HOUSE AND FOUND THE BOOKS WHERE MILDRED HAD STACKED THEM.

HE HID THEM IN THE BUSHES...

MILDRED?

AT THE DARKENED BEDROOM... THERE WAS NO SOUND.

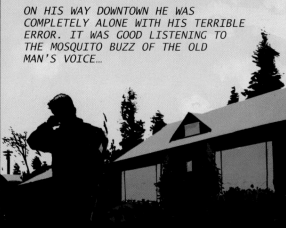

ON HIS WAY DOWNTOWN HE WAS COMPLETELY ALONE WITH HIS TERRIBLE ERROR. IT WAS GOOD LISTENING TO THE MOSQUITO BUZZ OF THE OLD MAN'S VOICE...

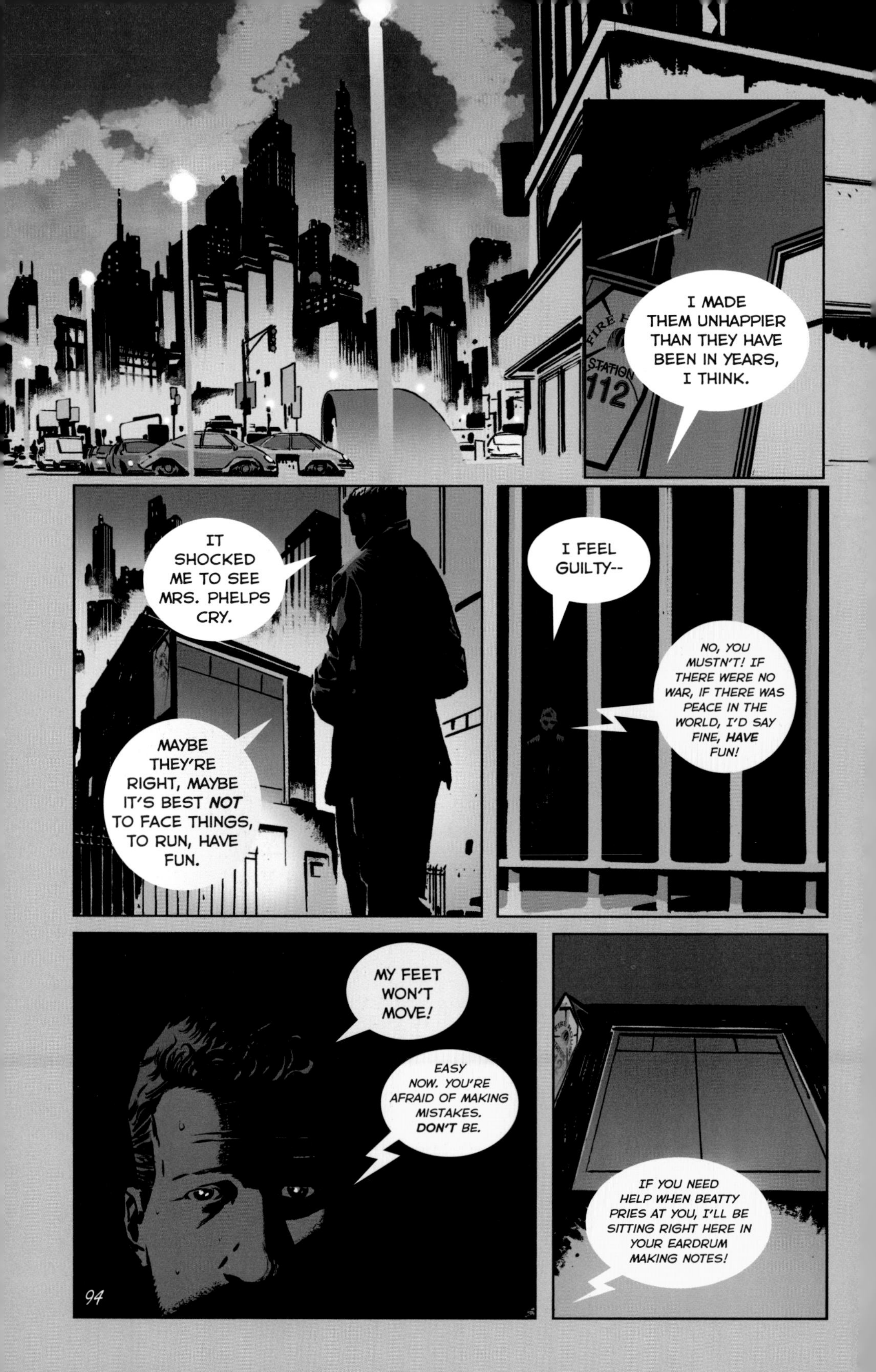
I MADE THEM UNHAPPIER THAN THEY HAVE BEEN IN YEARS, I THINK.
IT SHOCKED ME TO SEE MRS. PHELPS CRY.
MAYBE THEY'RE RIGHT, MAYBE IT'S BEST *NOT* TO FACE THINGS, TO RUN, HAVE FUN.
I FEEL GUILTY--
NO, YOU MUSTN'T! IF THERE WERE NO WAR, IF THERE WAS PEACE IN THE WORLD, I'D SAY FINE, **HAVE** FUN!
MY FEET WON'T MOVE!
EASY NOW. YOU'RE AFRAID OF MAKING MISTAKES. **DON'T** BE.
IF YOU NEED HELP WHEN BEATTY PRIES AT YOU, I'LL BE SITTING RIGHT HERE IN YOUR EARDRUM MAKING NOTES!

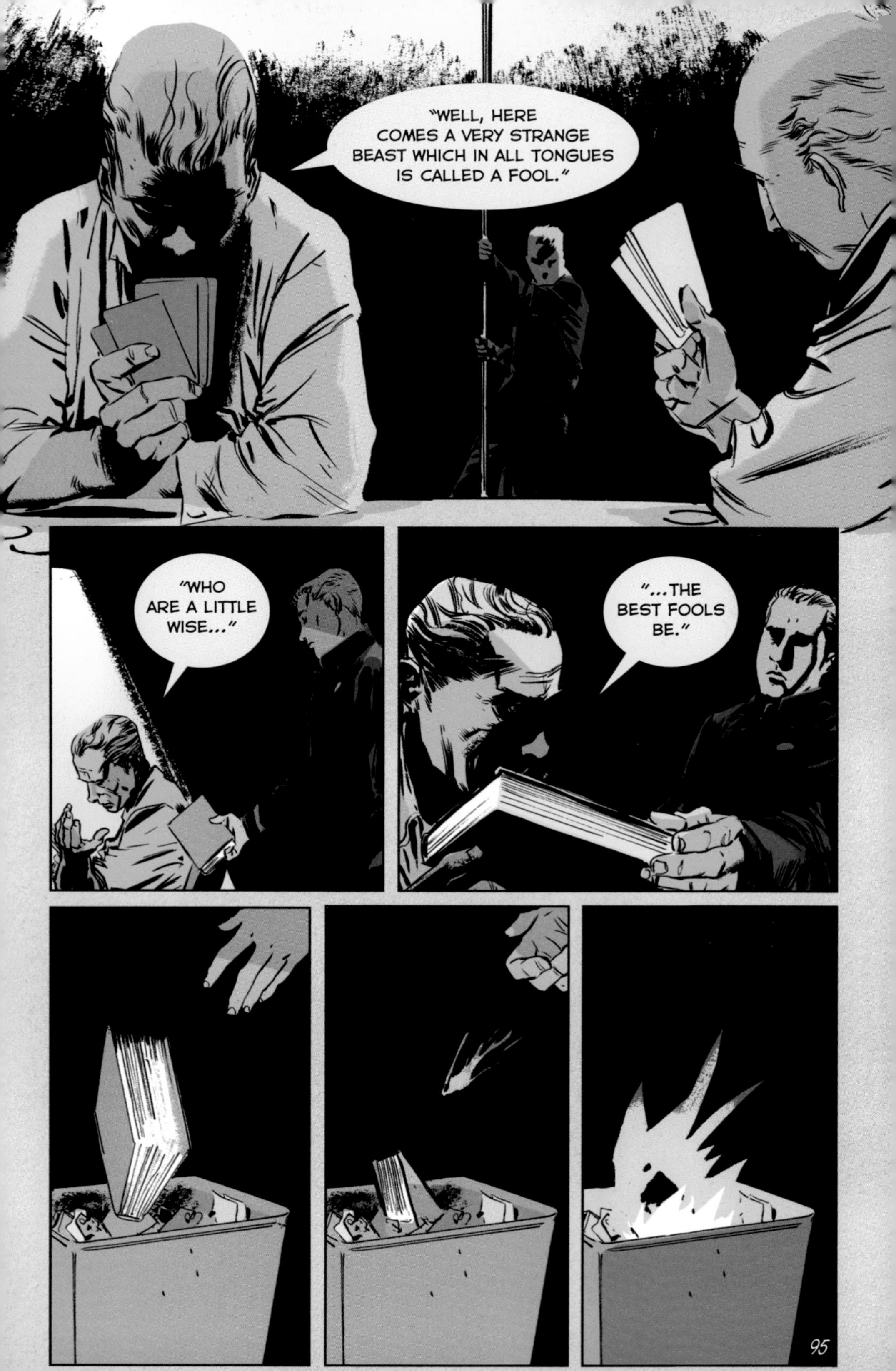
"WELL, HERE COMES A VERY STRANGE BEAST WHICH IN ALL TONGUES IS CALLED A FOOL."
"WHO ARE A LITTLE WISE..."
"...THE BEST FOOLS BE."

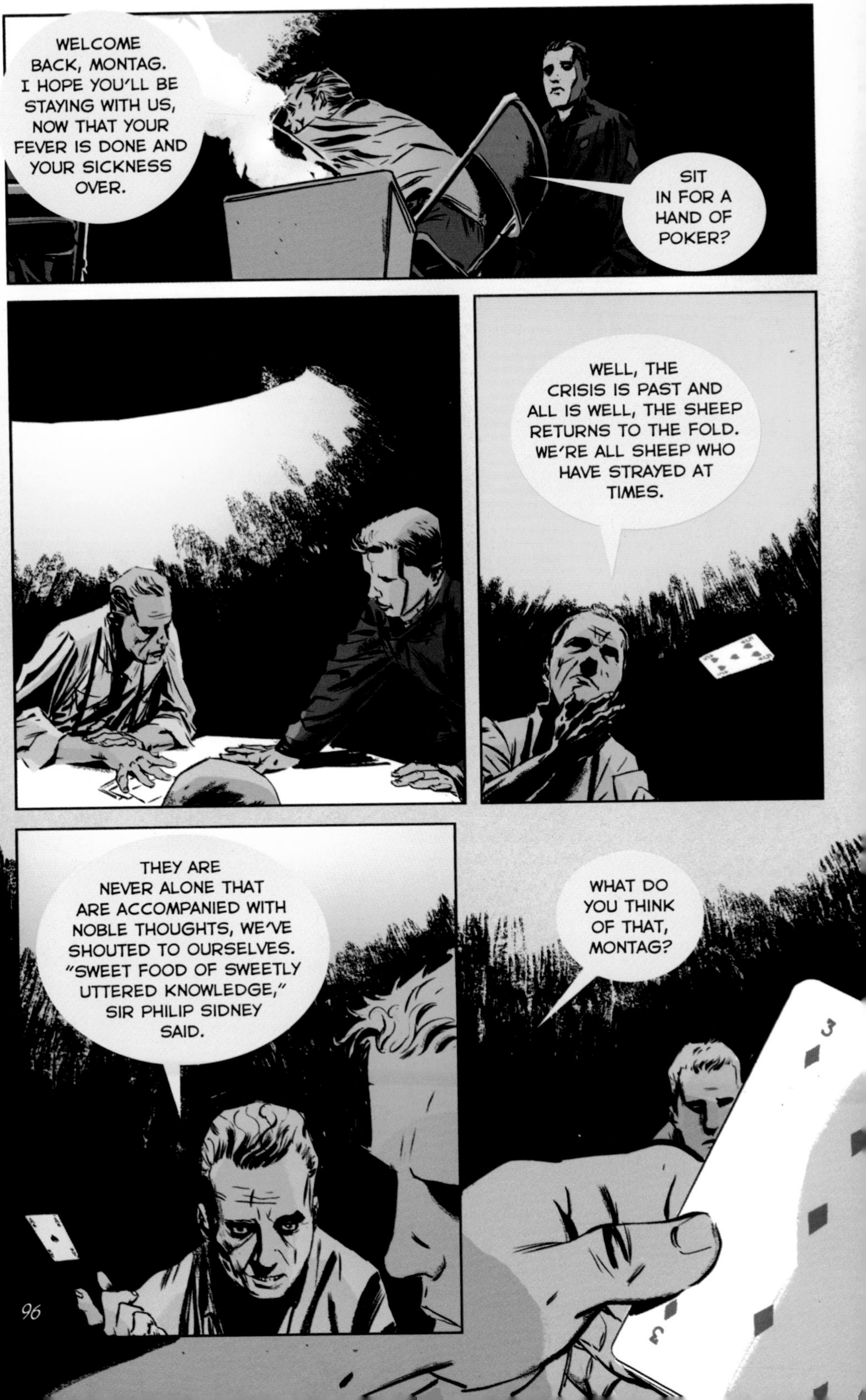
WELCOME BACK, MONTAG. I HOPE YOU'LL BE STAYING WITH US, NOW THAT YOUR FEVER IS DONE AND YOUR SICKNESS OVER.
SIT IN FOR A HAND OF POKER?
WELL, THE CRISIS IS PAST AND ALL IS WELL, THE SHEEP RETURNS TO THE FOLD. WE'RE ALL SHEEP WHO HAVE STRAYED AT TIMES.
THEY ARE NEVER ALONE THAT ARE ACCOMPANIED WITH NOBLE THOUGHTS, WE'VE SHOUTED TO OURSELVES. "SWEET FOOD OF SWEETLY UTTERED KNOWLEDGE," SIR PHILIP SIDNEY SAID.
WHAT DO YOU THINK OF THAT, MONTAG?

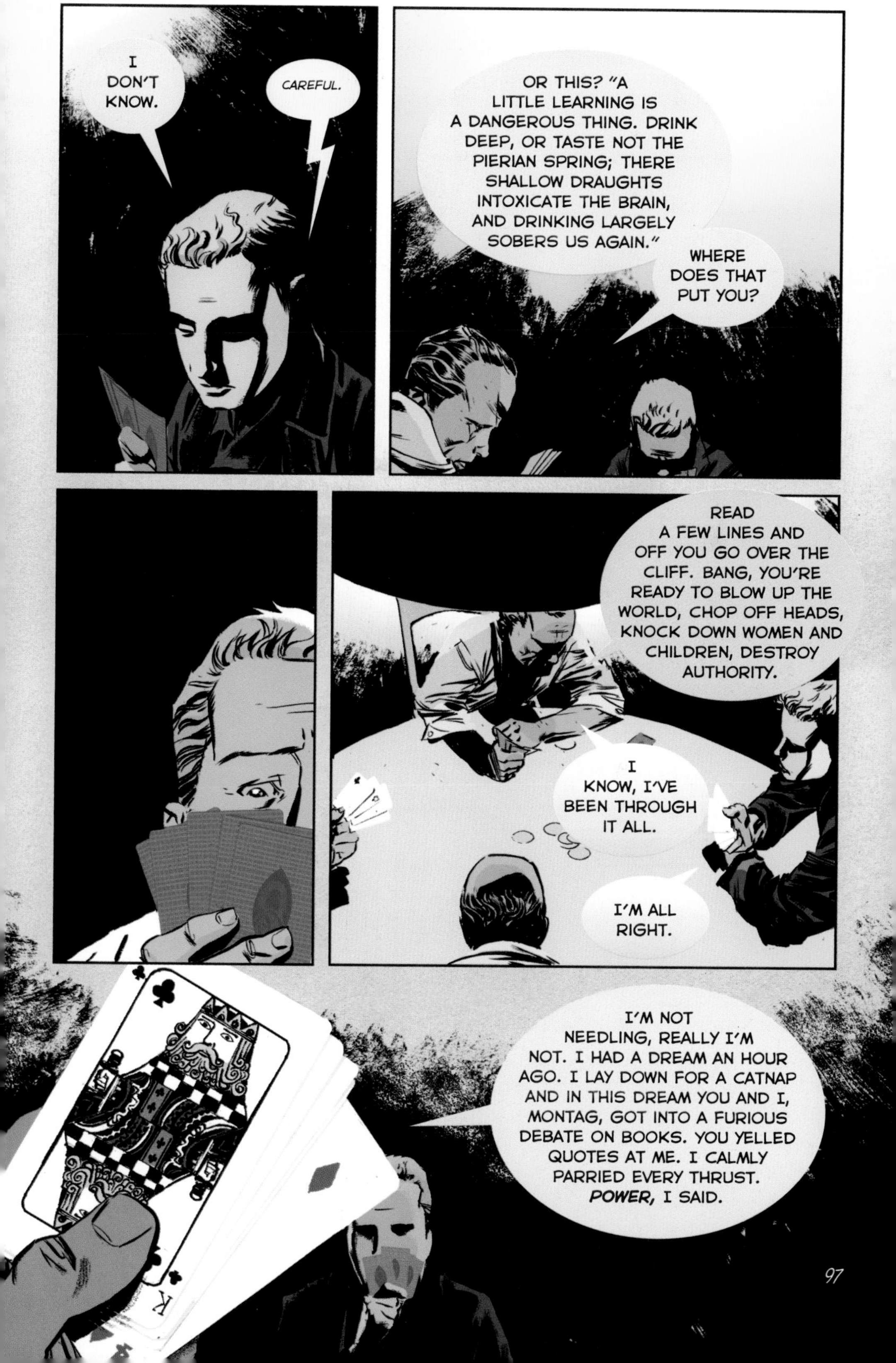
I DON'T KNOW.
CAREFUL.
OR THIS? "A LITTLE LEARNING IS A DANGEROUS THING. DRINK DEEP, OR TASTE NOT THE PIERIAN SPRING; THERE SHALLOW DRAUGHTS INTOXICATE THE BRAIN, AND DRINKING LARGELY SOBERS US AGAIN."
WHERE DOES THAT PUT YOU?
READ A FEW LINES AND OFF YOU GO OVER THE CLIFF. BANG, YOU'RE READY TO BLOW UP THE WORLD, CHOP OFF HEADS, KNOCK DOWN WOMEN AND CHILDREN, DESTROY AUTHORITY.
I KNOW, I'VE BEEN THROUGH IT ALL.
I'M ALL RIGHT.
I'M NOT NEEDLING, REALLY I'M NOT. I HAD A DREAM AN HOUR AGO. I LAY DOWN FOR A CATNAP AND IN THIS DREAM YOU AND I, MONTAG, GOT INTO A FURIOUS DEBATE ON BOOKS. YOU YELLED QUOTES AT ME. I CALMLY PARRIED EVERY THRUST. *POWER,* I SAID.

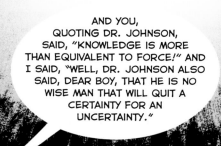

AND YOU, QUOTING DR. JOHNSON, SAID, "KNOWLEDGE IS MORE THAN EQUIVALENT TO FORCE!" AND I SAID, "WELL, DR. JOHNSON ALSO SAID, DEAR BOY, THAT HE IS NO WISE MAN THAT WILL QUIT A CERTAINTY FOR AN UNCERTAINTY."

STICK WITH THE FIREMEN, MONTAG. ALL ELSE IS DREARY CHAOS!

DON'T LISTEN.

AND YOU SAID QUOTING, "TRUTH WILL COME TO LIGHT, MURDER WILL NOT BE HID LONG!" AND I CRIED IN GOOD HUMOR, "OH GOD, HE SPEAKS ONLY OF HIS HORSE!" AND "THE DEVIL CAN CITE SCRIPTURE FOR HIS PURPOSE."

AND YOU YELLED, "THIS AGE THINKS BETTER OF A GILDED FOOL THAN OF A THREADBARE SAINT IN WISDOM'S SCHOOL!"

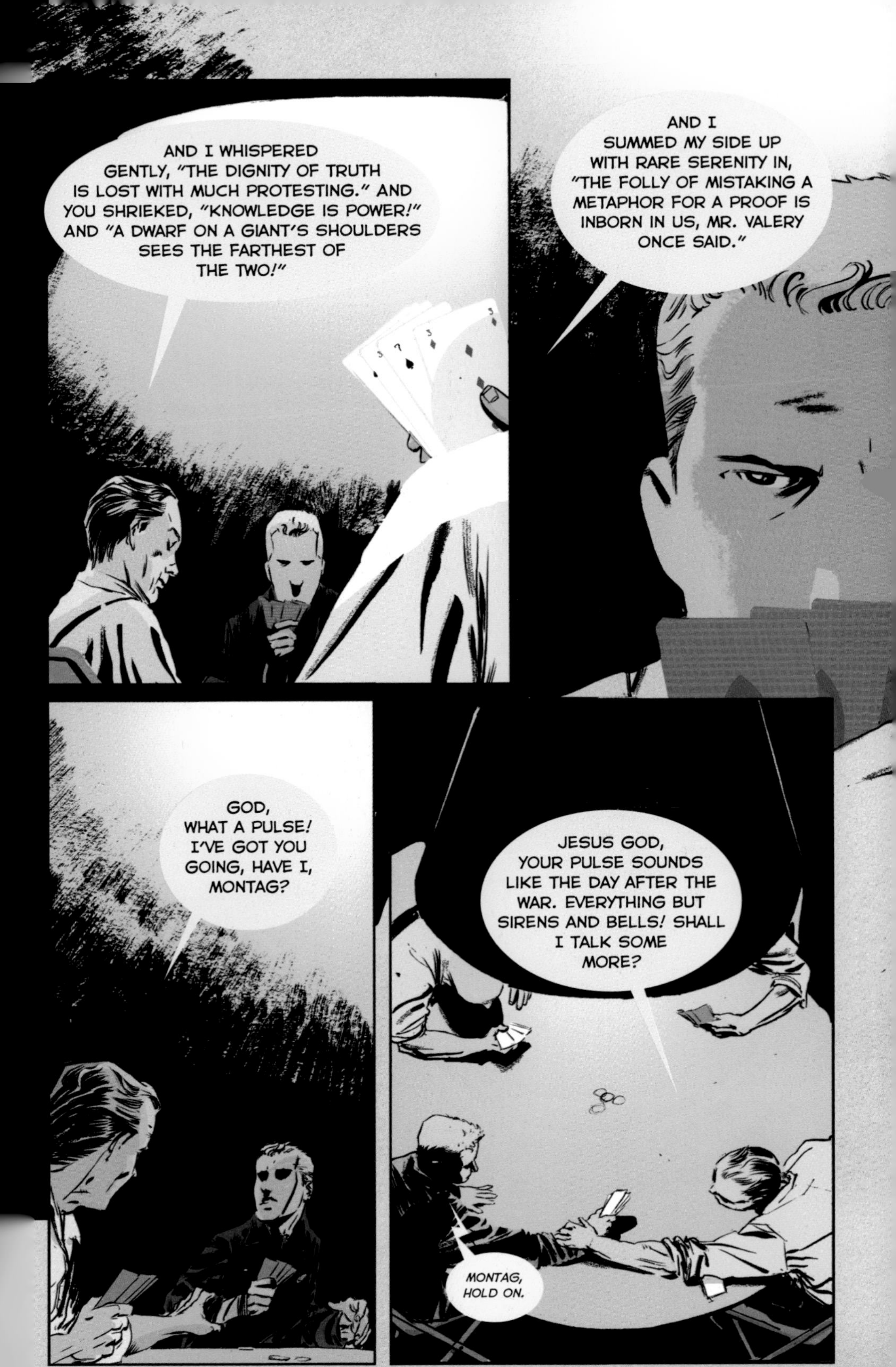
AND I WHISPERED GENTLY, "THE DIGNITY OF TRUTH IS LOST WITH MUCH PROTESTING." AND YOU SHRIEKED, "KNOWLEDGE IS POWER!" AND "A DWARF ON A GIANT'S SHOULDERS SEES THE FARTHEST OF THE TWO!"
AND I SUMMED MY SIDE UP WITH RARE SERENITY IN, "THE FOLLY OF MISTAKING A METAPHOR FOR A PROOF IS INBORN IN US, MR. VALERY ONCE SAID."
GOD, WHAT A PULSE! I'VE GOT YOU GOING, HAVE I, MONTAG?
JESUS GOD, YOUR PULSE SOUNDS LIKE THE DAY AFTER THE WAR. EVERYTHING BUT SIRENS AND BELLS! SHALL I TALK SOME MORE?
MONTAG, HOLD ON.

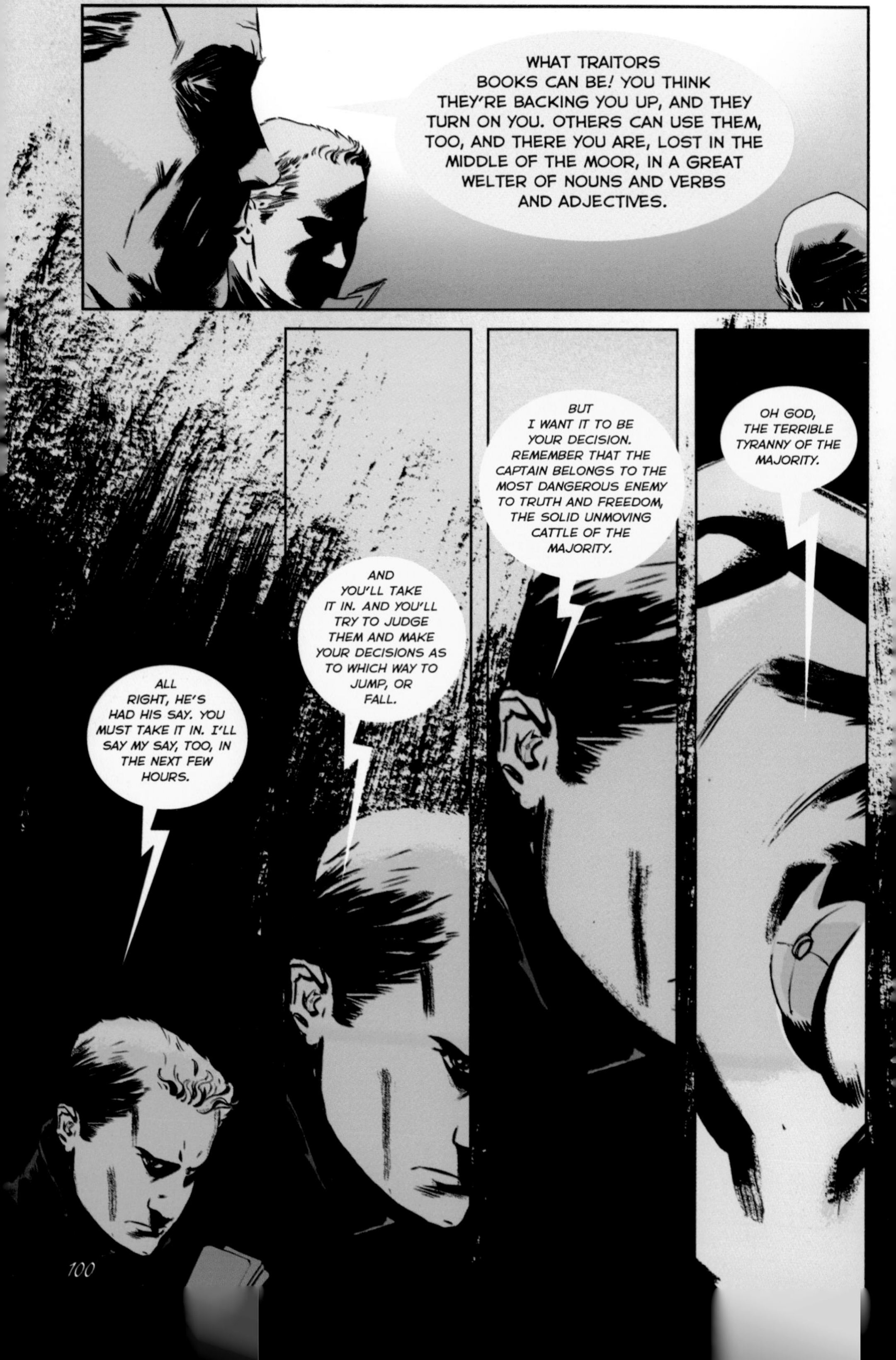
WHAT TRAITORS BOOKS CAN BE! YOU THINK THEY'RE BACKING YOU UP, AND THEY TURN ON YOU. OTHERS CAN USE THEM, TOO, AND THERE YOU ARE, LOST IN THE MIDDLE OF THE MOOR, IN A GREAT WELTER OF NOUNS AND VERBS AND ADJECTIVES.
ALL RIGHT, HE'S HAD HIS SAY. YOU MUST TAKE IT IN. I'LL SAY MY SAY, TOO, IN THE NEXT FEW HOURS.
AND YOU'LL TAKE IT IN. AND YOU'LL TRY TO JUDGE THEM AND MAKE YOUR DECISIONS AS TO WHICH WAY TO JUMP, OR FALL.
BUT I WANT IT TO BE YOUR DECISION. REMEMBER THAT THE CAPTAIN BELONGS TO THE MOST DANGEROUS ENEMY TO TRUTH AND FREEDOM, THE SOLID UNMOVING CATTLE OF THE MAJORITY.
OH GOD, THE TERRIBLE TYRANNY OF THE MAJORITY.

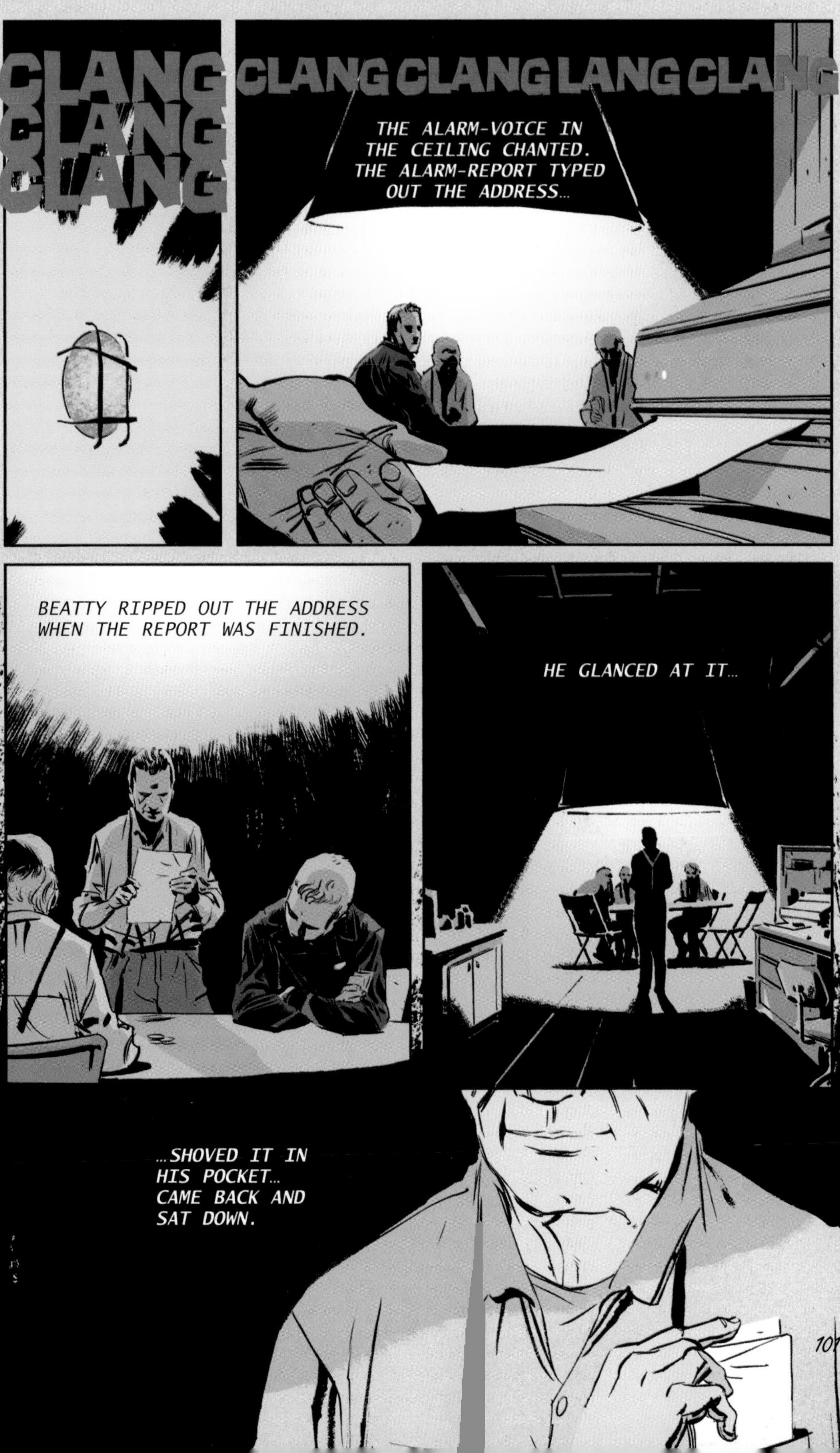
CLANG CLANG CLANG
CLANG CLANG CLANG LANG CLANG
THE ALARM-VOICE IN THE CEILING CHANTED. THE ALARM-REPORT TYPED OUT THE ADDRESS...
BEATTY RIPPED OUT THE ADDRESS WHEN THE REPORT WAS FINISHED.
HE GLANCED AT IT...
...SHOVED IT IN HIS POCKET... CAME BACK AND SAT DOWN.

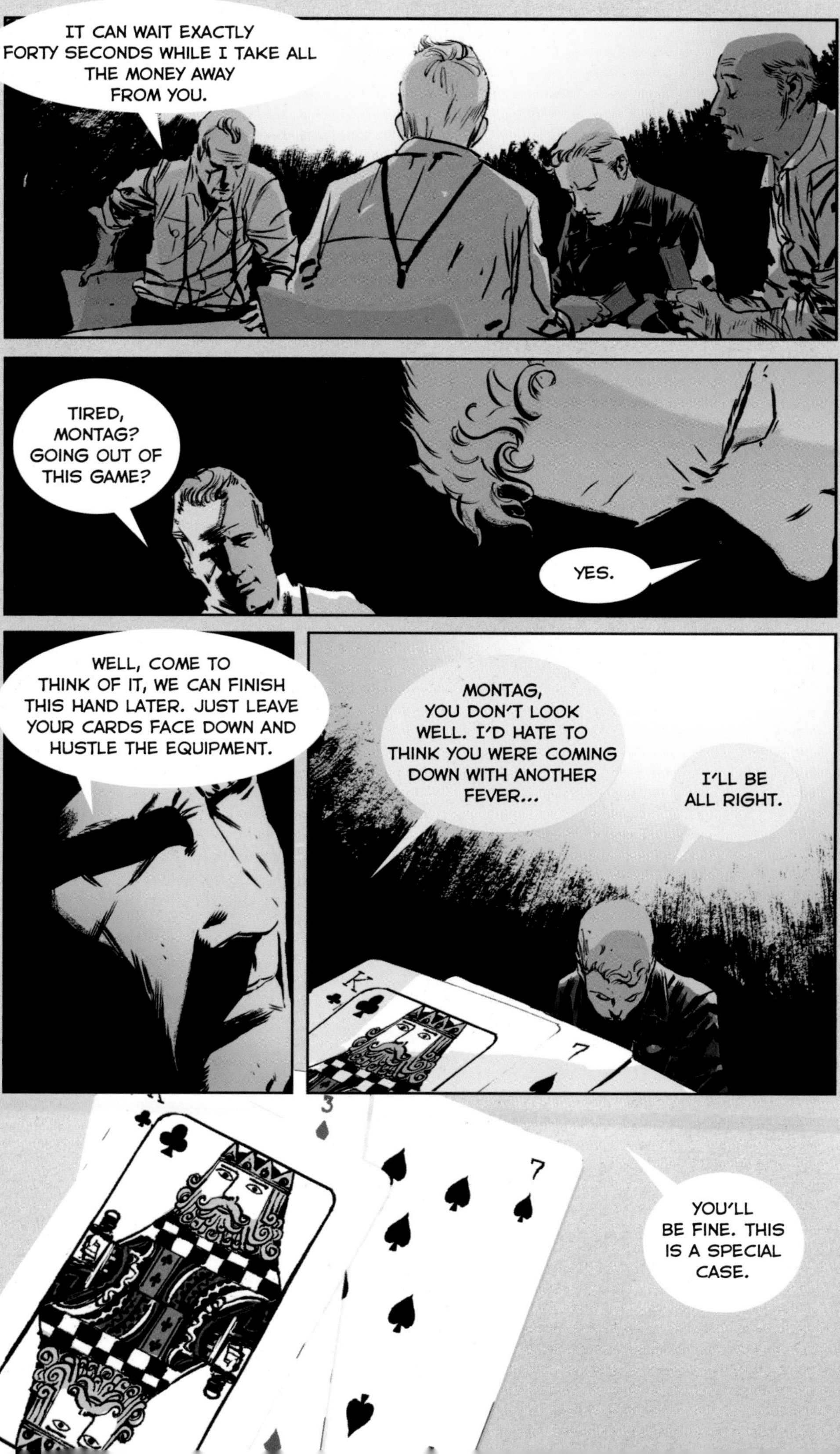
IT CAN WAIT EXACTLY FORTY SECONDS WHILE I TAKE ALL THE MONEY AWAY FROM YOU.
TIRED, MONTAG? GOING OUT OF THIS GAME?
YES.
WELL, COME TO THINK OF IT, WE CAN FINISH THIS HAND LATER. JUST LEAVE YOUR CARDS FACE DOWN AND HUSTLE THE EQUIPMENT.
MONTAG, YOU DON'T LOOK WELL. I'D HATE TO THINK YOU WERE COMING DOWN WITH ANOTHER FEVER...
I'LL BE ALL RIGHT.
YOU'LL BE FINE. THIS IS A SPECIAL CASE.

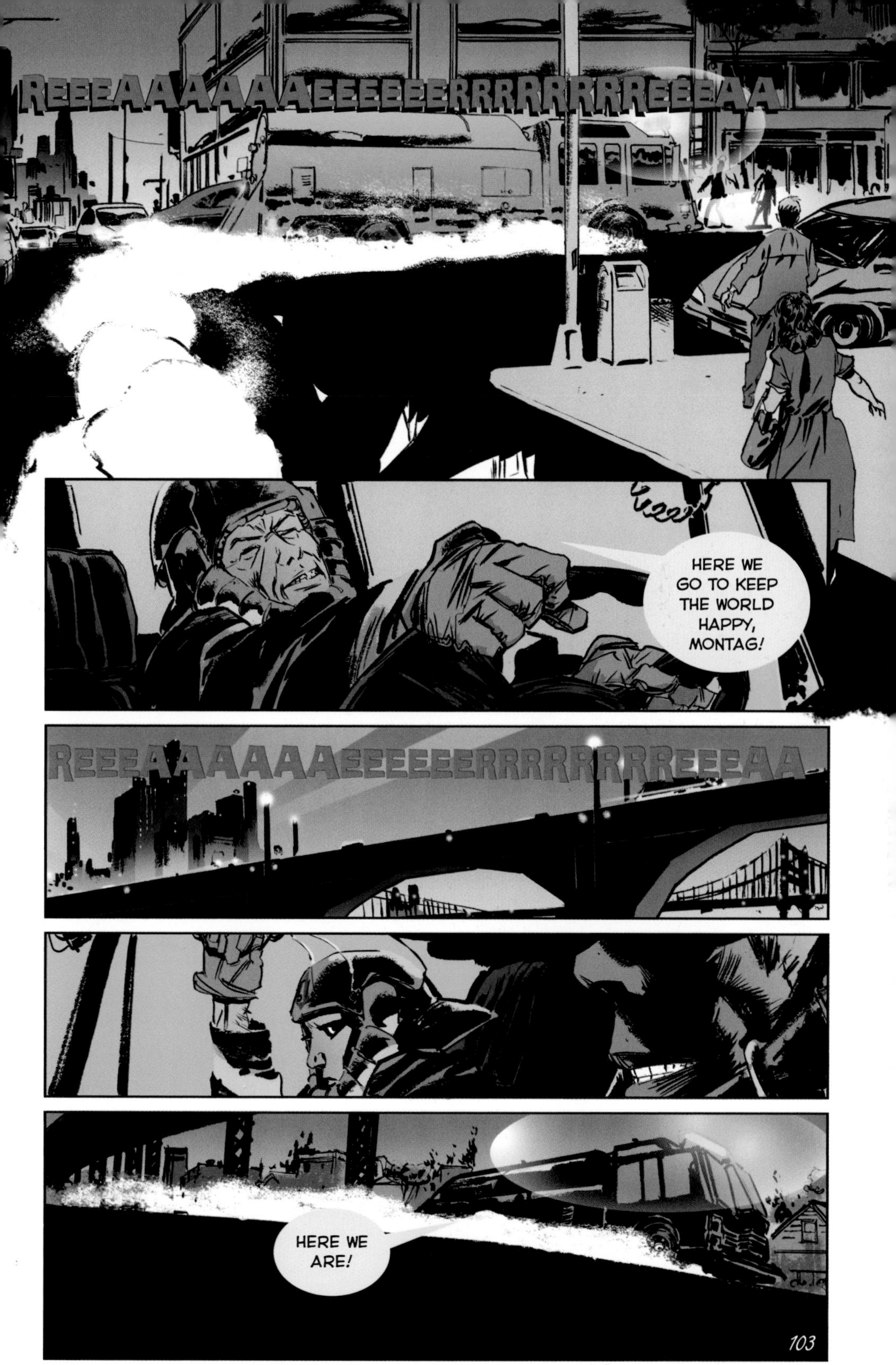
REEEAAAAAAEEEEEEERRRRRRRREEEAA
HERE WE GO TO KEEP THE WORLD HAPPY, MONTAG!
REEEAAAAAAEEEEEEERRRRRRRREEEAA
HERE WE ARE!

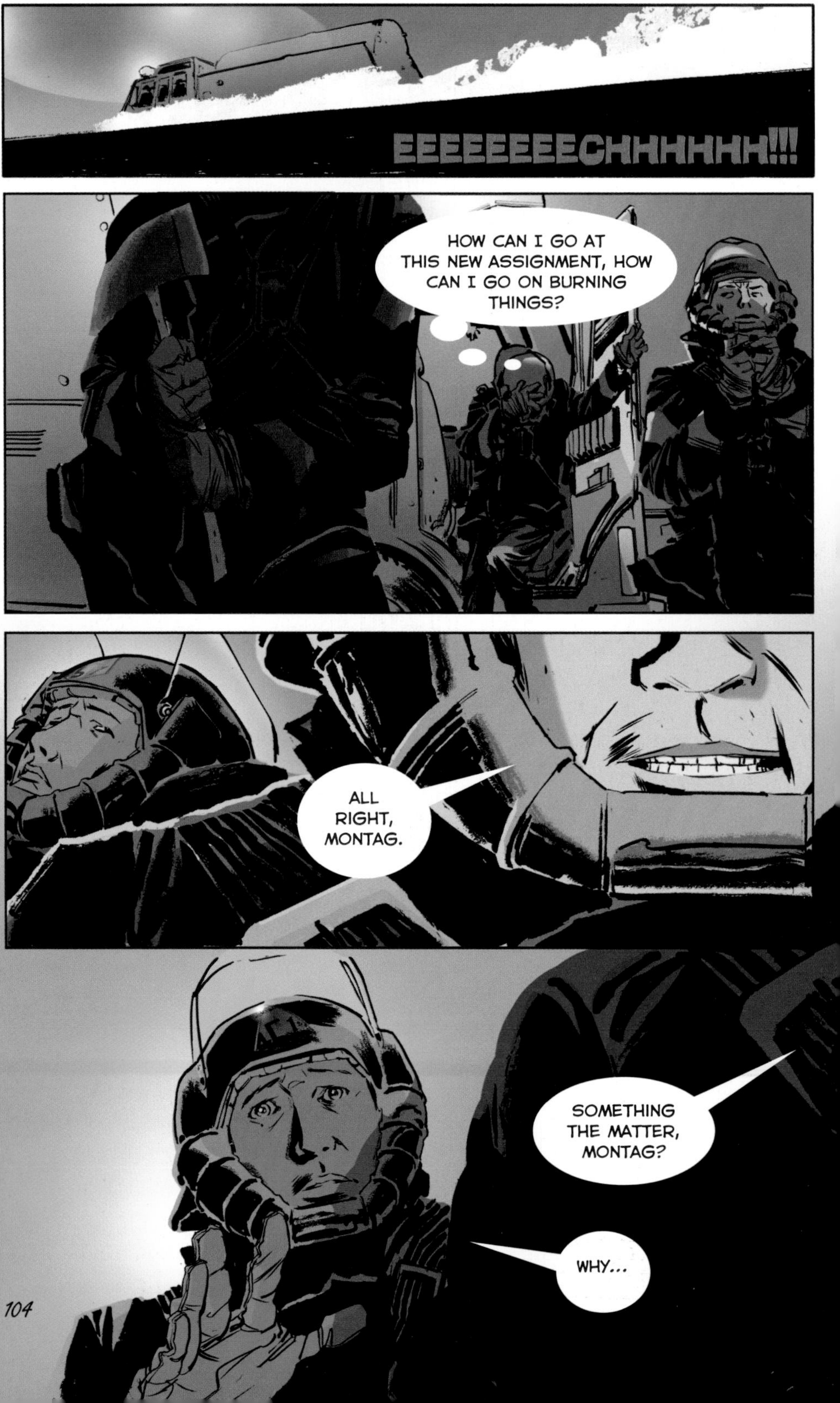
EEEEEEEEECHHHHHH!!!
HOW CAN I GO AT THIS NEW ASSIGNMENT, HOW CAN I GO ON BURNING THINGS?
ALL RIGHT, MONTAG.
SOMETHING THE MATTER, MONTAG?
WHY...

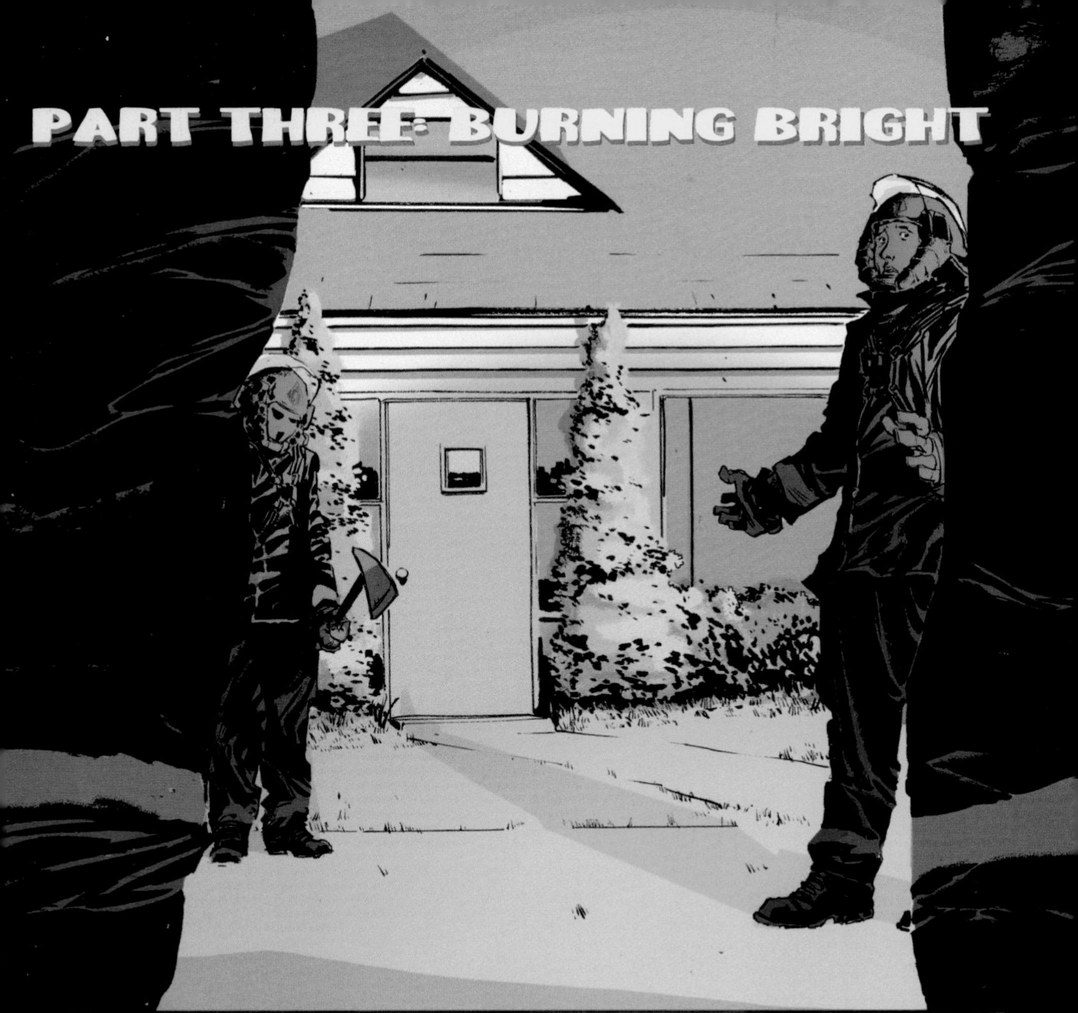
PART THREE: BURNING BRIGHT

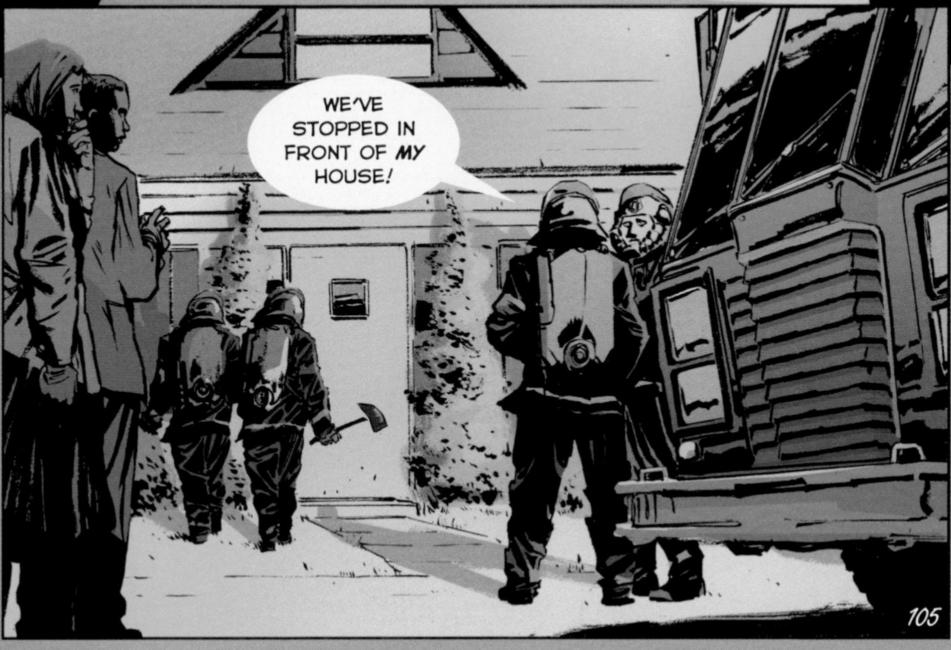
WE'VE STOPPED IN FRONT OF MY HOUSE!

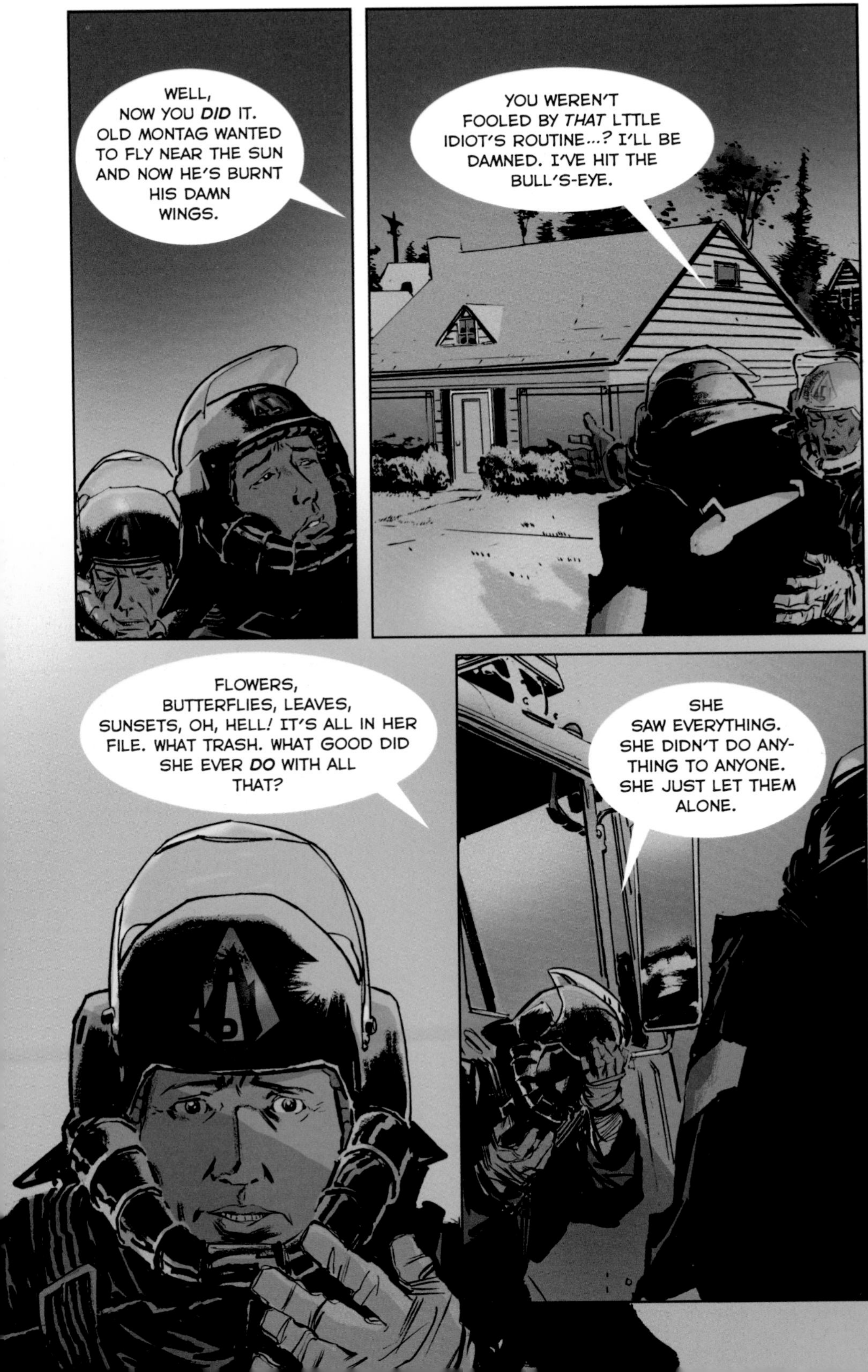
WELL, NOW YOU *DID* IT. OLD MONTAG WANTED TO FLY NEAR THE SUN AND NOW HE'S BURNT HIS DAMN WINGS.
YOU WEREN'T FOOLED BY *THAT* LTTLE IDIOT'S ROUTINE...? I'LL BE DAMNED. I'VE HIT THE BULL'S-EYE.
FLOWERS, BUTTERFLIES, LEAVES, SUNSETS, OH, HELL! IT'S ALL IN HER FILE. WHAT TRASH. WHAT GOOD DID SHE EVER *DO* WITH ALL THAT?
SHE SAW EVERYTHING. SHE DIDN'T DO ANY-THING TO ANYONE. SHE JUST LET THEM ALONE.

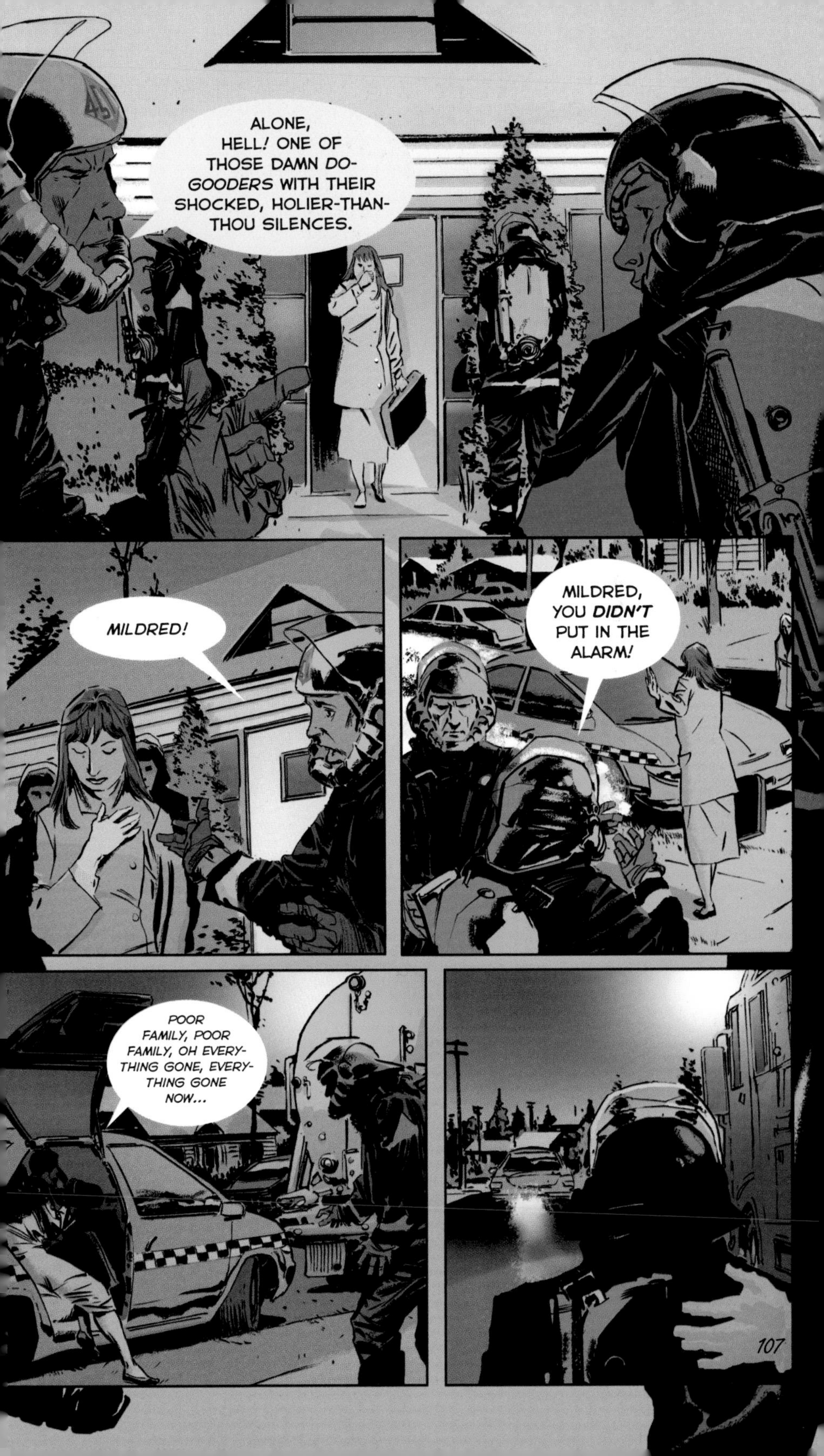
ALONE, HELL! ONE OF THOSE DAMN DO-GOODERS WITH THEIR SHOCKED, HOLIER-THAN-THOU SILENCES.
MILDRED!
MILDRED, YOU DIDN'T PUT IN THE ALARM!
POOR FAMILY, POOR FAMILY, OH EVERY-THING GONE, EVERY-THING GONE NOW...

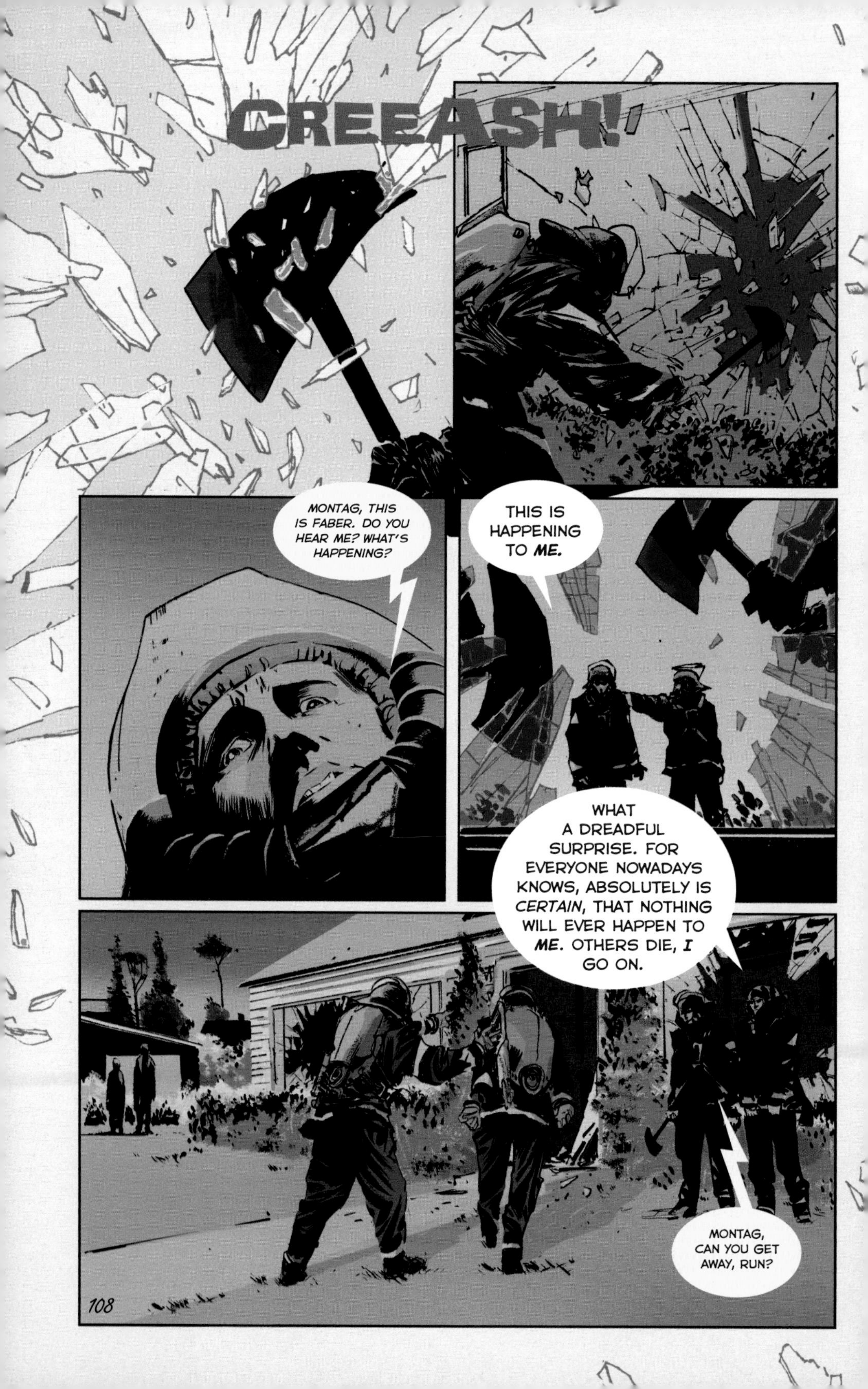
CREEASH!
MONTAG, THIS IS FABER. DO YOU HEAR ME? WHAT'S HAPPENING?
THIS IS HAPPENING TO *ME.*
WHAT A DREADFUL SURPRISE. FOR EVERYONE NOWADAYS KNOWS, ABSOLUTELY IS *CERTAIN*, THAT NOTHING WILL EVER HAPPEN TO *ME*. OTHERS DIE, *I* GO ON.
MONTAG, CAN YOU GET AWAY, RUN?

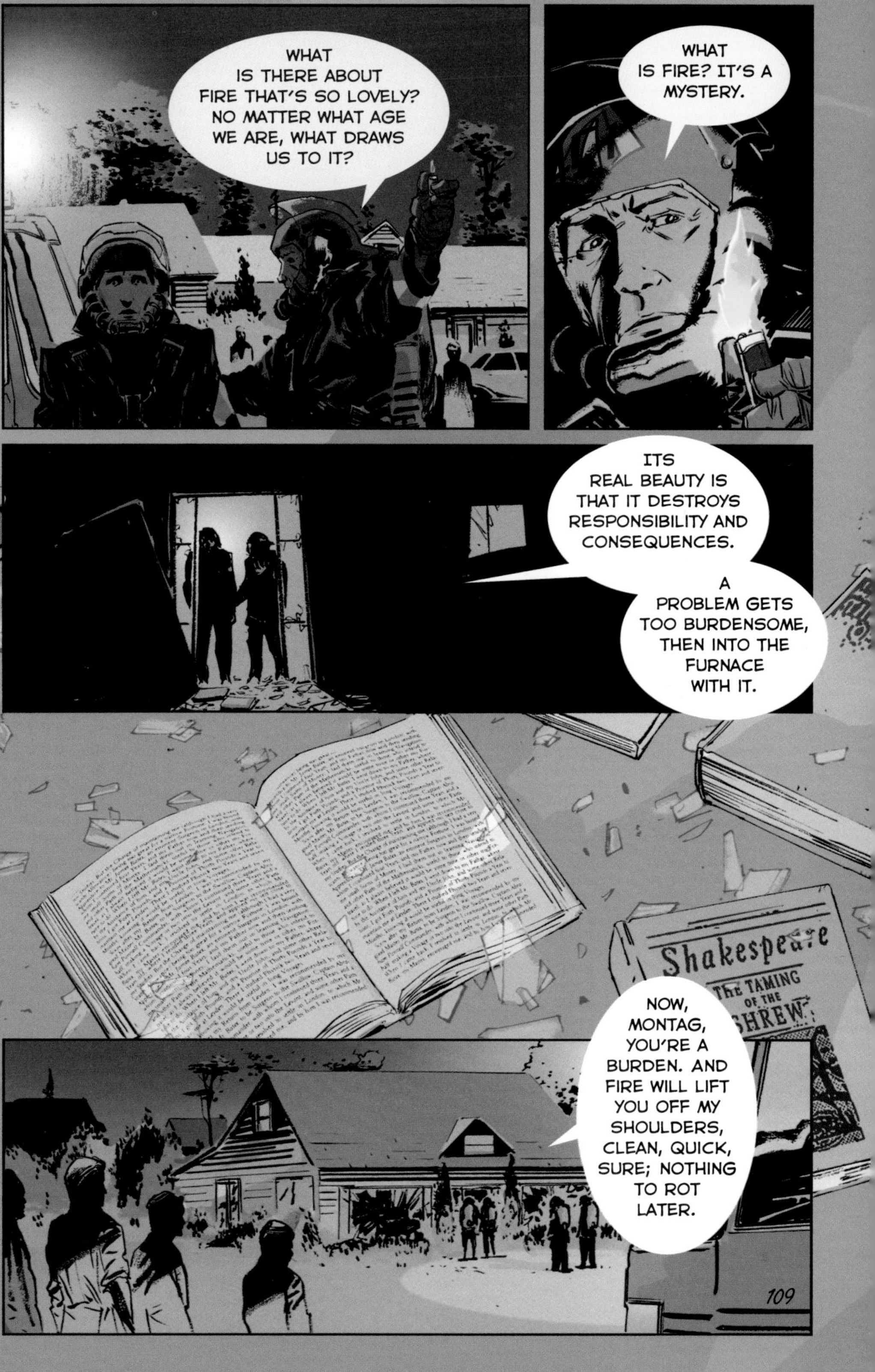
WHAT IS THERE ABOUT FIRE THAT'S SO LOVELY? NO MATTER WHAT AGE WE ARE, WHAT DRAWS US TO IT?
WHAT IS FIRE? IT'S A MYSTERY.
ITS REAL BEAUTY IS THAT IT DESTROYS RESPONSIBILITY AND CONSEQUENCES.
A PROBLEM GETS TOO BURDENSOME, THEN INTO THE FURNACE WITH IT.
Shakespeare
THE TAMING OF THE SHREW
NOW, MONTAG, YOU'RE A BURDEN. AND FIRE WILL LIFT YOU OFF MY SHOULDERS, CLEAN, QUICK, SURE; NOTHING TO ROT LATER.

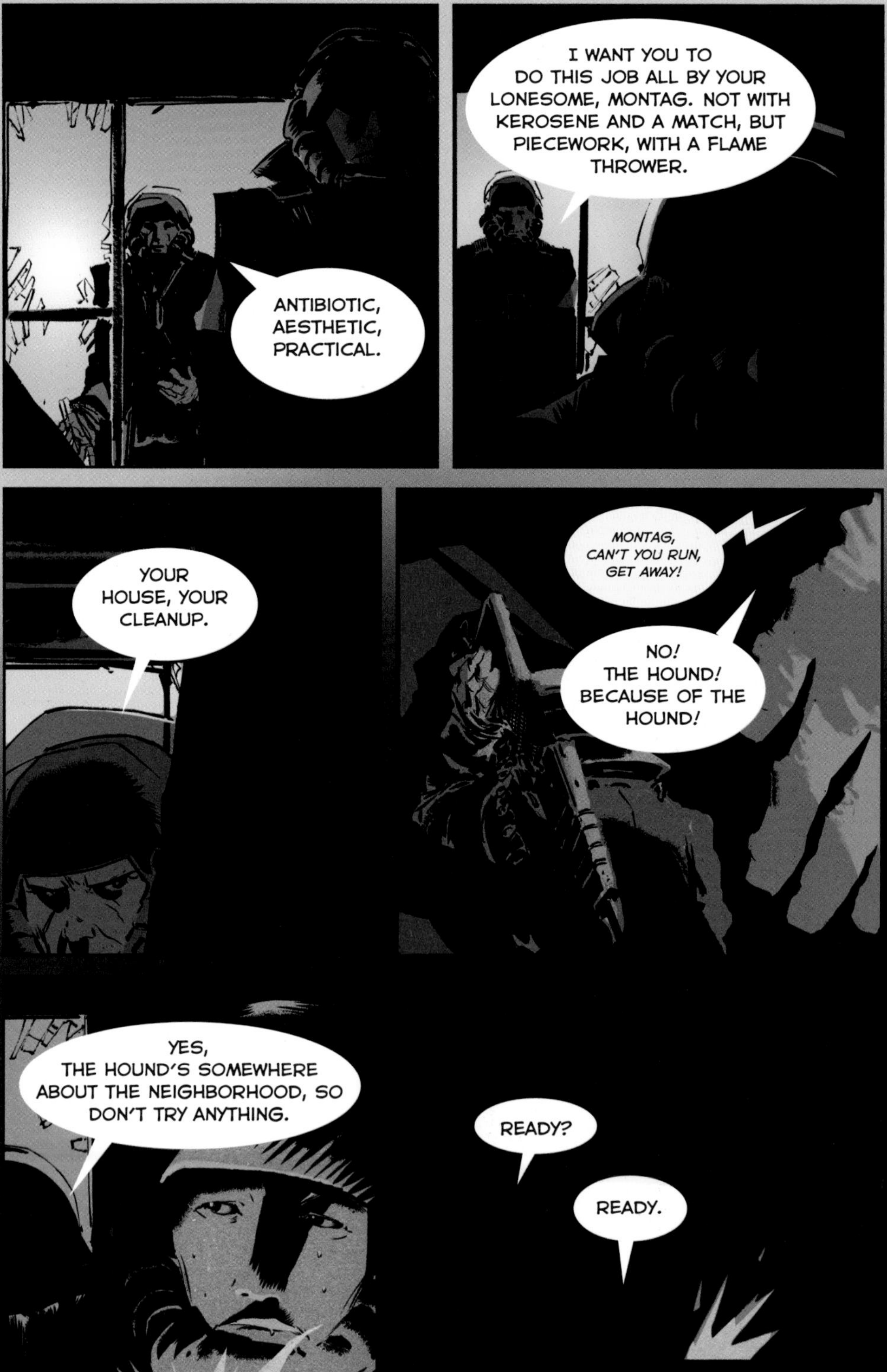
ANTIBIOTIC, AESTHETIC, PRACTICAL.
I WANT YOU TO DO THIS JOB ALL BY YOUR LONESOME, MONTAG. NOT WITH KEROSENE AND A MATCH, BUT PIECEWORK, WITH A FLAME THROWER.
YOUR HOUSE, YOUR CLEANUP.
MONTAG, CAN'T YOU RUN, GET AWAY!
NO*!* THE HOUND*!* BECAUSE OF THE HOUND*!*
YES, THE HOUND'S SOMEWHERE ABOUT THE NEIGHBORHOOD, SO DON'T TRY ANYTHING.
READY?
READY.

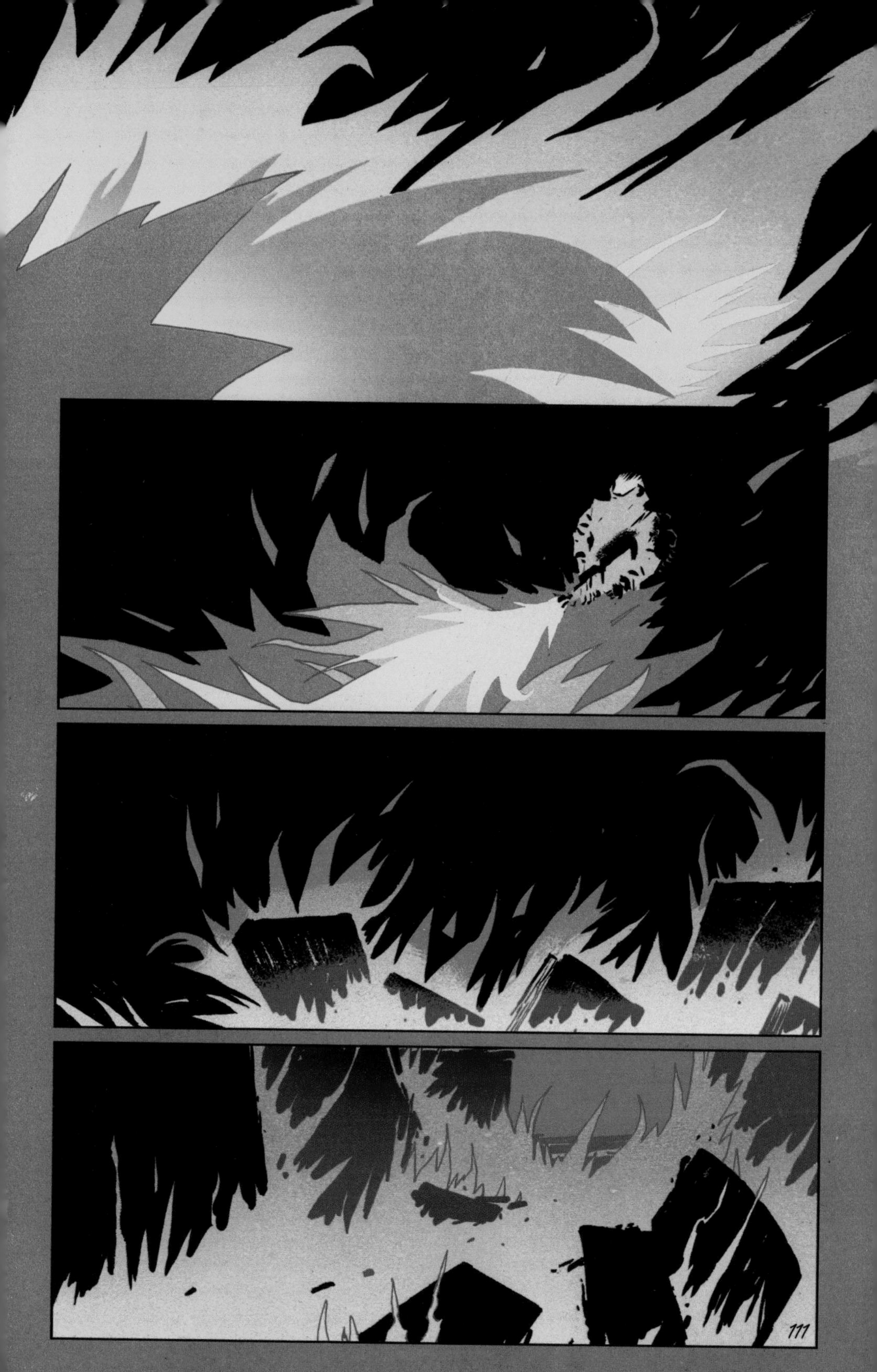

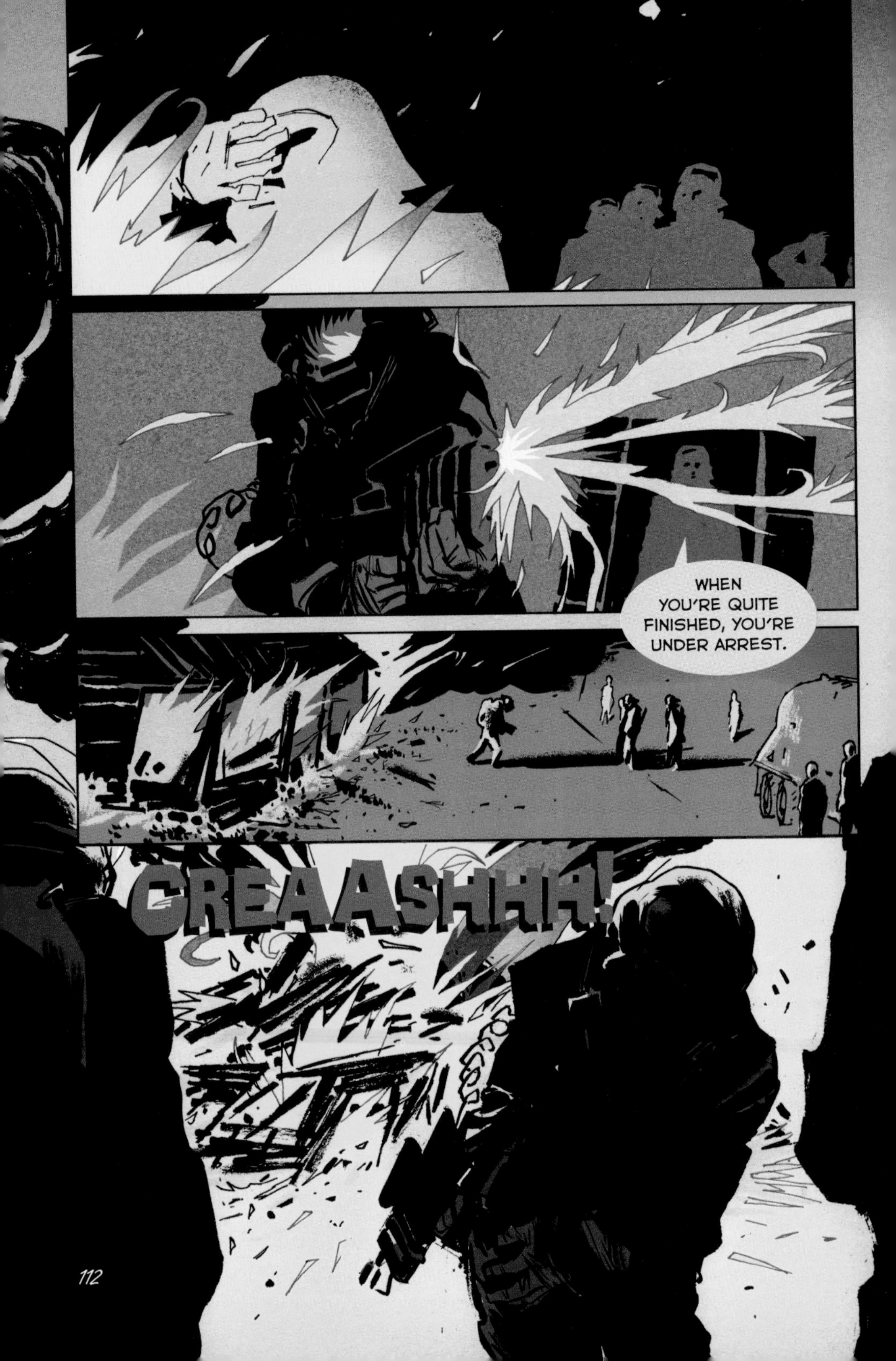
WHEN YOU'RE QUITE FINISHED, YOU'RE UNDER ARREST.
CREAASHHH!

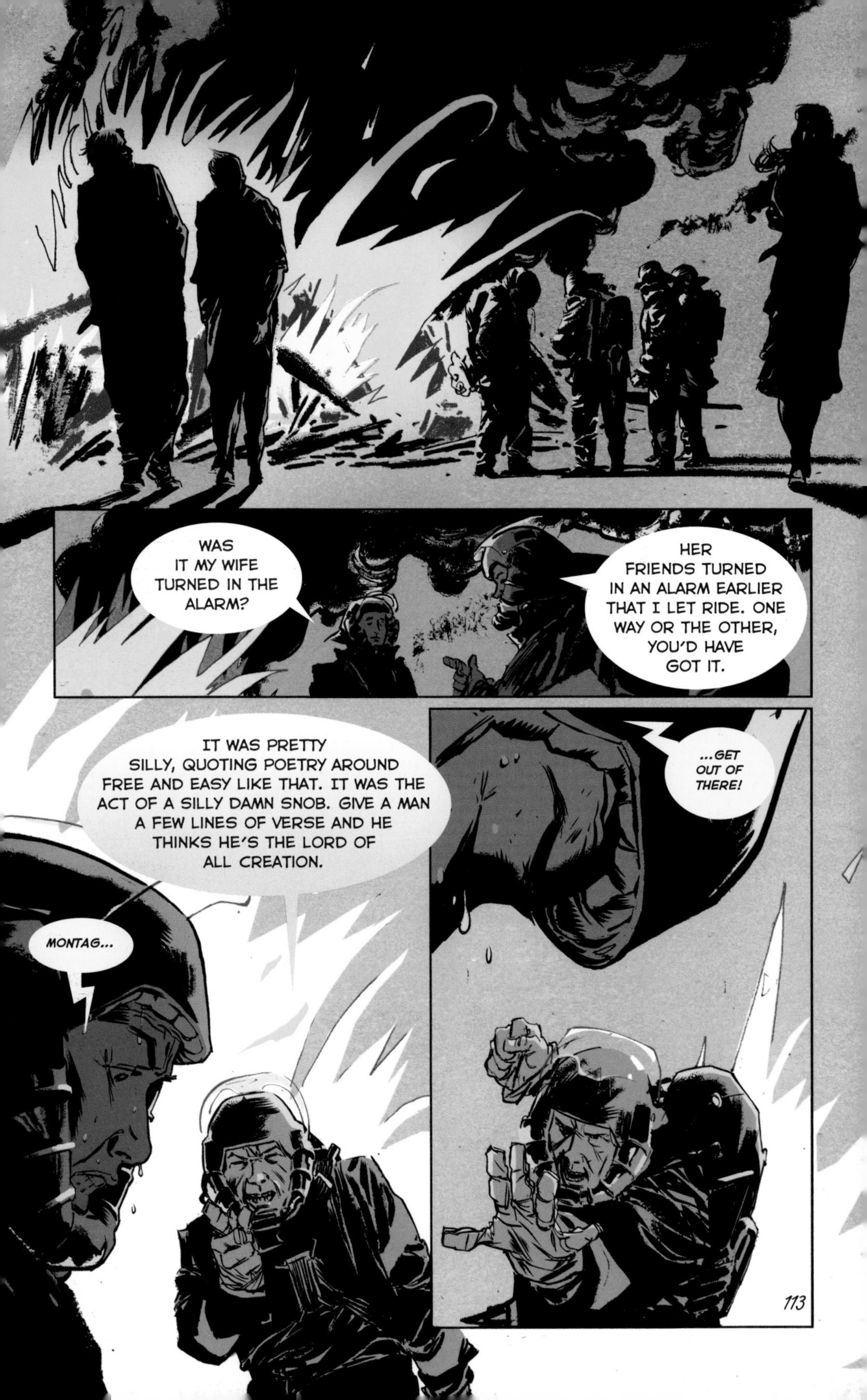
WAS IT MY WIFE TURNED IN THE ALARM?
HER FRIENDS TURNED IN AN ALARM EARLIER THAT I LET RIDE. ONE WAY OR THE OTHER, YOU'D HAVE GOT IT.
IT WAS PRETTY SILLY, QUOTING POETRY AROUND FREE AND EASY LIKE THAT. IT WAS THE ACT OF A SILLY DAMN SNOB. GIVE A MAN A FEW LINES OF VERSE AND HE THINKS HE'S THE LORD OF ALL CREATION.
MONTAG...
...GET OUT OF THERE!

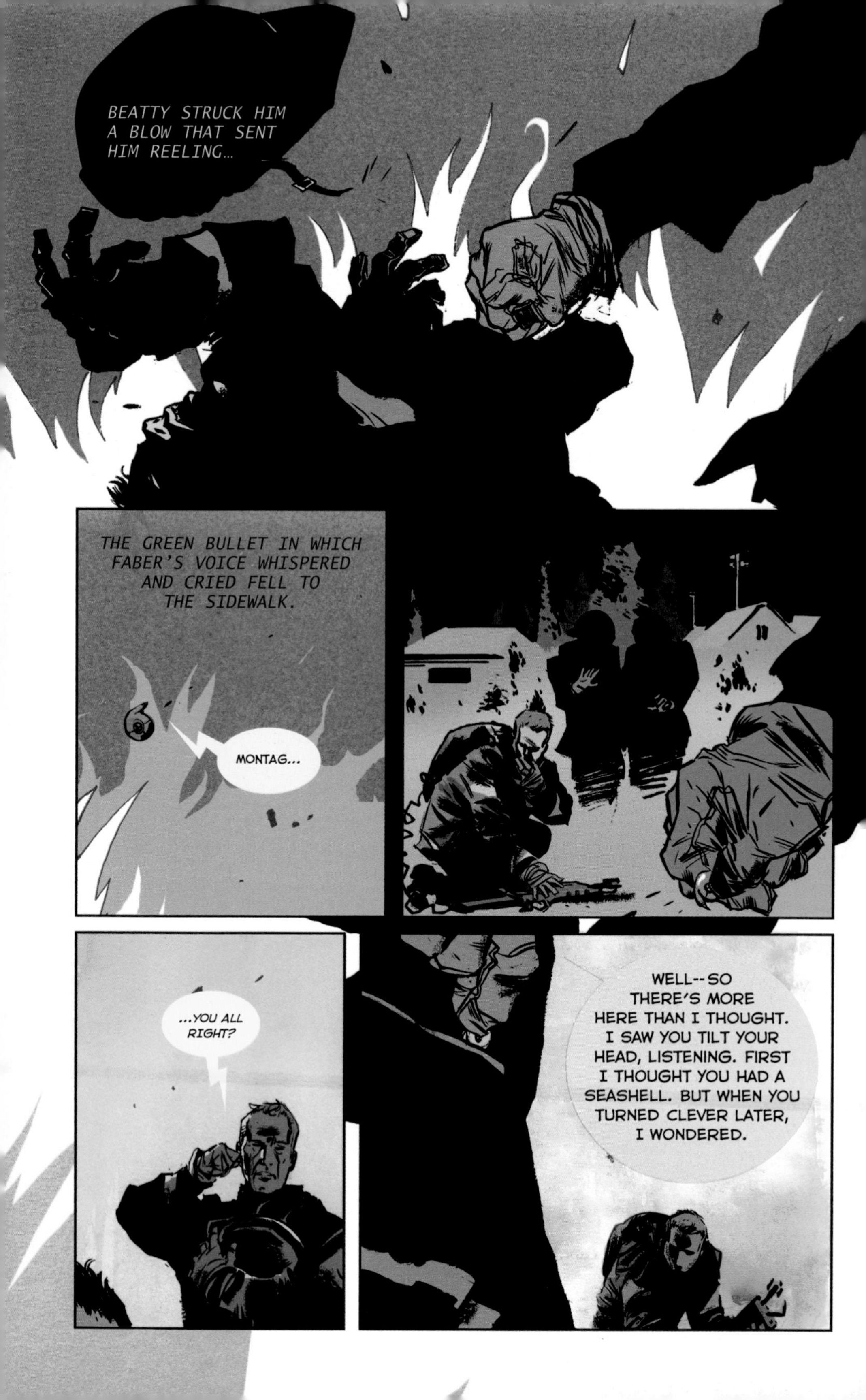
BEATTY STRUCK HIM A BLOW THAT SENT HIM REELING...
THE GREEN BULLET IN WHICH FABER'S VOICE WHISPERED AND CRIED FELL TO THE SIDEWALK.
MONTAG...
...YOU ALL RIGHT?
WELL--SO THERE'S MORE HERE THAN I THOUGHT. I SAW YOU TILT YOUR HEAD, LISTENING. FIRST I THOUGHT YOU HAD A SEASHELL. BUT WHEN YOU TURNED CLEVER LATER, I WONDERED.

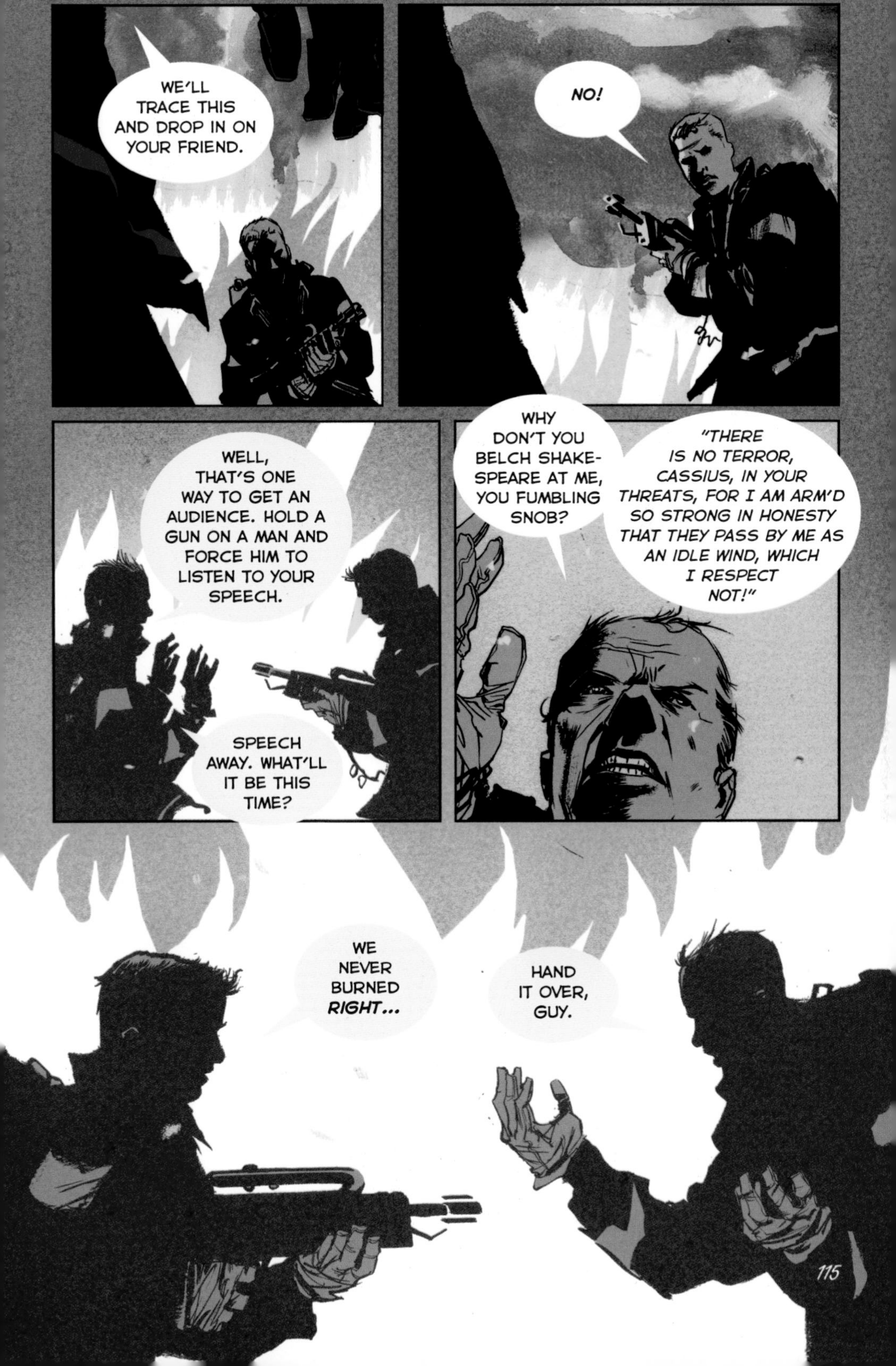
WE'LL TRACE THIS AND DROP IN ON YOUR FRIEND.
NO!
WELL, THAT'S ONE WAY TO GET AN AUDIENCE. HOLD A GUN ON A MAN AND FORCE HIM TO LISTEN TO YOUR SPEECH.
SPEECH AWAY. WHAT'LL IT BE THIS TIME?
WHY DON'T YOU BELCH SHAKE-SPEARE AT ME, YOU FUMBLING SNOB?
"THERE IS NO TERROR, CASSIUS, IN YOUR THREATS, FOR I AM ARM'D SO STRONG IN HONESTY THAT THEY PASS BY ME AS AN IDLE WIND, WHICH I RESPECT NOT!"
WE NEVER BURNED *RIGHT*...
HAND IT OVER, GUY.

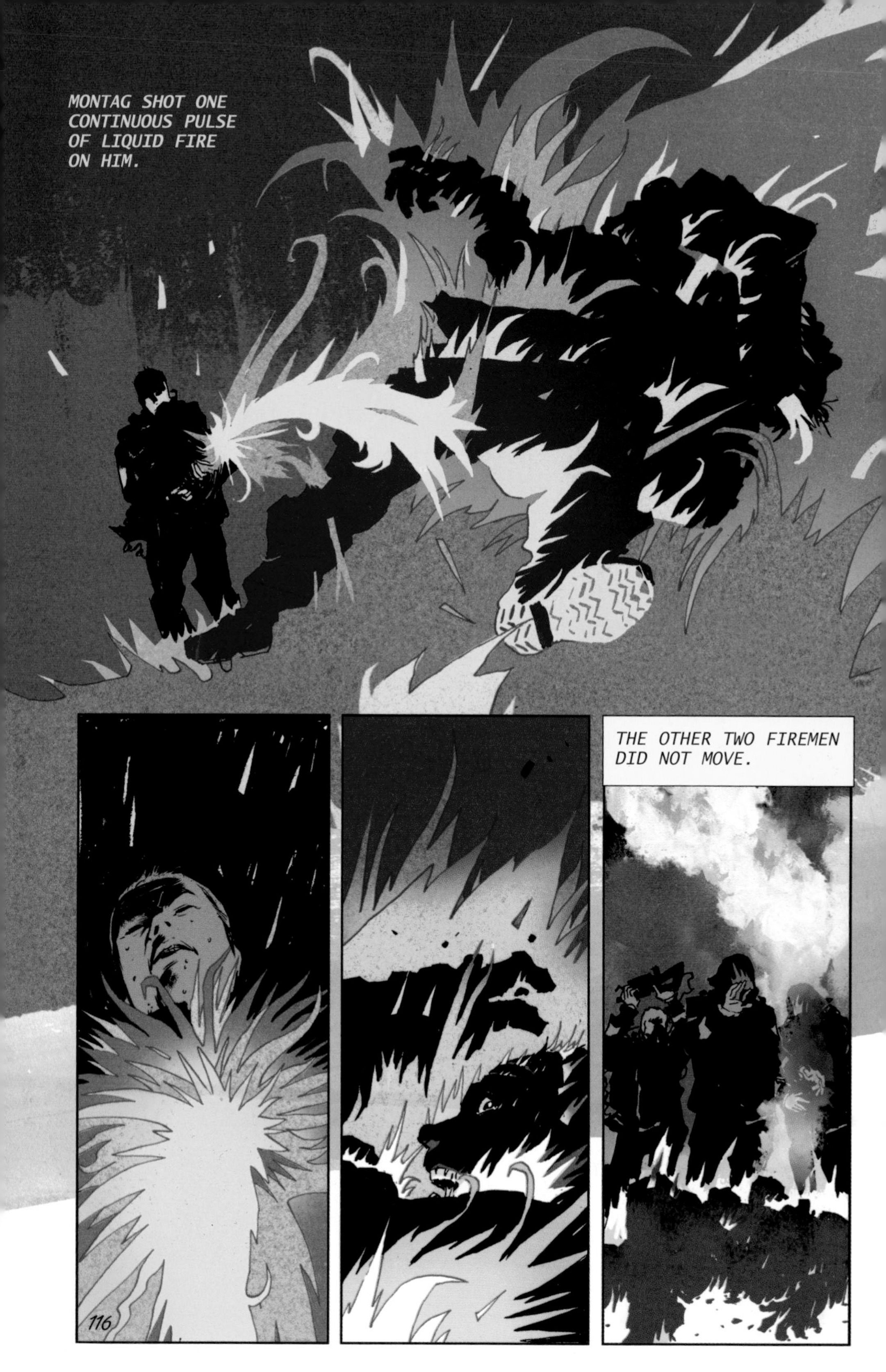
MONTAG SHOT ONE CONTINUOUS PULSE OF LIQUID FIRE ON HIM.
THE OTHER TWO FIREMEN DID NOT MOVE.

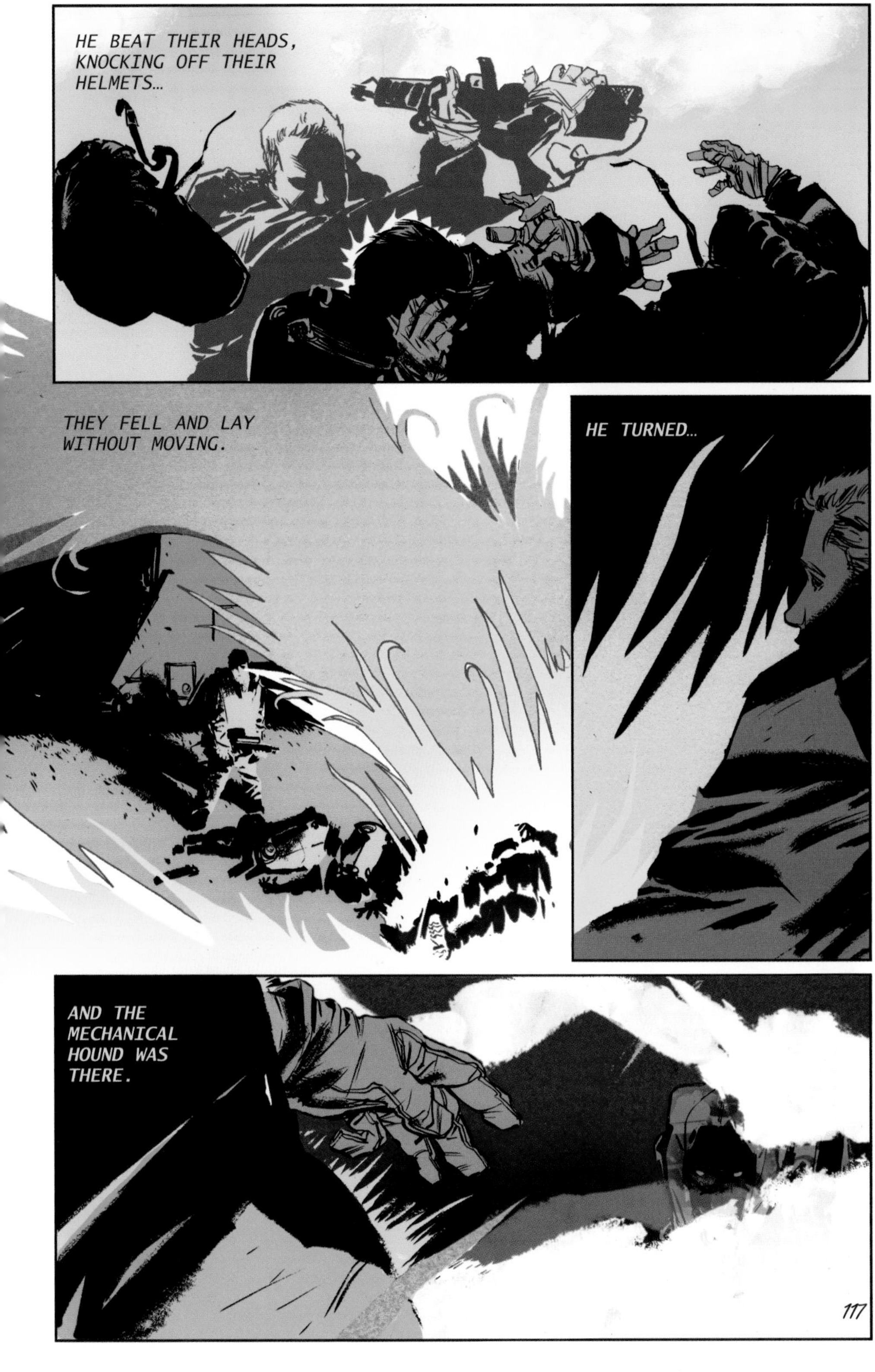
HE BEAT THEIR HEADS, KNOCKING OFF THEIR HELMETS...
THEY FELL AND LAY WITHOUT MOVING.
HE TURNED...
AND THE MECHANICAL HOUND WAS THERE.

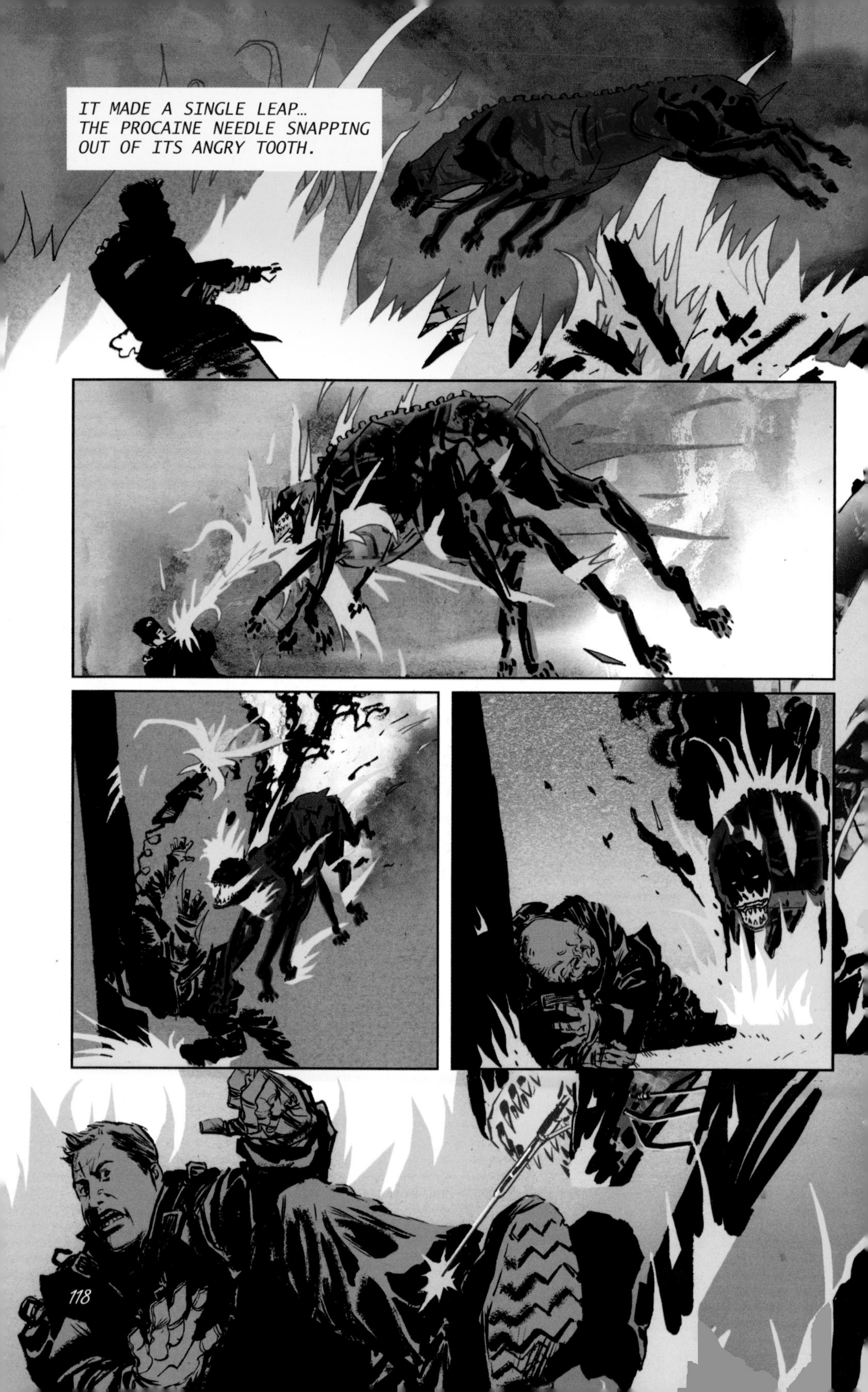
IT MADE A SINGLE LEAP… THE PROCAINE NEEDLE SNAPPING OUT OF ITS ANGRY TOOTH.

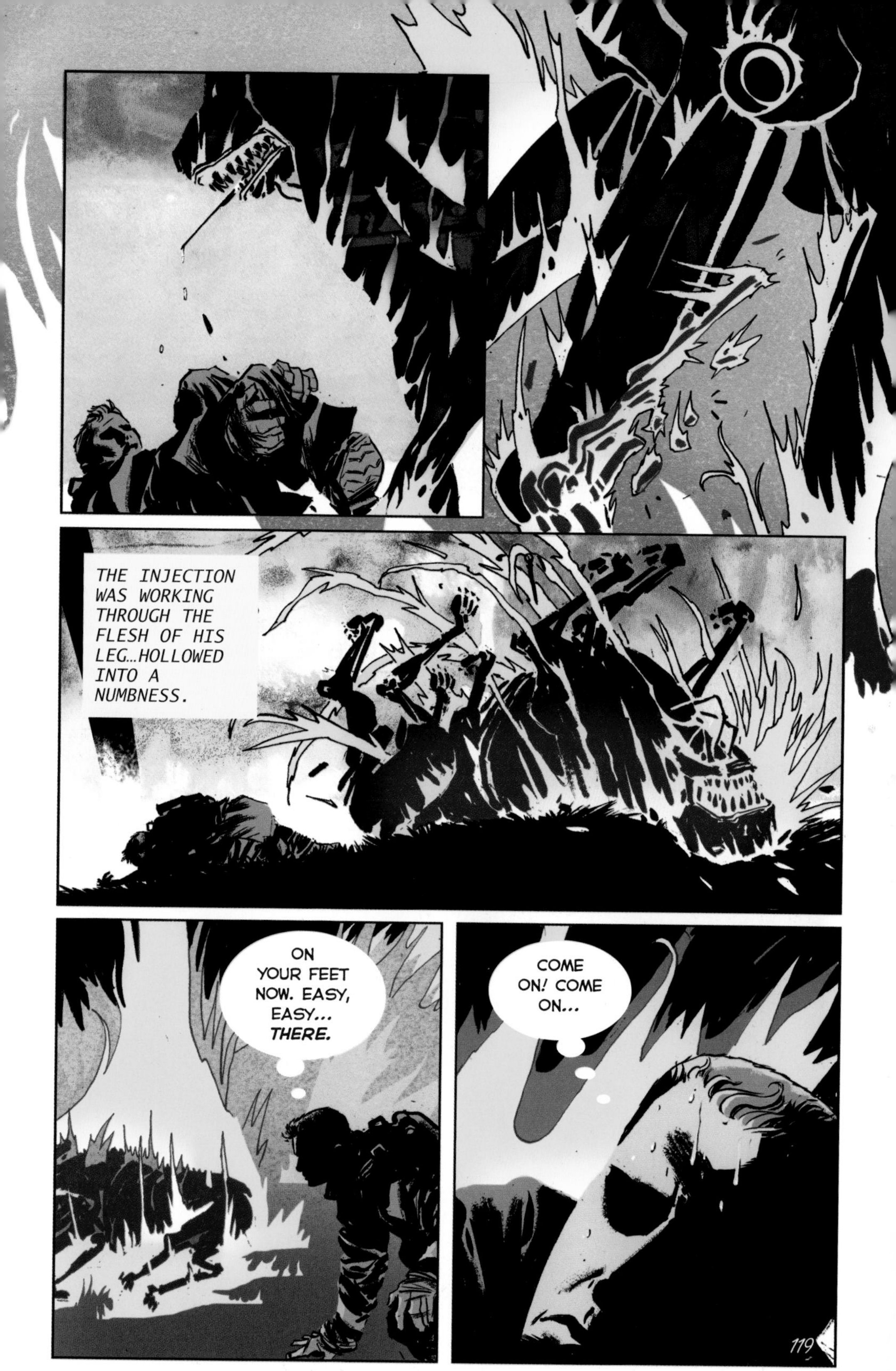
THE INJECTION WAS WORKING THROUGH THE FLESH OF HIS LEG...HOLLOWED INTO A NUMBNESS.
ON YOUR FEET NOW. EASY, EASY... *THERE.*
COME ON! COME ON...

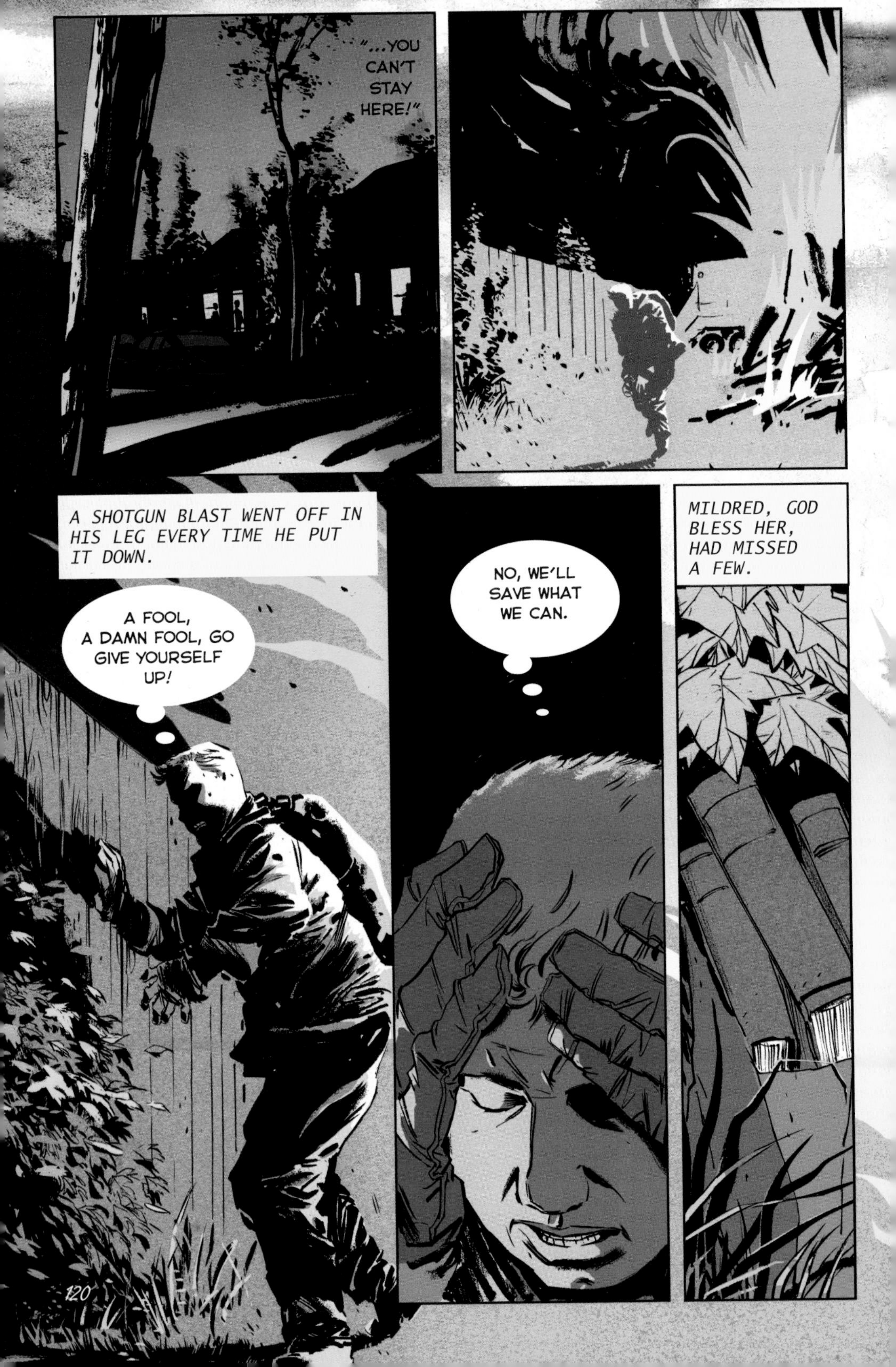
"...YOU CAN'T STAY HERE!"
A SHOTGUN BLAST WENT OFF IN HIS LEG EVERY TIME HE PUT IT DOWN.
A FOOL, A DAMN FOOL, GO GIVE YOURSELF UP!
NO, WE'LL SAVE WHAT WE CAN.
MILDRED, GOD BLESS HER, HAD MISSED A FEW.

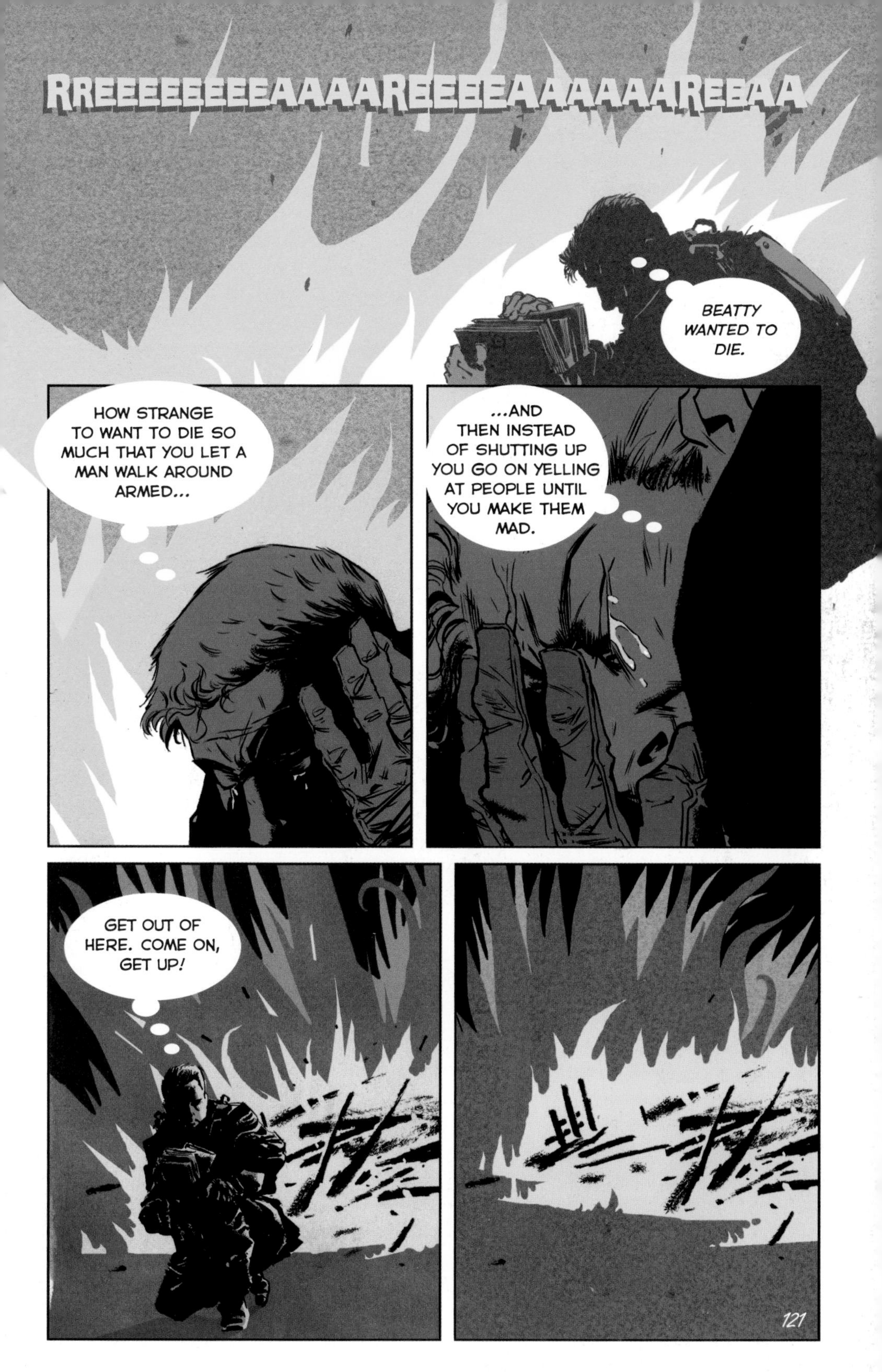
RREEEEEEEEAAAAREEEEEAAAAAAREEAA
BEATTY WANTED TO DIE.
HOW STRANGE TO WANT TO DIE SO MUCH THAT YOU LET A MAN WALK AROUND ARMED...
...AND THEN INSTEAD OF SHUTTING UP YOU GO ON YELLING AT PEOPLE UNTIL YOU MAKE THEM MAD.
GET OUT OF HERE. COME ON, GET UP!

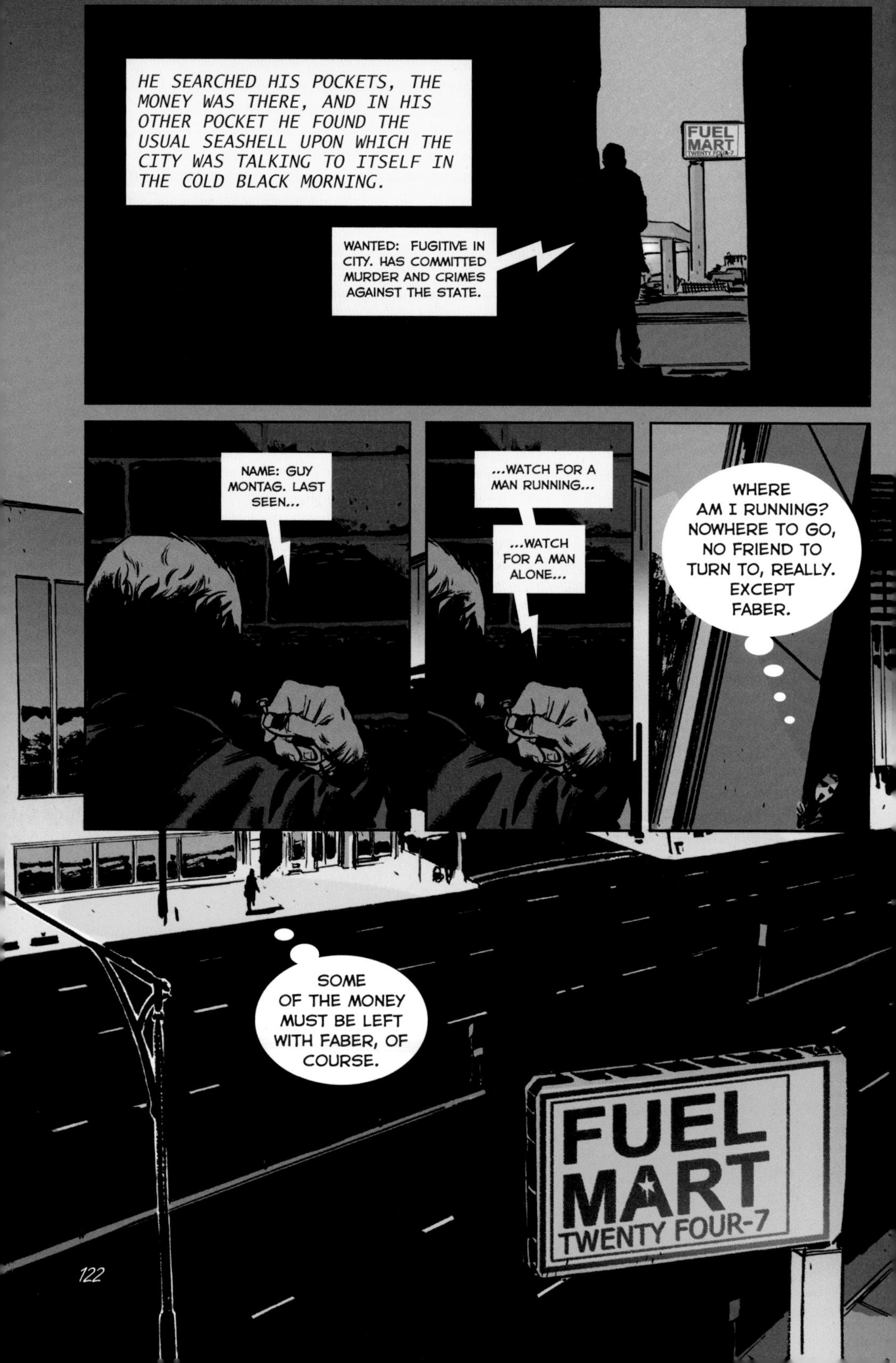
HE SEARCHED HIS POCKETS, THE MONEY WAS THERE, AND IN HIS OTHER POCKET HE FOUND THE USUAL SEASHELL UPON WHICH THE CITY WAS TALKING TO ITSELF IN THE COLD BLACK MORNING.
WANTED: FUGITIVE IN CITY. HAS COMMITTED MURDER AND CRIMES AGAINST THE STATE.
FUEL MART TWENTY FOUR-7
NAME: GUY MONTAG. LAST SEEN...
...WATCH FOR A MAN RUNNING...
...WATCH FOR A MAN ALONE...
WHERE AM I RUNNING? NOWHERE TO GO, NO FRIEND TO TURN TO, REALLY. EXCEPT FABER.
SOME OF THE MONEY MUST BE LEFT WITH FABER, OF COURSE.
FUEL MART TWENTY FOUR-7

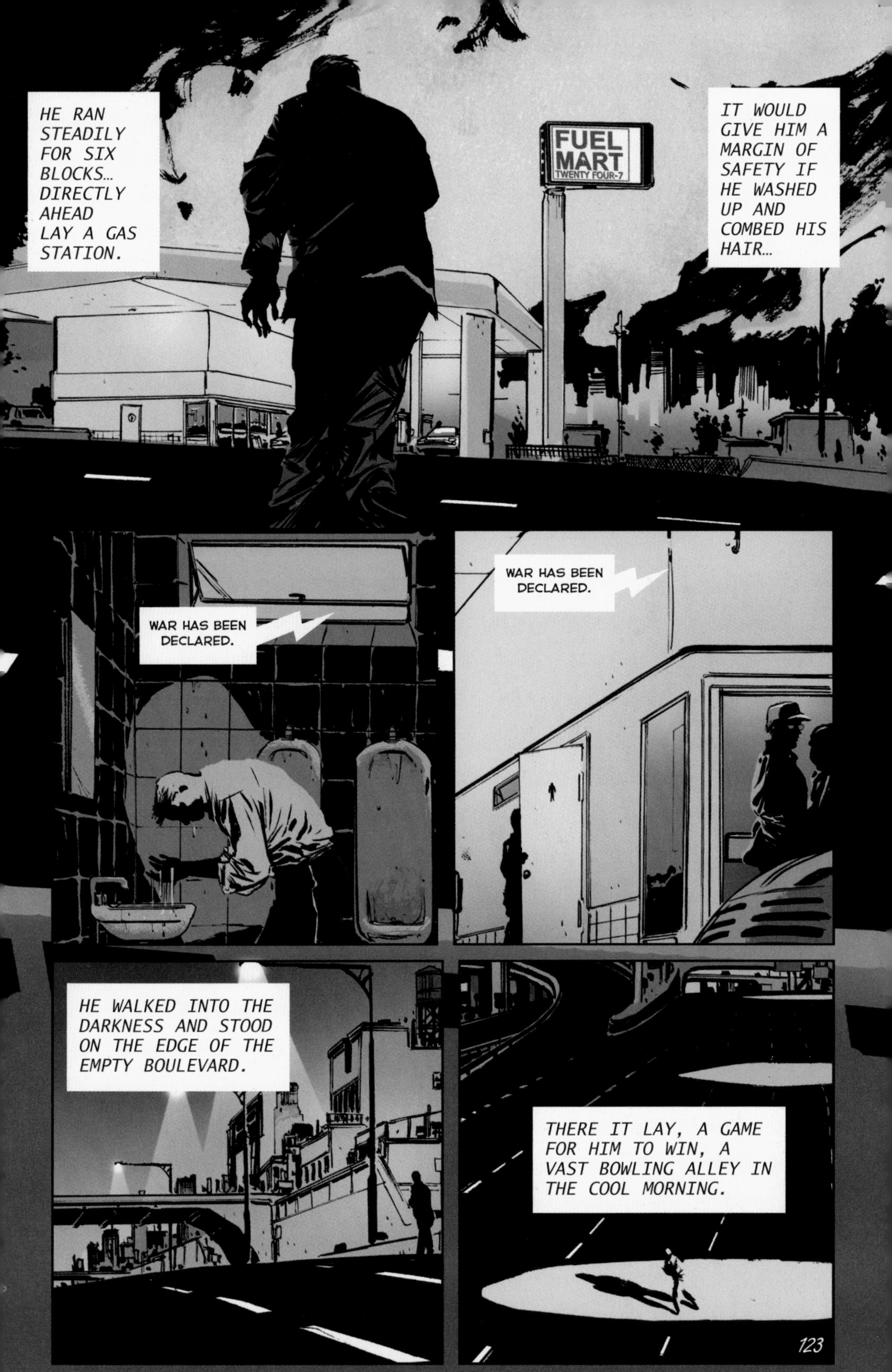
HE RAN STEADILY FOR SIX BLOCKS... DIRECTLY AHEAD LAY A GAS STATION.
FUEL MART TWENTY FOUR-7
IT WOULD GIVE HIM A MARGIN OF SAFETY IF HE WASHED UP AND COMBED HIS HAIR...
WAR HAS BEEN DECLARED.
WAR HAS BEEN DECLARED.
HE WALKED INTO THE DARKNESS AND STOOD ON THE EDGE OF THE EMPTY BOULEVARD.
THERE IT LAY, A GAME FOR HIM TO WIN, A VAST BOWLING ALLEY IN THE COOL MORNING.

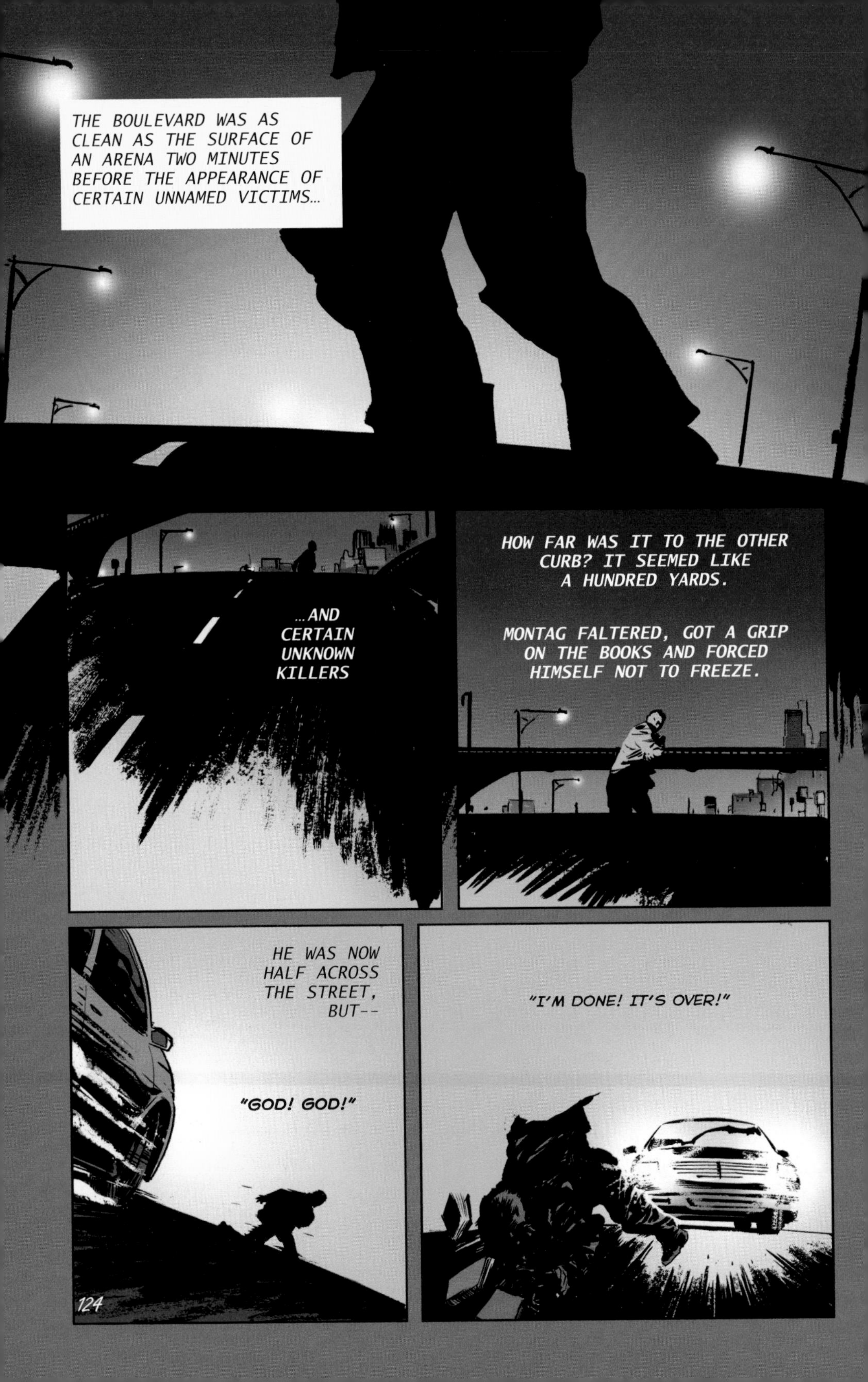
THE BOULEVARD WAS AS CLEAN AS THE SURFACE OF AN ARENA TWO MINUTES BEFORE THE APPEARANCE OF CERTAIN UNNAMED VICTIMS...
...AND CERTAIN UNKNOWN KILLERS
HOW FAR WAS IT TO THE OTHER CURB? IT SEEMED LIKE A HUNDRED YARDS.
MONTAG FALTERED, GOT A GRIP ON THE BOOKS AND FORCED HIMSELF NOT TO FREEZE.
HE WAS NOW HALF ACROSS THE STREET, BUT--
"GOD! GOD!"
"I'M DONE! IT'S OVER!"

"WASN'T THE POLICE. A CARFUL OF CHILDREN, ALL AGES."

"FOR NO REASON AT ALL IN THE WORLD THEY WOULD HAVE KILLED ME."

"I WONDER IF THEY WERE THE ONES WHO KILLED CLARISSE?"

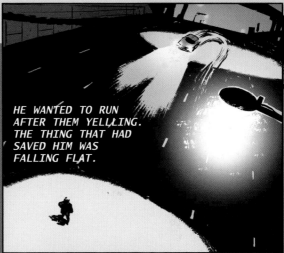

HE WANTED TO RUN AFTER THEM YELLING. THE THING THAT HAD SAVED HIM WAS FALLING FLAT.

THE DRIVER OF THAT CAR, SEEING MONTAG DOWN, INSTINCTIVELY CONSIDERED THE PROBABILITY THAT RUNNING OVER A BODY AT SUCH A HIGH SPEED...

...MIGHT TURN THE CAR UPSIDE DOWN AND SPILL THEM OUT.

IF MONTAG HAD REMAINED AN **UPRIGHT** TARGET?...

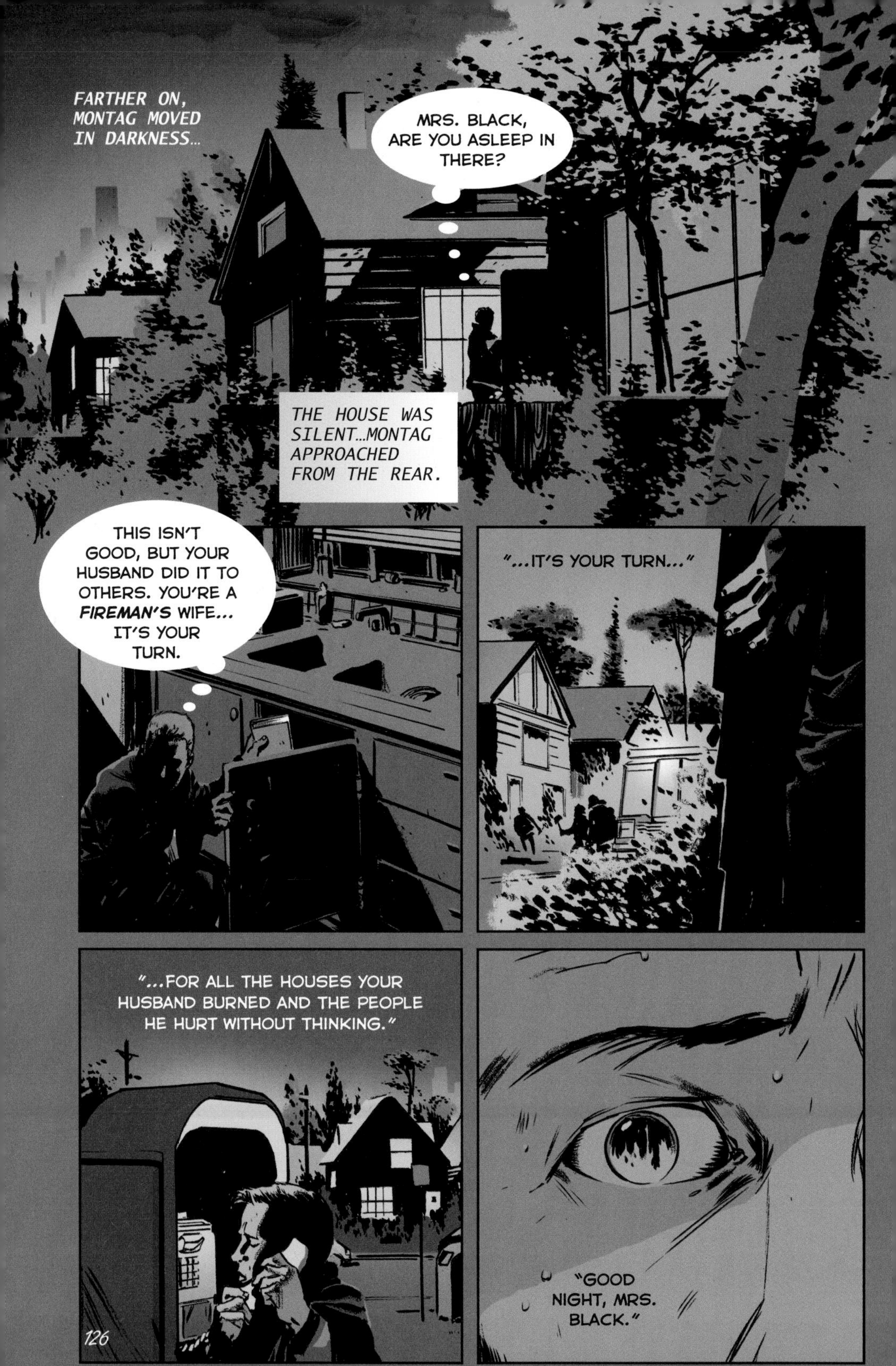
FARTHER ON, MONTAG MOVED IN DARKNESS...
MRS. BLACK, ARE YOU ASLEEP IN THERE?
THE HOUSE WAS SILENT...MONTAG APPROACHED FROM THE REAR.
THIS ISN'T GOOD, BUT YOUR HUSBAND DID IT TO OTHERS. YOU'RE A FIREMAN'S WIFE... IT'S YOUR TURN.
"...IT'S YOUR TURN..."
"...FOR ALL THE HOUSES YOUR HUSBAND BURNED AND THE PEOPLE HE HURT WITHOUT THINKING."
"GOOD NIGHT, MRS. BLACK."

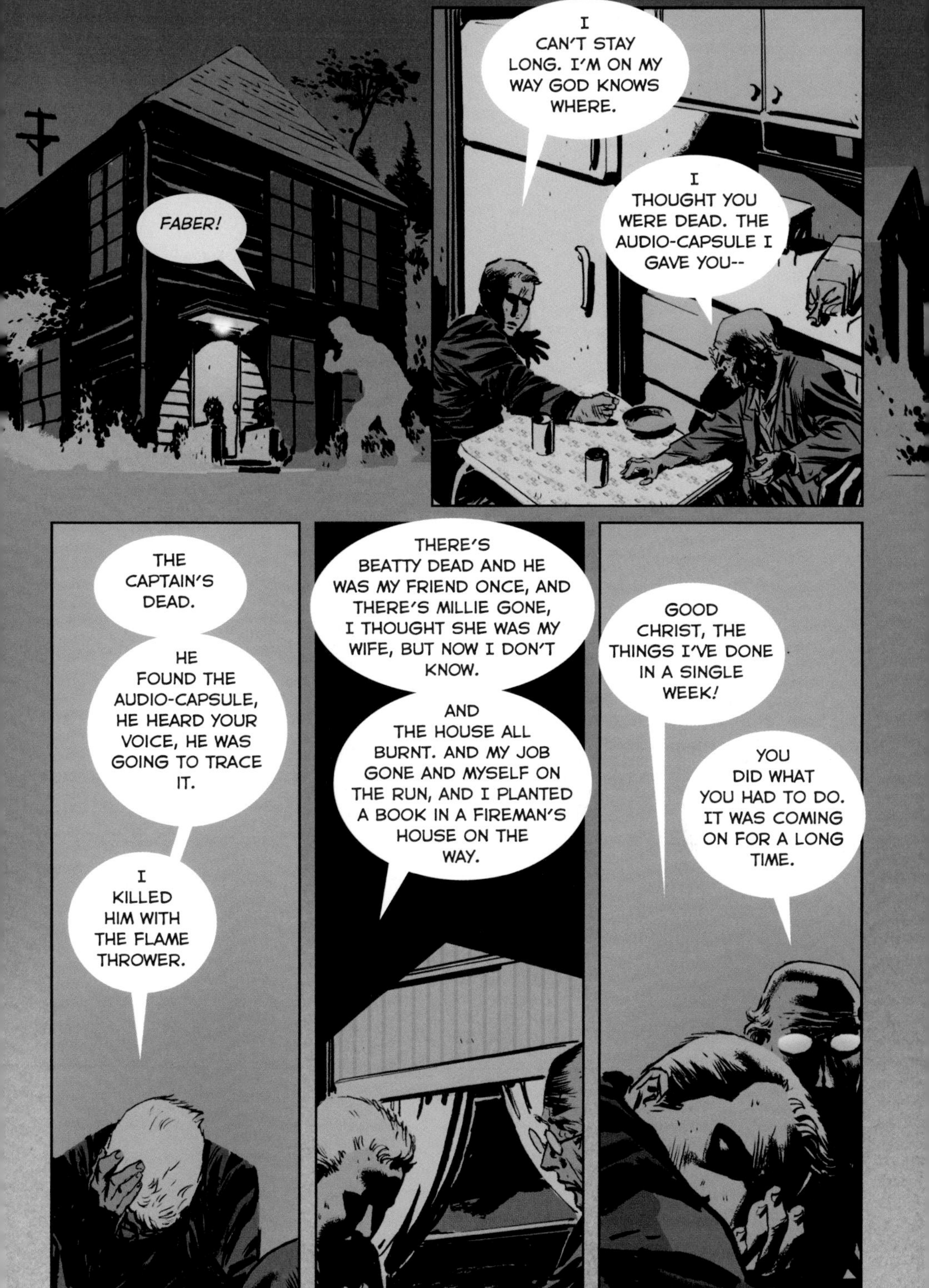
FABER!
I CAN'T STAY LONG. I'M ON MY WAY GOD KNOWS WHERE.
I THOUGHT YOU WERE DEAD. THE AUDIO-CAPSULE I GAVE YOU--
THE CAPTAIN'S DEAD.
HE FOUND THE AUDIO-CAPSULE, HE HEARD YOUR VOICE, HE WAS GOING TO TRACE IT.
I KILLED HIM WITH THE FLAME THROWER.
THERE'S BEATTY DEAD AND HE WAS MY FRIEND ONCE, AND THERE'S MILLIE GONE, I THOUGHT SHE WAS MY WIFE, BUT NOW I DON'T KNOW.
AND THE HOUSE ALL BURNT. AND MY JOB GONE AND MYSELF ON THE RUN, AND I PLANTED A BOOK IN A FIREMAN'S HOUSE ON THE WAY.
GOOD CHRIST, THE THINGS I'VE DONE IN A SINGLE WEEK!
YOU DID WHAT YOU HAD TO DO. IT WAS COMING ON FOR A LONG TIME.

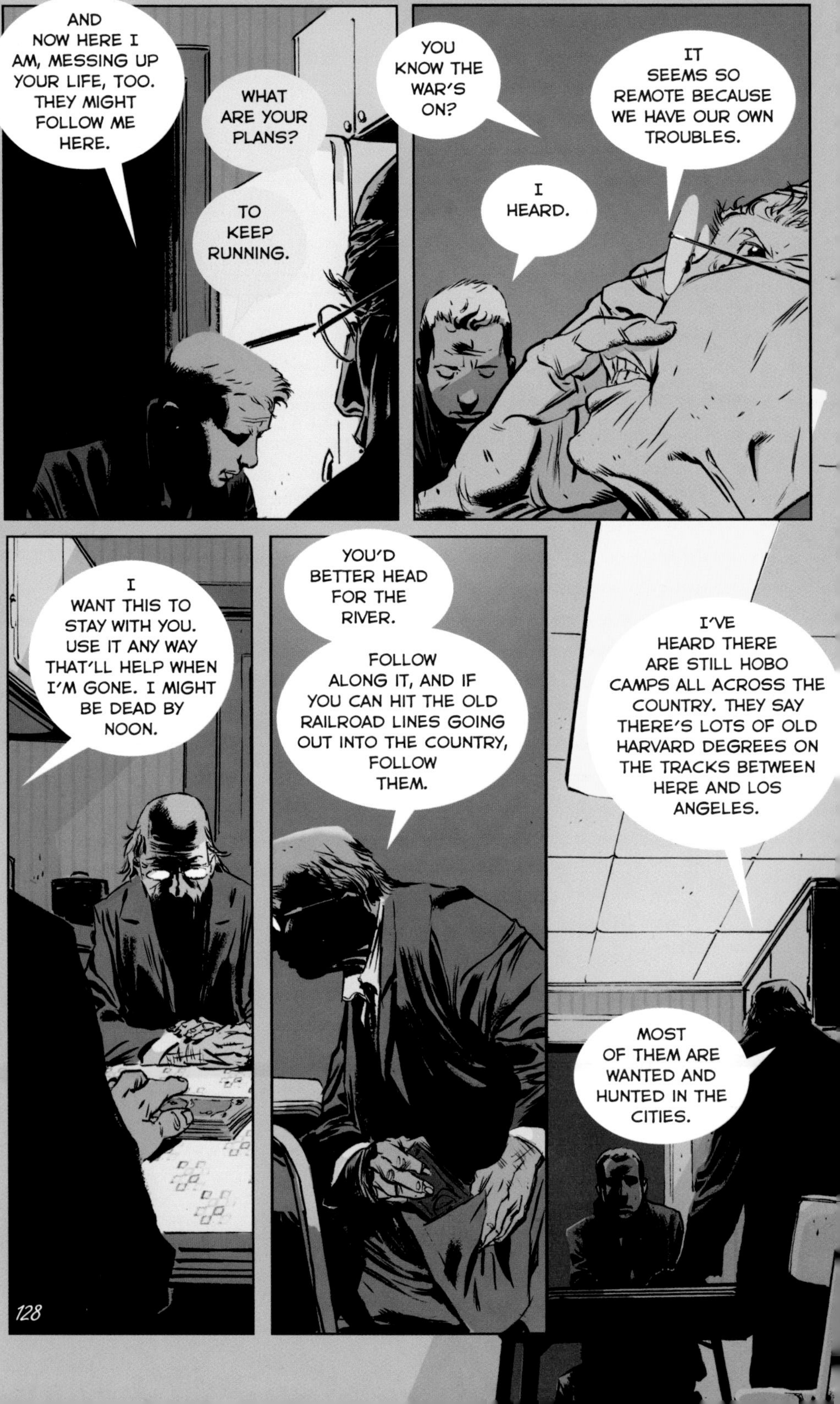

AND NOW HERE I AM, MESSING UP YOUR LIFE, TOO. THEY MIGHT FOLLOW ME HERE.
WHAT ARE YOUR PLANS?
TO KEEP RUNNING.
YOU KNOW THE WAR'S ON?
I HEARD.
IT SEEMS SO REMOTE BECAUSE WE HAVE OUR OWN TROUBLES.
I WANT THIS TO STAY WITH YOU. USE IT ANY WAY THAT'LL HELP WHEN I'M GONE. I MIGHT BE DEAD BY NOON.
YOU'D BETTER HEAD FOR THE RIVER.
FOLLOW ALONG IT, AND IF YOU CAN HIT THE OLD RAILROAD LINES GOING OUT INTO THE COUNTRY, FOLLOW THEM.
I'VE HEARD THERE ARE STILL HOBO CAMPS ALL ACROSS THE COUNTRY. THEY SAY THERE'S LOTS OF OLD HARVARD DEGREES ON THE TRACKS BETWEEN HERE AND LOS ANGELES.
MOST OF THEM ARE WANTED AND HUNTED IN THE CITIES.

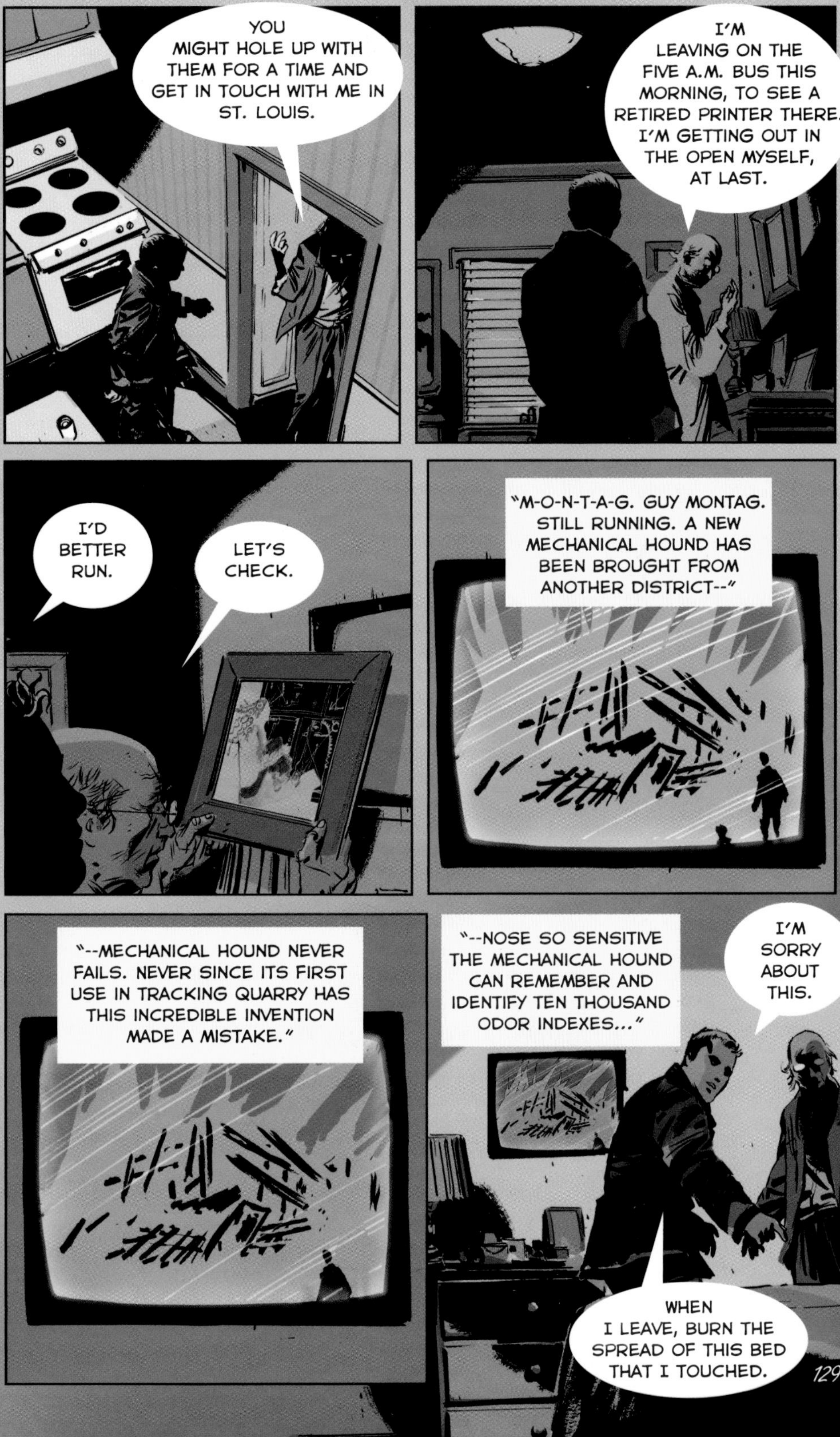
YOU MIGHT HOLE UP WITH THEM FOR A TIME AND GET IN TOUCH WITH ME IN ST. LOUIS.
I'M LEAVING ON THE FIVE A.M. BUS THIS MORNING, TO SEE A RETIRED PRINTER THERE. I'M GETTING OUT IN THE OPEN MYSELF, AT LAST.
I'D BETTER RUN.
LET'S CHECK.
"M-O-N-T-A-G. GUY MONTAG. STILL RUNNING. A NEW MECHANICAL HOUND HAS BEEN BROUGHT FROM ANOTHER DISTRICT--"
"--MECHANICAL HOUND NEVER FAILS. NEVER SINCE ITS FIRST USE IN TRACKING QUARRY HAS THIS INCREDIBLE INVENTION MADE A MISTAKE."
"--NOSE SO SENSITIVE THE MECHANICAL HOUND CAN REMEMBER AND IDENTIFY TEN THOUSAND ODOR INDEXES..."
I'M SORRY ABOUT THIS.
WHEN I LEAVE, BURN THE SPREAD OF THIS BED THAT I TOUCHED.

"BURN THE CHAIR IN THE LIVING ROOM. WIPE DOWN THE FURNITURE WITH ALCOHOL. WIPE THE DOORKNOBS. TURN ON YOUR SPRINKLERS AS HIGH AS THEY'LL GO AND HOSE OFF THE SIDEWALKS."

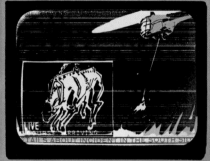

"ONE LAST THING. A SUITCASE, GET IT, FILL IT WITH YOUR DIRTIEST CLOTHES, A SHIRT, SOCKS..."

"SEAL THE VALISE WITH CLEAR TAPE. MAY I TAKE THIS WHISKEY? I'LL NEED IT LATER."

"CHRIST, I HOPE THIS WORKS!"

"GOOD-BYE!"

MONTAG RAN.

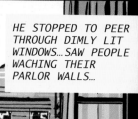

HE STOPPED TO PEER THROUGH DIMLY LIT WINDOWS... SAW PEOPLE WACHING THEIR PARLOR WALLS...

...ON THE WALLS THE MECHANICAL HOUND... SPIDERING ALONG... HERE AND GONE...

NOW AT ELM TERRACE, LINCOLN. OAK, PARK...

"FABER'S HOUSE! DON'T STOP, GO ON."

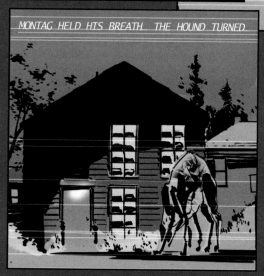

MONTAG HELD HIS BREATH. THE HOUND TURNED.

...AND PLUNGED AWAY FROM FABER'S HOUSE...

131

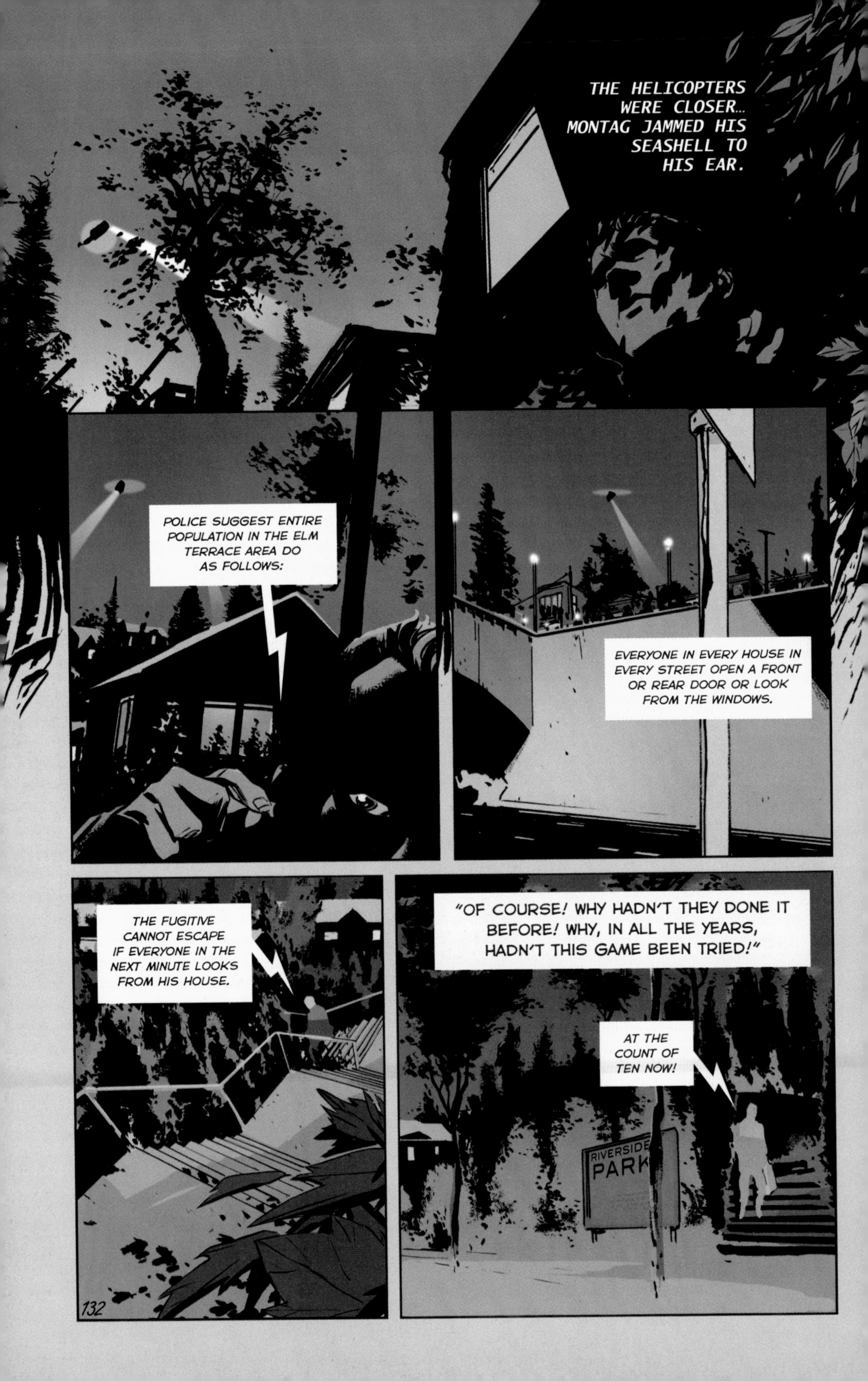
THE HELICOPTERS WERE CLOSER... MONTAG JAMMED HIS SEASHELL TO HIS EAR.
POLICE SUGGEST ENTIRE POPULATION IN THE ELM TERRACE AREA DO AS FOLLOWS:
EVERYONE IN EVERY HOUSE IN EVERY STREET OPEN A FRONT OR REAR DOOR OR LOOK FROM THE WINDOWS.
THE FUGITIVE CANNOT ESCAPE IF EVERYONE IN THE NEXT MINUTE LOOKS FROM HIS HOUSE.
"OF COURSE! WHY HADN'T THEY DONE IT BEFORE! WHY, IN ALL THE YEARS, HADN'T THIS GAME BEEN TRIED!"
AT THE COUNT OF TEN NOW!
RIVERSIDE PARK

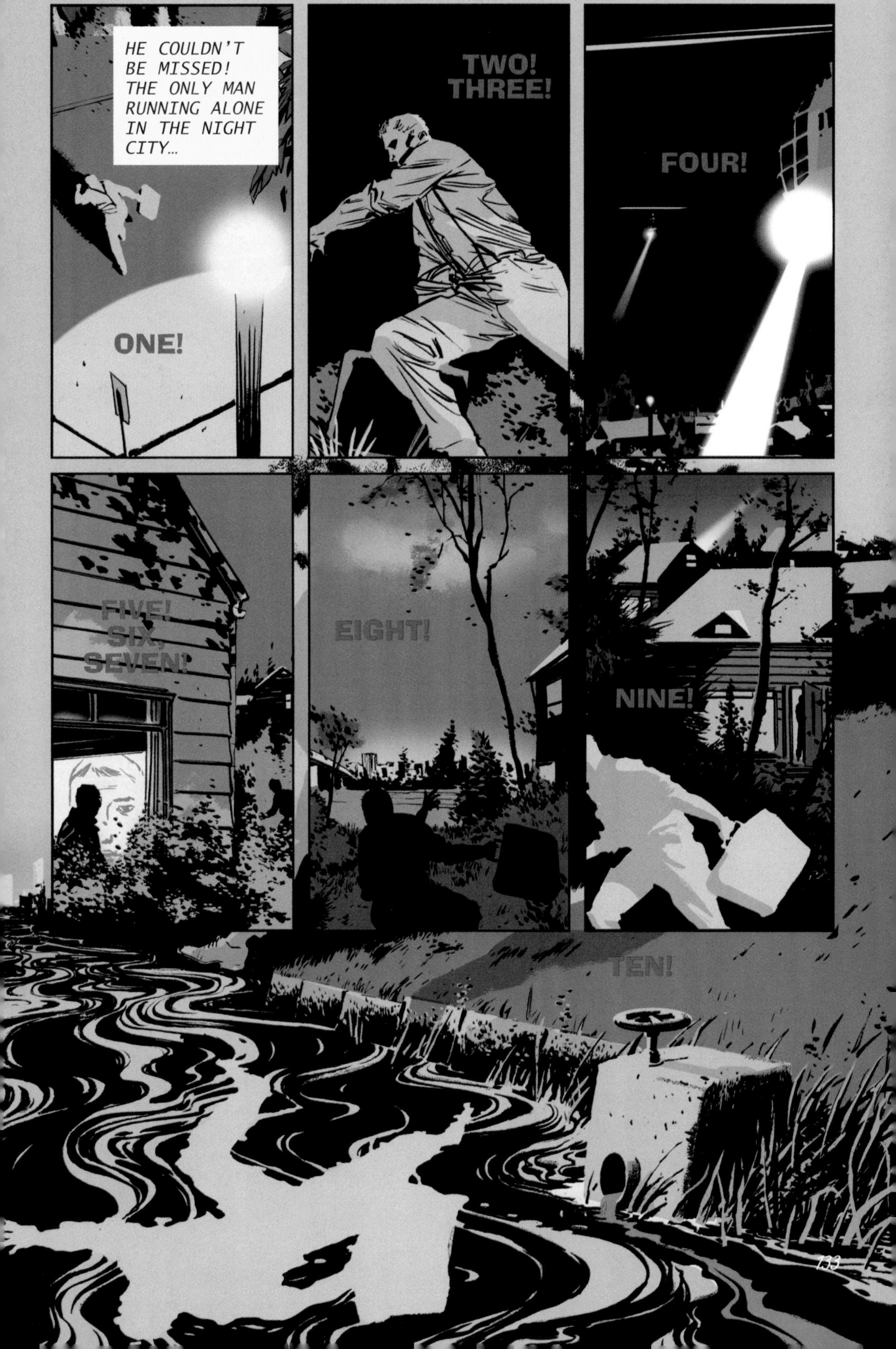
HE COULDN'T BE MISSED! THE ONLY MAN RUNNING ALONE IN THE NIGHT CITY...
ONE!
TWO! THREE!
FOUR!
FIVE! SIX, SEVEN!
EIGHT!
NINE!
TEN!

HE WAS AT THE RIVER.

OVERHEAD, THE
GREAT RACKETING
FANS OF THE
HELICOPTERS
HOVERED.

HE FELT THE
RIVER PULL HIM
FARTHER INTO
DARKNESS.

HE WAS THREE
HUNDRED YARDS
DOWNSTREAM WHEN
THE HOUND
REACHED THE
RIVER.

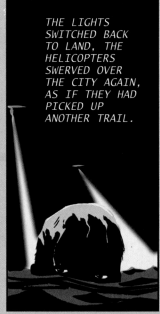

THE LIGHTS
SWITCHED BACK
TO LAND, THE
HELICOPTERS
SWERVED OVER
THE CITY AGAIN,
AS IF THEY HAD
PICKED UP
ANOTHER TRAIL.

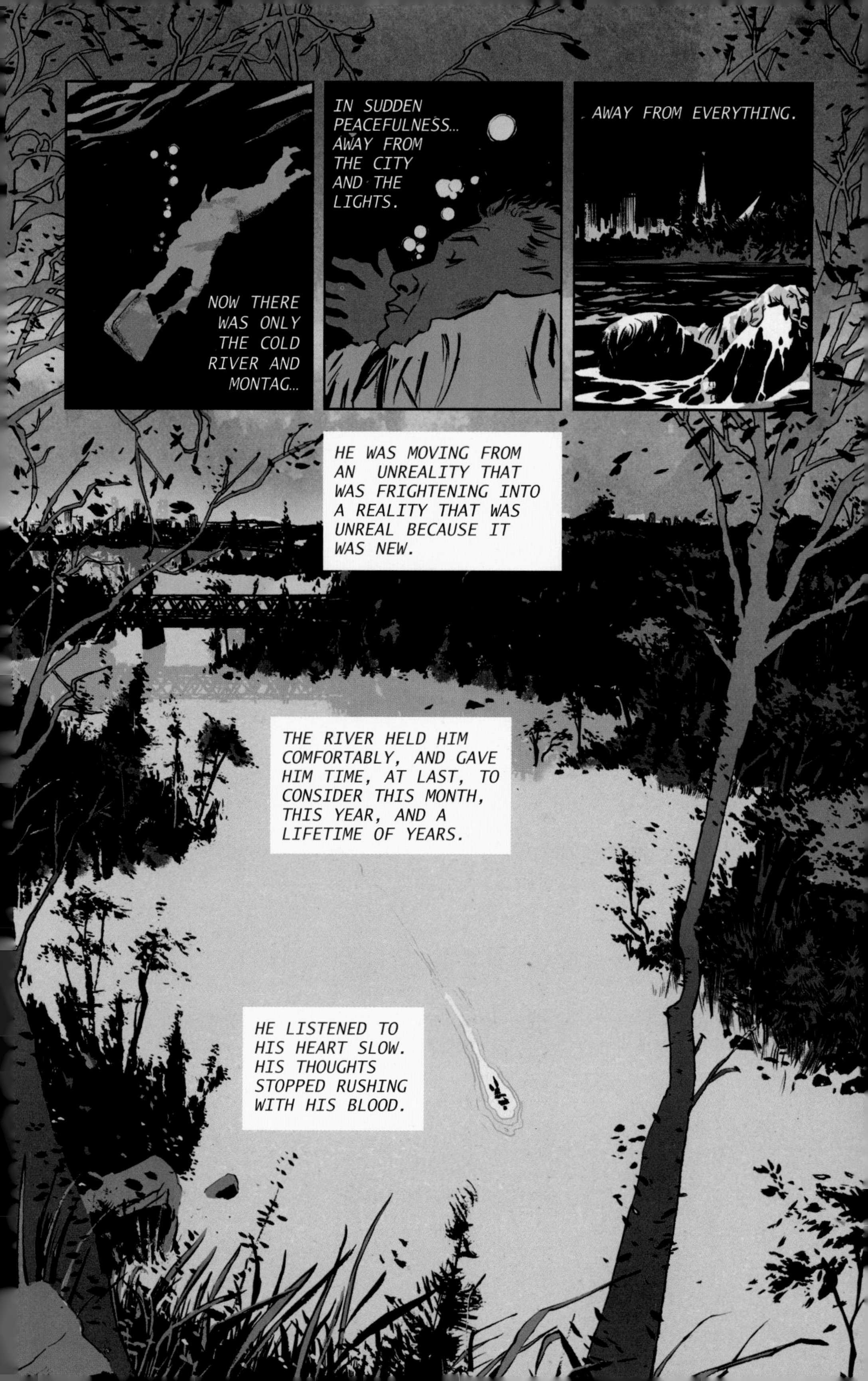
NOW THERE WAS ONLY THE COLD RIVER AND MONTAG...
IN SUDDEN PEACEFULNESS... AWAY FROM THE CITY AND THE LIGHTS.
...AWAY FROM EVERYTHING.
HE WAS MOVING FROM AN UNREALITY THAT WAS FRIGHTENING INTO A REALITY THAT WAS UNREAL BECAUSE IT WAS NEW.
THE RIVER HELD HIM COMFORTABLY, AND GAVE HIM TIME, AT LAST, TO CONSIDER THIS MONTH, THIS YEAR, AND A LIFETIME OF YEARS.
HE LISTENED TO HIS HEART SLOW. HIS THOUGHTS STOPPED RUSHING WITH HIS BLOOD.

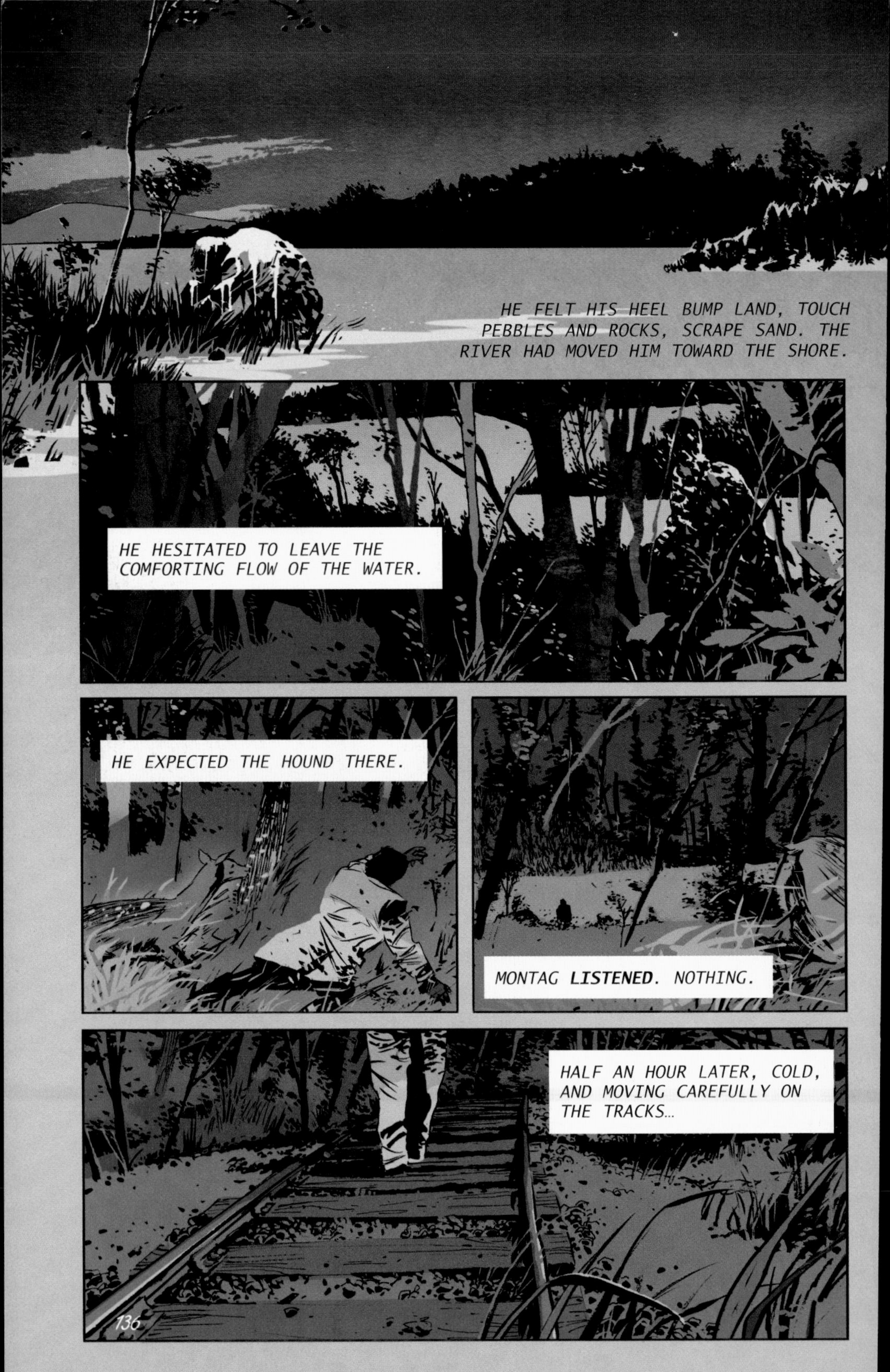
HE FELT HIS HEEL BUMP LAND, TOUCH PEBBLES AND ROCKS, SCRAPE SAND. THE RIVER HAD MOVED HIM TOWARD THE SHORE.
HE HESITATED TO LEAVE THE COMFORTING FLOW OF THE WATER.
HE EXPECTED THE HOUND THERE.
MONTAG **LISTENED**. NOTHING.
HALF AN HOUR LATER, COLD, AND MOVING CAREFULLY ON THE TRACKS...

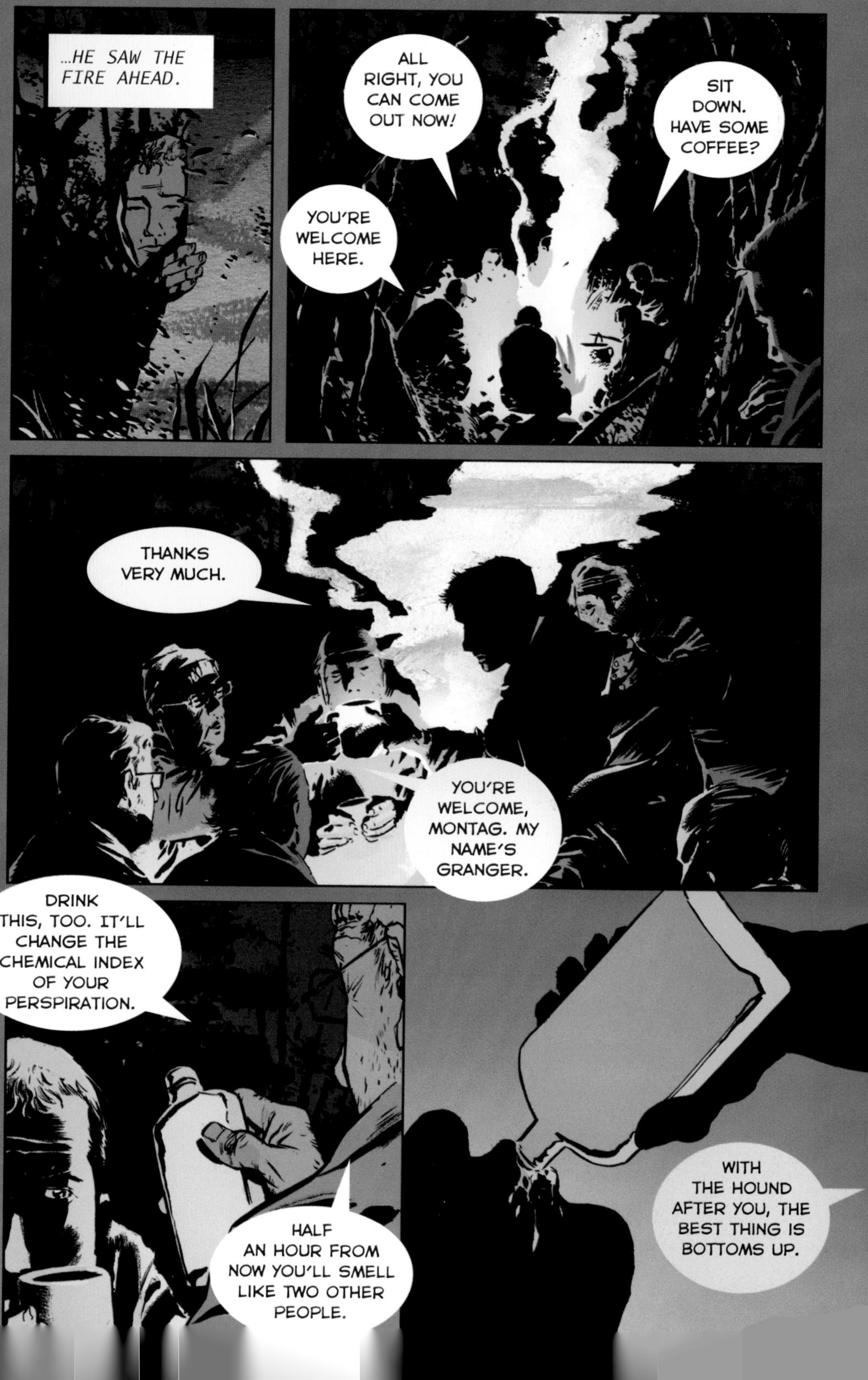
...HE SAW THE FIRE AHEAD.
ALL RIGHT, YOU CAN COME OUT NOW!
YOU'RE WELCOME HERE.
SIT DOWN. HAVE SOME COFFEE?
THANKS VERY MUCH.
YOU'RE WELCOME, MONTAG. MY NAME'S GRANGER.
DRINK THIS, TOO. IT'LL CHANGE THE CHEMICAL INDEX OF YOUR PERSPIRATION.
HALF AN HOUR FROM NOW YOU'LL SMELL LIKE TWO OTHER PEOPLE.
WITH THE HOUND AFTER YOU, THE BEST THING IS BOTTOMS UP.

YOU KNOW MY NAME.

WE'VE WATCHED THE CHASE. FIGURED YOU'D WIND UP SOUTH ALONG THE RIVER. THE CHASE IS STILL RUNNING. THE OTHER WAY, THOUGH.

THE OTHER WAY?

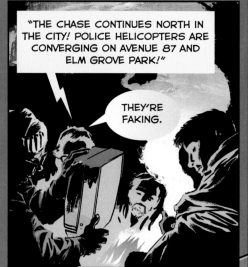

"THE CHASE CONTINUES NORTH IN THE CITY! POLICE HELICOPTERS ARE CONVERGING ON AVENUE 87 AND ELM GROVE PARK!"

THEY'RE FAKING.

YOU THREW THEM OFF AT THE RIVER. THEY CAN'T ADMIT IT. THEY'LL CATCH MONTAG IN THE NEXT FIVE MINUTES!

BUT HOW--

SEE THAT? IT'LL BE *YOU*; RIGHT UP AT THE END OF THAT STREET... OUR VICTIM.

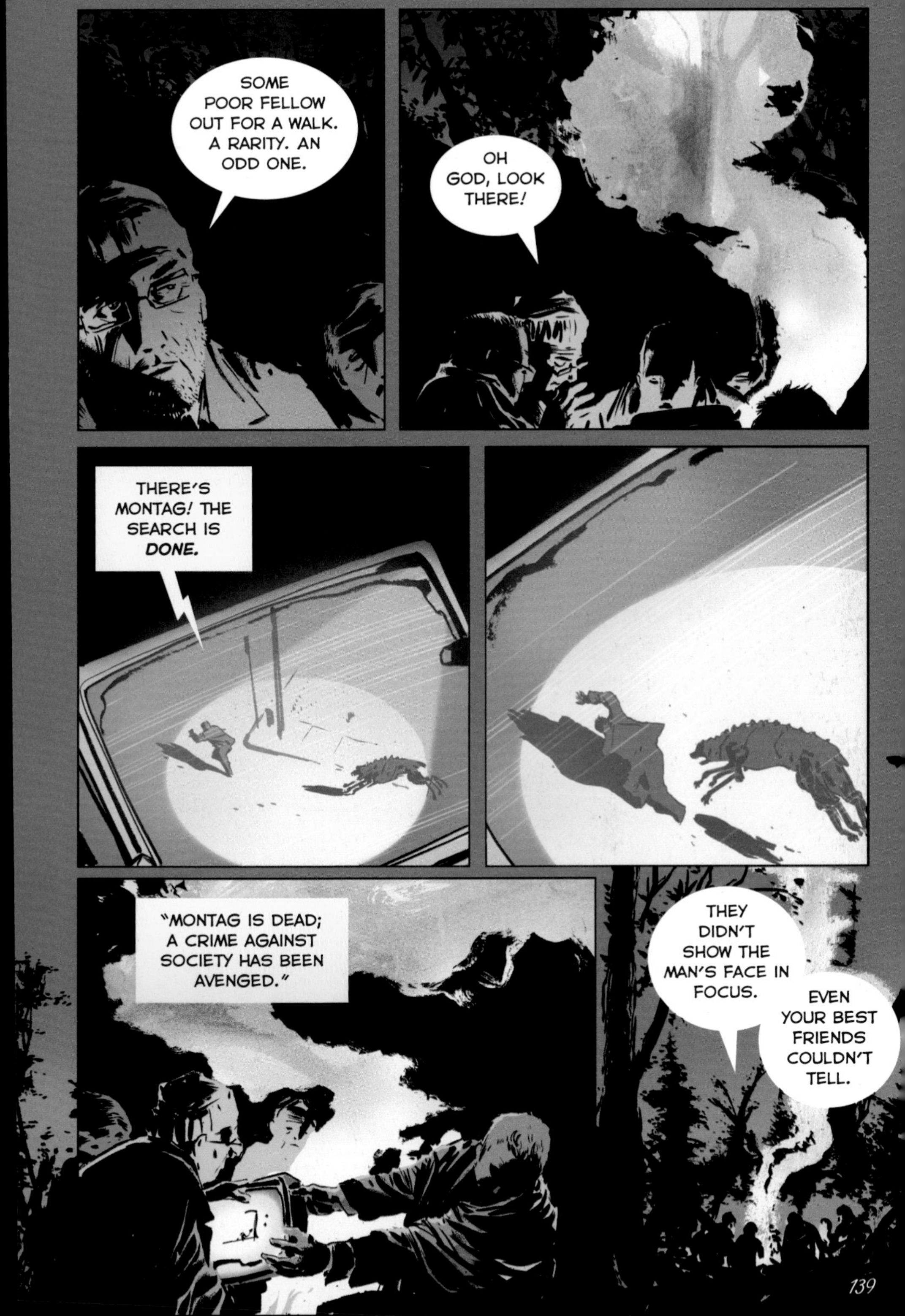
SOME POOR FELLOW OUT FOR A WALK. A RARITY. AN ODD ONE.
OH GOD, LOOK THERE!
THERE'S MONTAG! THE SEARCH IS DONE.
"MONTAG IS DEAD; A CRIME AGAINST SOCIETY HAS BEEN AVENGED."
THEY DIDN'T SHOW THE MAN'S FACE IN FOCUS.
EVEN YOUR BEST FRIENDS COULDN'T TELL.

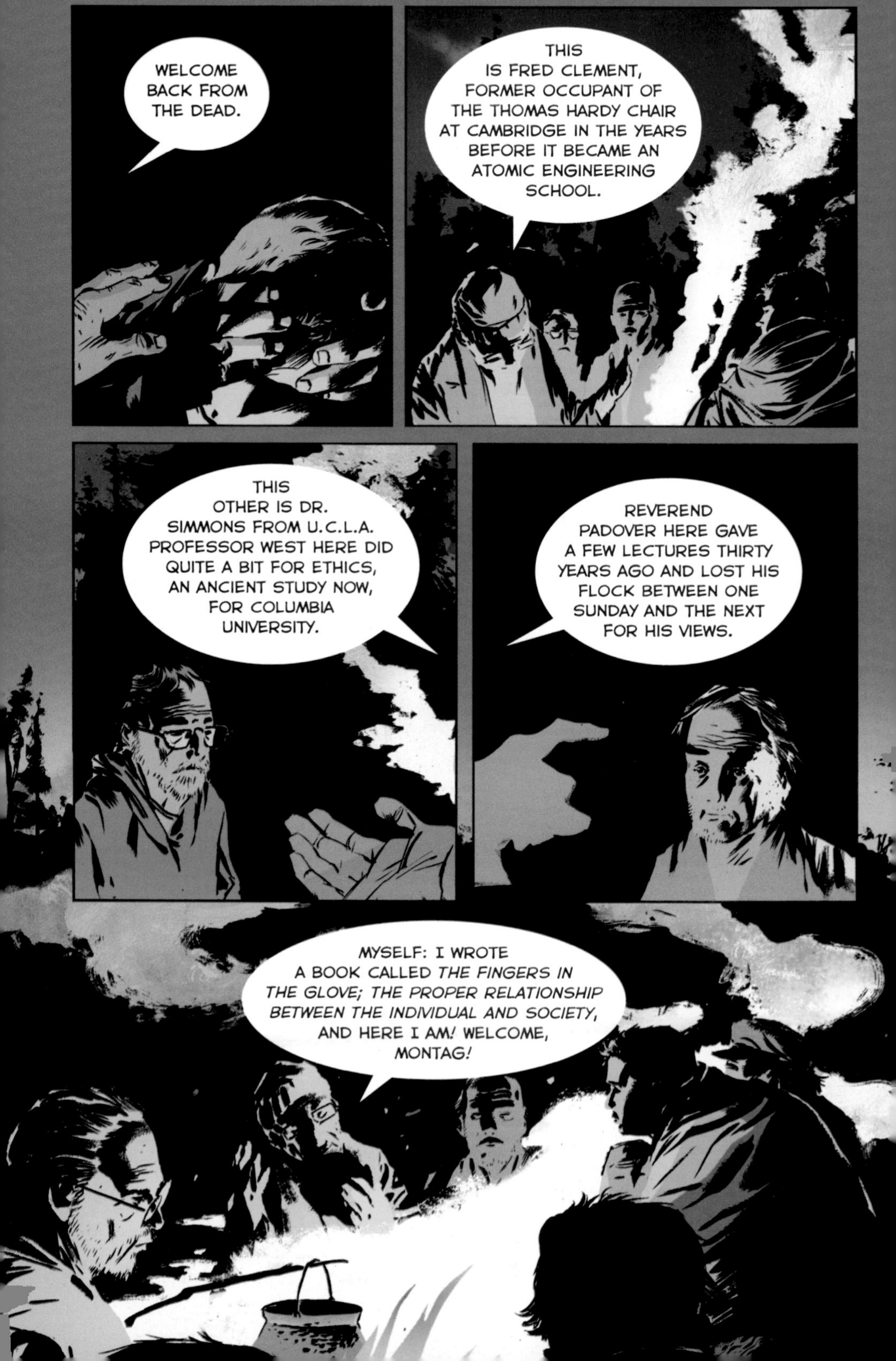
WELCOME BACK FROM THE DEAD.
THIS IS FRED CLEMENT, FORMER OCCUPANT OF THE THOMAS HARDY CHAIR AT CAMBRIDGE IN THE YEARS BEFORE IT BECAME AN ATOMIC ENGINEERING SCHOOL.
THIS OTHER IS DR. SIMMONS FROM U.C.L.A. PROFESSOR WEST HERE DID QUITE A BIT FOR ETHICS, AN ANCIENT STUDY NOW, FOR COLUMBIA UNIVERSITY.
REVEREND PADOVER HERE GAVE A FEW LECTURES THIRTY YEARS AGO AND LOST HIS FLOCK BETWEEN ONE SUNDAY AND THE NEXT FOR HIS VIEWS.
MYSELF: I WROTE A BOOK CALLED *THE FINGERS IN THE GLOVE; THE PROPER RELATIONSHIP BETWEEN THE INDIVIDUAL AND SOCIETY*, AND HERE I AM! WELCOME, MONTAG!

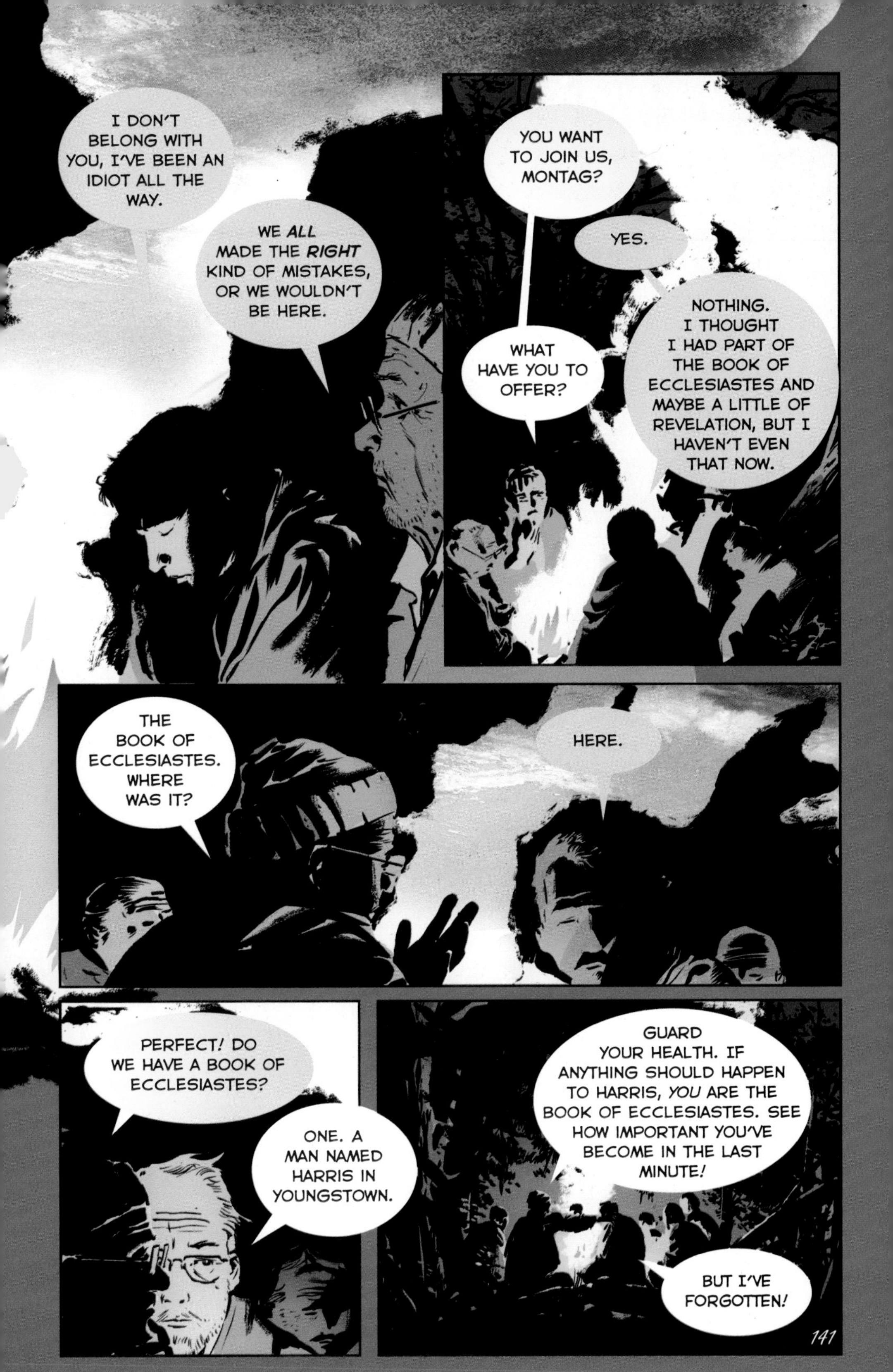
I DON'T BELONG WITH YOU, I'VE BEEN AN IDIOT ALL THE WAY.
WE *ALL* MADE THE *RIGHT* KIND OF MISTAKES, OR WE WOULDN'T BE HERE.
YOU WANT TO JOIN US, MONTAG?
YES.
WHAT HAVE YOU TO OFFER?
NOTHING. I THOUGHT I HAD PART OF THE BOOK OF ECCLESIASTES AND MAYBE A LITTLE OF REVELATION, BUT I HAVEN'T EVEN THAT NOW.
THE BOOK OF ECCLESIASTES. WHERE WAS IT?
HERE.
PERFECT! DO WE HAVE A BOOK OF ECCLESIASTES?
ONE. A MAN NAMED HARRIS IN YOUNGSTOWN.
GUARD YOUR HEALTH. IF ANYTHING SHOULD HAPPEN TO HARRIS, *YOU* ARE THE BOOK OF ECCLESIASTES. SEE HOW IMPORTANT YOU'VE BECOME IN THE LAST MINUTE!
BUT I'VE FORGOTTEN!

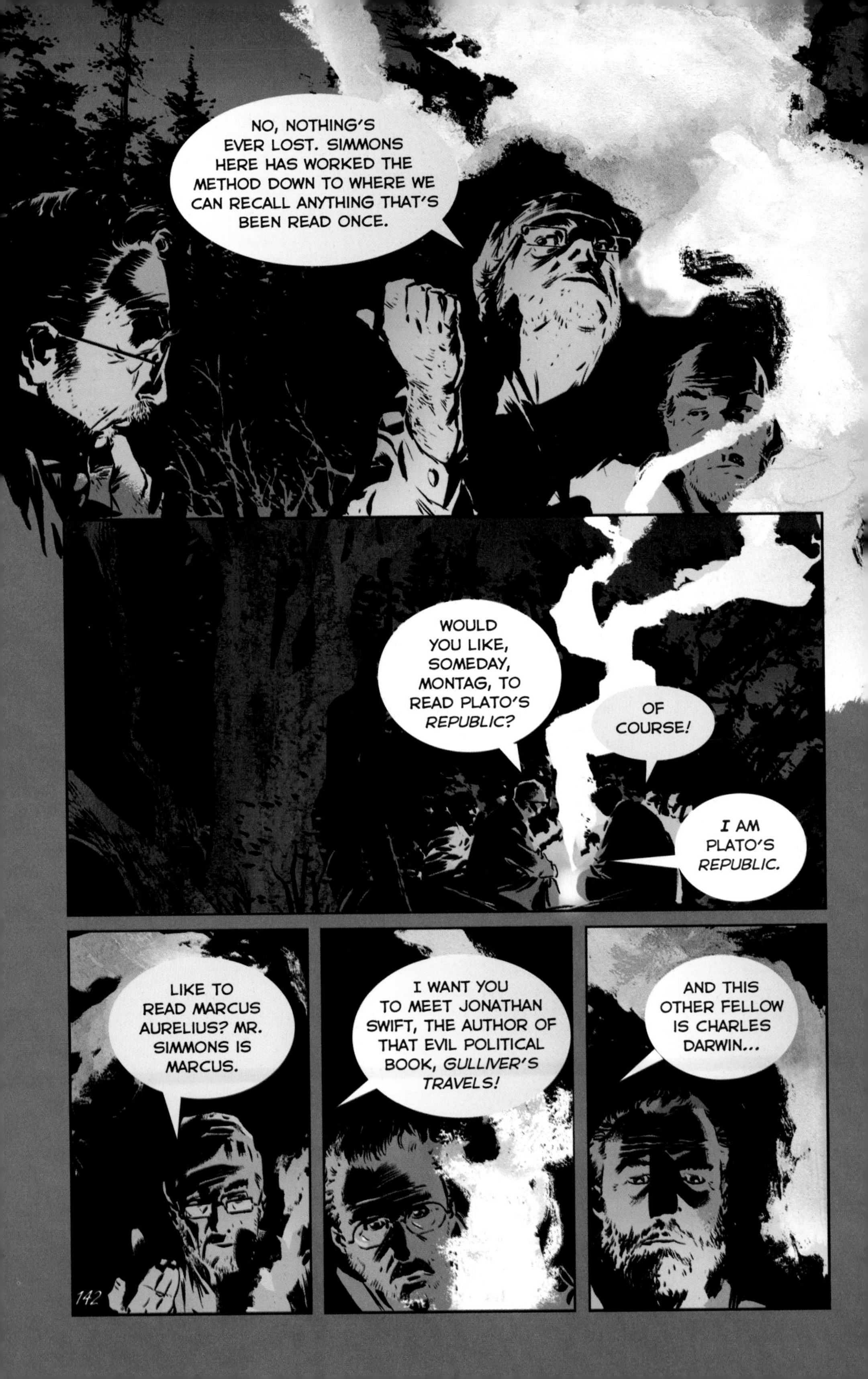
NO, NOTHING'S EVER LOST. SIMMONS HERE HAS WORKED THE METHOD DOWN TO WHERE WE CAN RECALL ANYTHING THAT'S BEEN READ ONCE.
WOULD YOU LIKE, SOMEDAY, MONTAG, TO READ PLATO'S *REPUBLIC*?
OF COURSE!
I AM PLATO'S *REPUBLIC.*
LIKE TO READ MARCUS AURELIUS? MR. SIMMONS IS MARCUS.
I WANT YOU TO MEET JONATHAN SWIFT, THE AUTHOR OF THAT EVIL POLITICAL BOOK, *GULLIVER'S TRAVELS!*
AND THIS OTHER FELLOW IS CHARLES DARWIN...

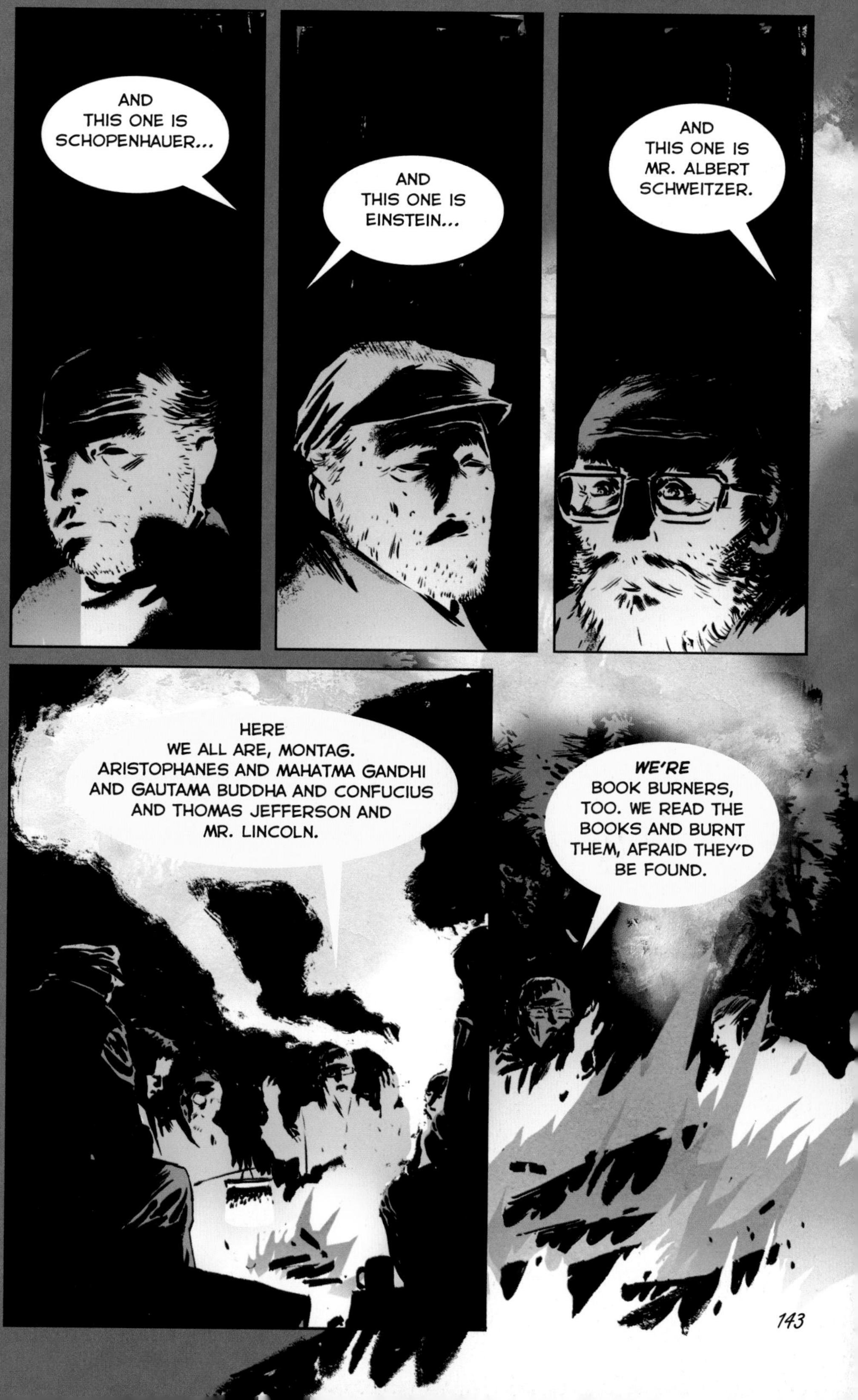
AND THIS ONE IS SCHOPENHAUER...
AND THIS ONE IS EINSTEIN...
AND THIS ONE IS MR. ALBERT SCHWEITZER.
HERE WE ALL ARE, MONTAG. ARISTOPHANES AND MAHATMA GANDHI AND GAUTAMA BUDDHA AND CONFUCIUS AND THOMAS JEFFERSON AND MR. LINCOLN.
WE'RE BOOK BURNERS, TOO. WE READ THE BOOKS AND BURNT THEM, AFRAID THEY'D BE FOUND.

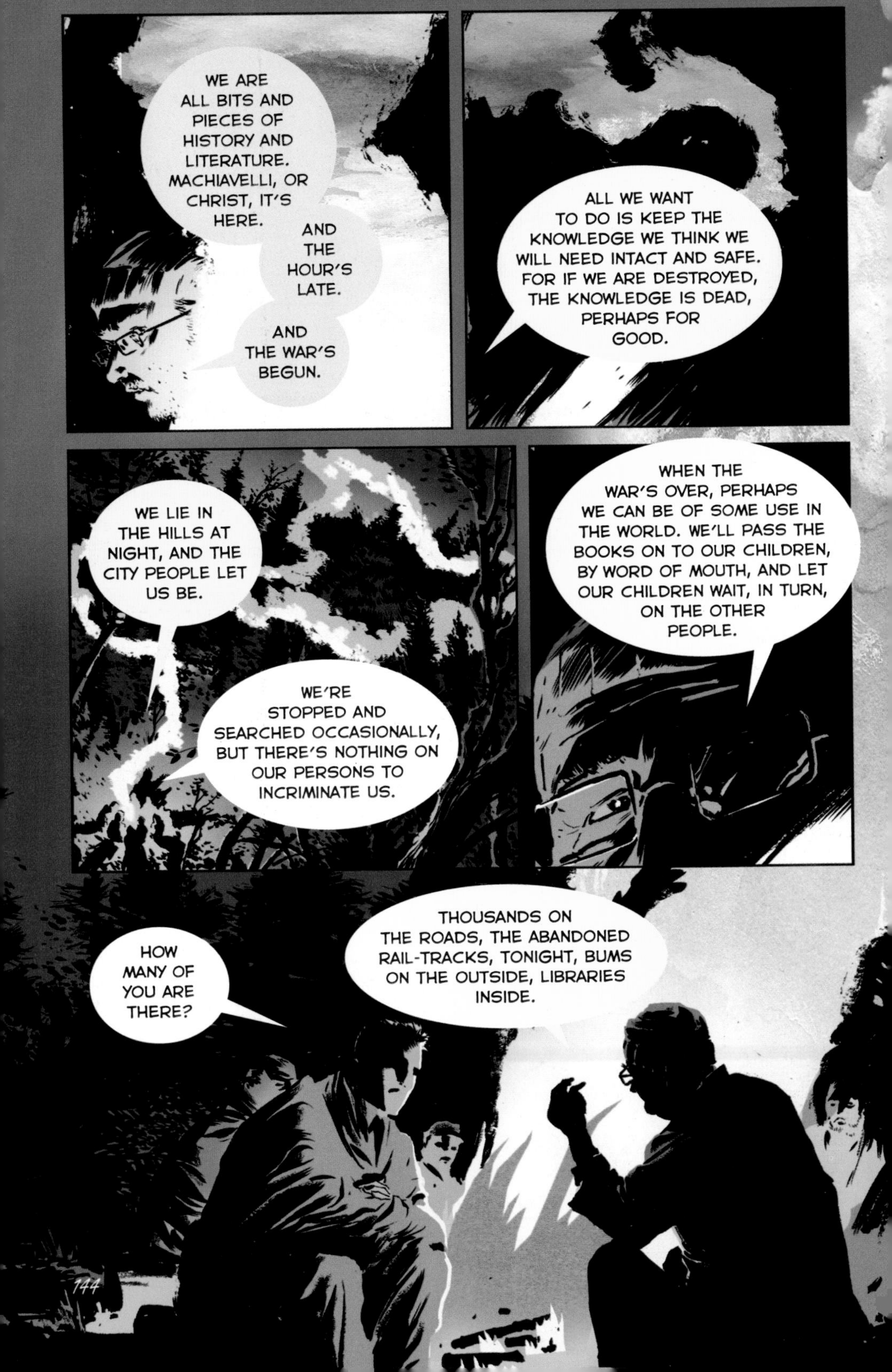
WE ARE ALL BITS AND PIECES OF HISTORY AND LITERATURE. MACHIAVELLI, OR CHRIST, IT'S HERE.
AND THE HOUR'S LATE.
AND THE WAR'S BEGUN.
ALL WE WANT TO DO IS KEEP THE KNOWLEDGE WE THINK WE WILL NEED INTACT AND SAFE. FOR IF WE ARE DESTROYED, THE KNOWLEDGE IS DEAD, PERHAPS FOR GOOD.
WE LIE IN THE HILLS AT NIGHT, AND THE CITY PEOPLE LET US BE.
WE'RE STOPPED AND SEARCHED OCCASIONALLY, BUT THERE'S NOTHING ON OUR PERSONS TO INCRIMINATE US.
WHEN THE WAR'S OVER, PERHAPS WE CAN BE OF SOME USE IN THE WORLD. WE'LL PASS THE BOOKS ON TO OUR CHILDREN, BY WORD OF MOUTH, AND LET OUR CHILDREN WAIT, IN TURN, ON THE OTHER PEOPLE.
HOW MANY OF YOU ARE THERE?
THOUSANDS ON THE ROADS, THE ABANDONED RAIL-TRACKS, TONIGHT, BUMS ON THE OUTSIDE, LIBRARIES INSIDE.

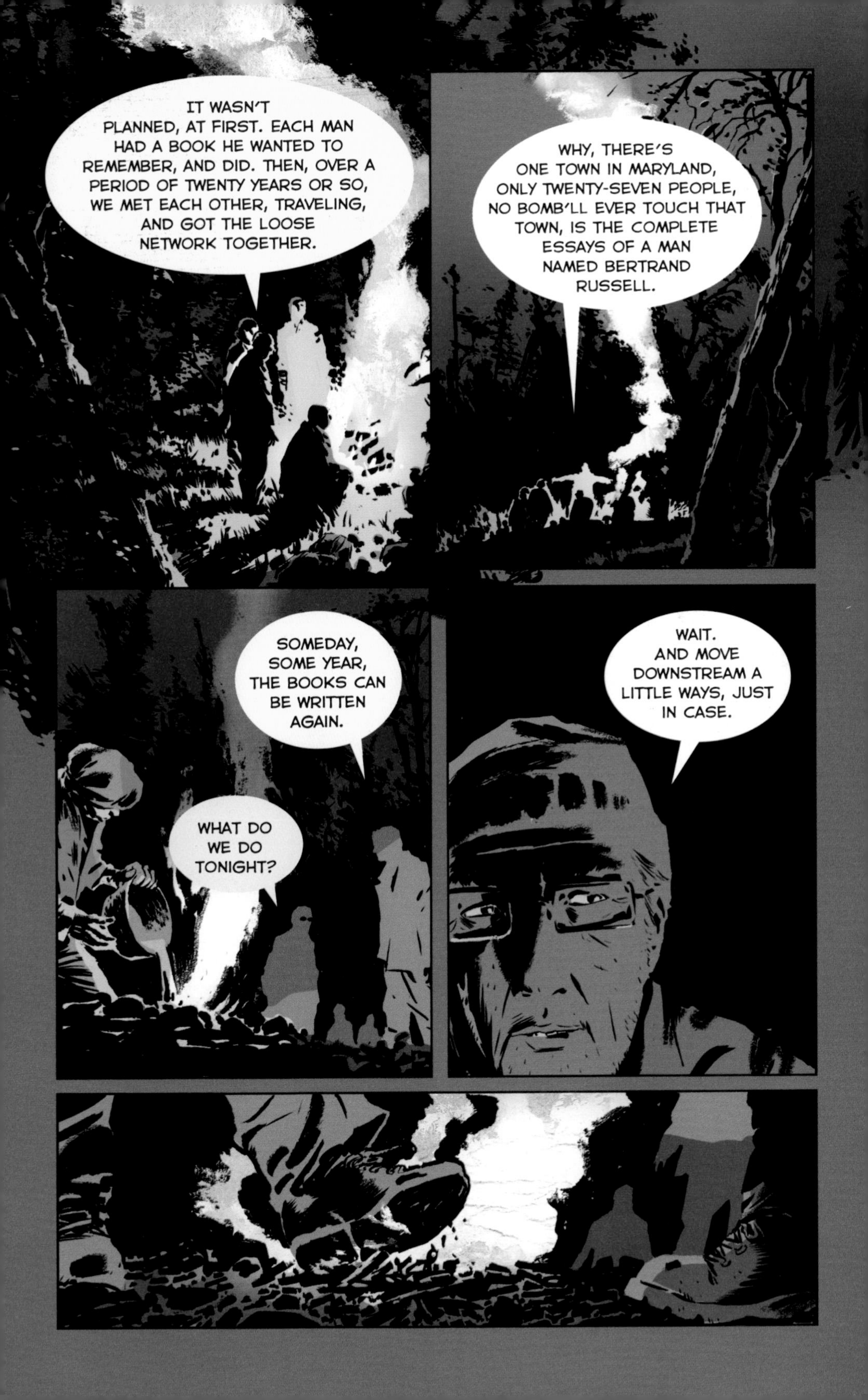
IT WASN'T PLANNED, AT FIRST. EACH MAN HAD A BOOK HE WANTED TO REMEMBER, AND DID. THEN, OVER A PERIOD OF TWENTY YEARS OR SO, WE MET EACH OTHER, TRAVELING, AND GOT THE LOOSE NETWORK TOGETHER.
WHY, THERE'S ONE TOWN IN MARYLAND, ONLY TWENTY-SEVEN PEOPLE, NO BOMB'LL EVER TOUCH THAT TOWN, IS THE COMPLETE ESSAYS OF A MAN NAMED BERTRAND RUSSELL.
SOMEDAY, SOME YEAR, THE BOOKS CAN BE WRITTEN AGAIN.
WHAT DO WE DO TONIGHT?
WAIT. AND MOVE DOWNSTREAM A LITTLE WAYS, JUST IN CASE.

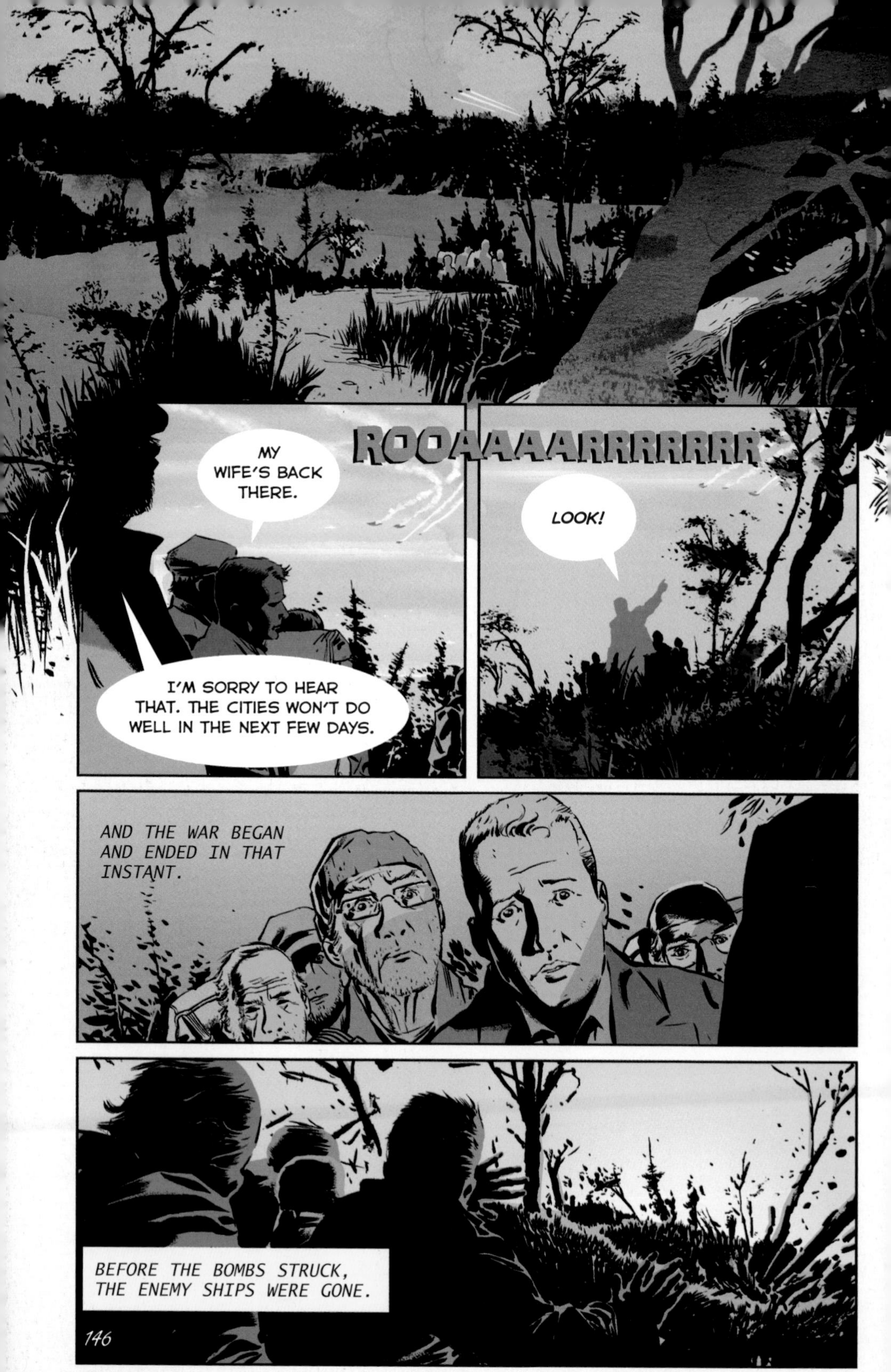
MY WIFE'S BACK THERE.
I'M SORRY TO HEAR THAT. THE CITIES WON'T DO WELL IN THE NEXT FEW DAYS.
ROOAAAAARRRRRRR
LOOK!
AND THE WAR BEGAN AND ENDED IN THAT INSTANT.
BEFORE THE BOMBS STRUCK, THE ENEMY SHIPS WERE GONE.

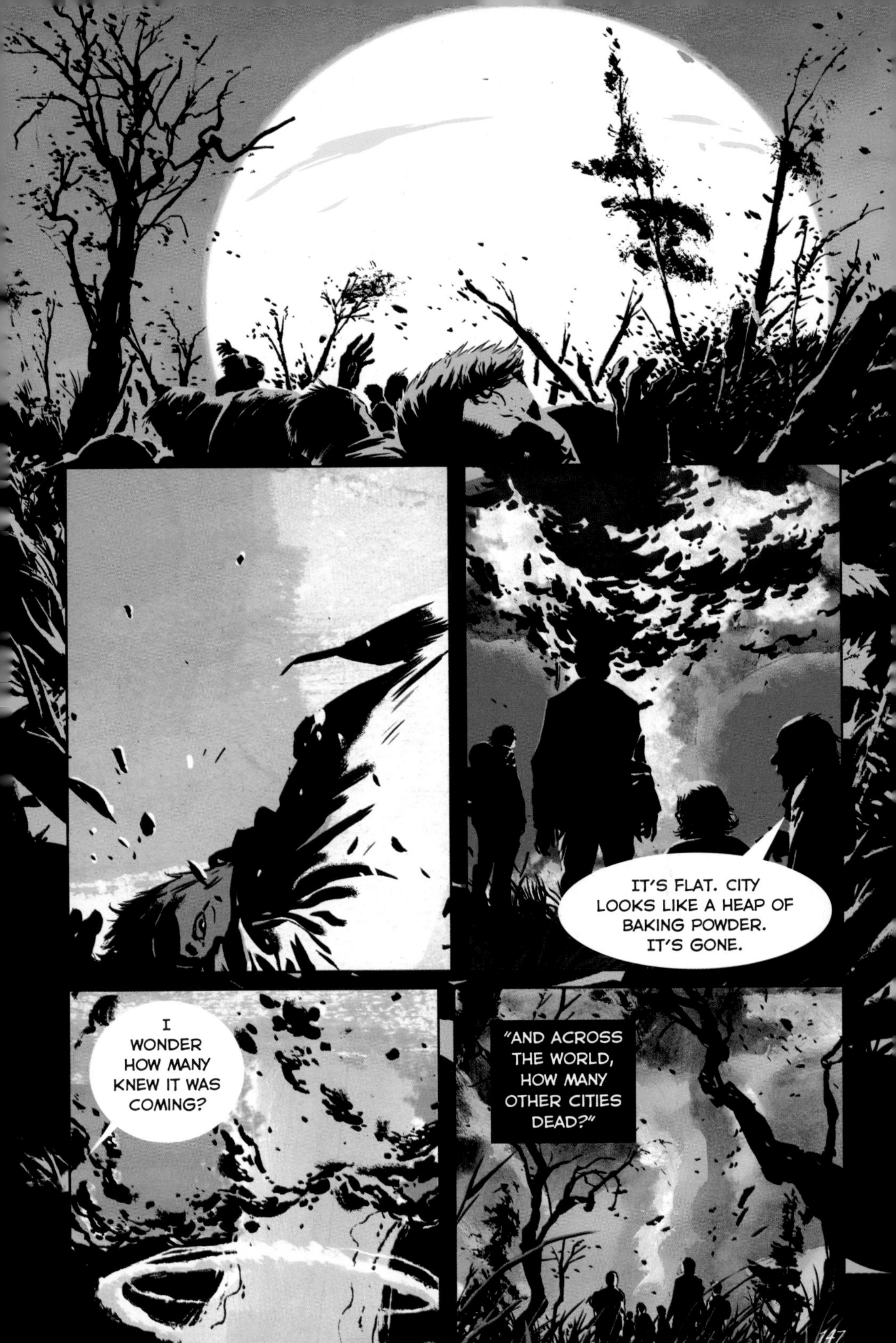
IT'S FLAT. CITY LOOKS LIKE A HEAP OF BAKING POWDER. IT'S GONE.
I WONDER HOW MANY KNEW IT WAS COMING?
"AND ACROSS THE WORLD, HOW MANY OTHER CITIES DEAD?"

THERE WAS A SILLY DAMN BIRD CALLED A PHOENIX BACK BEFORE CHRIST, EVERY FEW HUNDRED YEARS HE BUILT A PYRE AND BURNT HIMSELF UP.

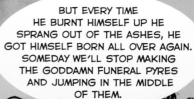

BUT EVERY TIME HE BURNT HIMSELF UP HE SPRANG OUT OF THE ASHES, HE GOT HIMSELF BORN ALL OVER AGAIN. SOMEDAY WE'LL STOP MAKING THE GODDAMN FUNERAL PYRES AND JUMPING IN THE MIDDLE OF THEM.

NOW, LET'S GET ON UPSTREAM, AND HOLD ON TO ONE THOUGHT: YOU'RE NOT IMPORTANT. YOU'RE NOT ANYTHING.

SOMEDAY THE LOAD WE'RE CARRYING WITH US MAY HELP SOMEONE. BUT EVEN WHEN WE HAD THE BOOKS ON HAND, WE DIDN'T USE WHAT WE GOT OUT OF THEM.

WE'RE GOING TO MEET A LOT OF LONELY PEOPLE IN THE NEXT WEEK AND THE NEXT MONTH AND THE NEXT YEAR.

AND WHEN THEY ASK US WHAT WE'RE DOING, YOU CAN SAY, *WE'RE REMEMBERING.*

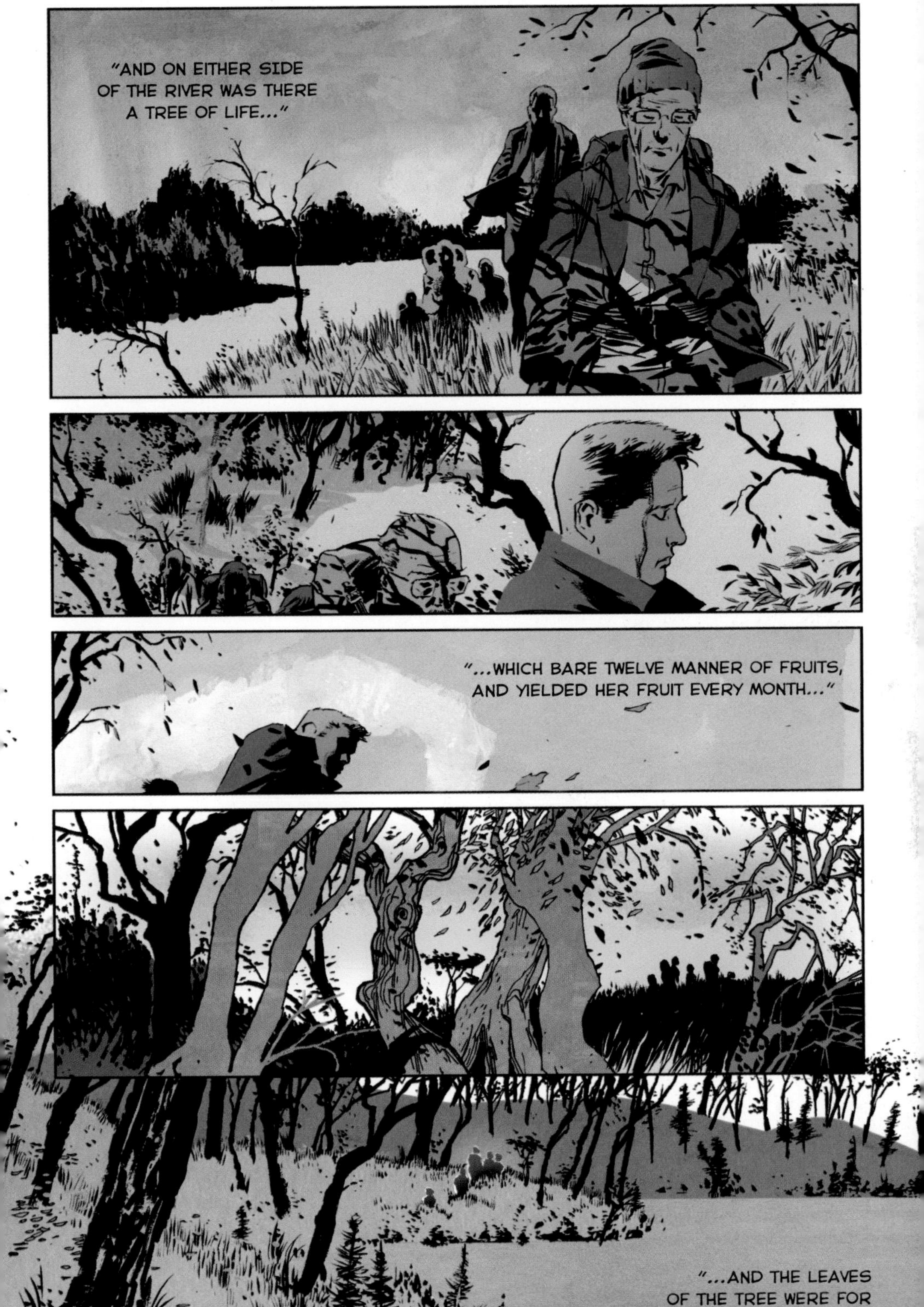
"AND ON EITHER SIDE OF THE RIVER WAS THERE A TREE OF LIFE..."
"...WHICH BARE TWELVE MANNER OF FRUITS, AND YIELDED HER FRUIT EVERY MONTH..."
"...AND THE LEAVES OF THE TREE WERE FOR THE HEALING OF THE NATIONS."

A NOTE ABOUT THE AUTHOR

RAY BRADBURY IS A WRITER OF MYSTERIES, SCIENCE FICTION, HORROR, FANTASY, AND MAINSTREAM FICTION, AND IS WIDELY CONSIDERED ONE OF THE GREATEST AND MOST POPULAR AMERICAN WRITERS OF THE TWENTIETH CENTURY. HE HAS WRITTEN NOVELS, SHORT STORIES, PLAYS, POETRY, SCREENPLAYS, AND TELEPLAYS. MANY OF HIS WORKS HAVE BEEN ADAPTED FOR TELEVISION AND FILM.

HIS MOST POPULAR BOOKS ARE THE NOVELS *FAHRENHEIT 451* AND *SOMETHING WICKED THIS WAY COMES*, AND THE STORY COLLECTION *THE MARTIAN CHRONICLES*. SINCE HIS WORK WAS FIRST PUBLISHED IN THE 1940s, BRADBURY HAS RECEIVED MANY AWARDS. AMONG THESE ARE A SPECIAL CITATION FROM THE PULITZER PRIZE BOARD IN 2007 FOR HIS "DISTINGUISHED, PROLIFIC, AND DEEPLY INFLUENTIAL CAREER AS AN UNMATCHED AUTHOR OF SCIENCE FICTION AND FANTASY." HE HAS ALSO RECEIVED THE NATIONAL MEDAL OF ARTS, A WORLD FANTASY AWARD, THE SCIENCE FICTION AND FANTASY WRITERS OF AMERICA GRAND MASTER AWARD, AND AN EMMY AWARD, AMONG OTHERS.

MORE INFORMATION ABOUT THE AUTHOR, HIS CAREER, AND HIS CURRENT PROJECTS CAN BE FOUND AT RAYBRADBURY.COM

A NOTE ABOUT THE ARTIST

TIM HAMILTON HAS PRODUCED ART FOR *THE NEW YORK TIMES BOOK REVIEW, CICADA* MAGAZINE, KING FEATURES, BOOM STUDIOS, *MAD* MAGAZINE, DC COMICS, DARK HORSE COMICS, TOYBIZ, AND *NICKELODEON* MAGAZINE. HAMILTON IS ALSO A FOUNDING MEMBER OF THE ONLINE COMICS COLLABORATIVE ACTIVATECOMIX.COM, WHERE HE HAS SERIALIZED HIS STORIES *PET SITTER* AND *ADVENTURES OF THE FLOATING ELEPHANT*. HE RECENTLY ADAPTED ROBERT LOUIS STEVENSON'S *TREASURE ISLAND* INTO A GRAPHIC NOVEL.